New World
MYTHOLOGY

New World
MYTHOLOGY

Myths and Legends of Oceania and the Americas

CHIEF CONSULTANT
Dr. Alice Mills

GLOBAL BOOK PUBLISHING

Managing director	Chryl Campbell
Publishing director	Sarah Anderson
Project manager	Dannielle Doggett
Art directors	Stan Lamond
	Kylie Mulquin
New title development manager	David Kidd
Chief consultant	Dr. Alice Mills
Commissioning editors	Dannielle Doggett
	Jody Lee
Picture research	Dannielle Doggett
	Jody Lee
Cover design	Kylie Mulquin
Designers	Wendy Farley
	Kerry Klinner
Cartographer	John Frith
Typesetting	Dee Rogers
Index	Glenda Browne
	Jon Jermey
Production	Ian Coles
Foreign rights	Belinda Vance
Publishing assistant	Jessica Luca

First published in 2003 by
Global Book Publishing
Level 8, 15 Orion Road, Lane Cove,
NSW 2066, Australia
Ph: (612) 9425 5800   Fax: (612) 9425 5804
Email: rightsmanager@globalpub.com.au

ISBN 9781740480222

Printed in China by SNP Leefung Printers Limited
Film separation Pica Digital Pte Ltd, Singapore

Photographers
Global Book Publishing would be pleased to hear from photographers interested in supplying photographs.

Captions for preliminary pages and section openers
Page 1: Reconstruction of the Aztec Calendar Stone
Page 2: Maori sculpture, Auckland, New Zealand
Page 5: Mayan Pyramid of the Magician with Chac the rain god, Uxmal, Mexico
Pages 6–7: Native American totem poles, Vancouver, Canada
Pages 8–9: Wandjina rock art, Kimberley region, Western Australia
Pages 10–11: Maori war pirogue (canoe)
Pages 58–59: Fresco from the Mayan Temple of Bonampak

CONTRIBUTORS

Dr. Philip Clarke has an academic background in biology, geography, and anthropology. After studying at the University of Adelaide in Australia, he started working in the Aboriginal ethnographical collections at the South Australian Museum in 1982. Dr. Clarke's research interests back then were chiefly Aboriginal use of plants as foods, medicines, and materials for making artifacts. This eventually broadened out to Aboriginal perception and use of the land, with a particular focus on the cultural geography of southern Australia. This research produced a number of publications on Aboriginal mythology. From the early 1990s, Dr. Clarke has mainly worked in central and northern Australia, investigating Aboriginal links to the land. A major project at the South Australian Museum was the repatriation of Aboriginal men's secret sacred objects back to senior cultural custodians. During 1998–2000 his major task was curating the Australian Aboriginal Cultures Gallery Project. Dr. Clarke is presently the Head of Anthropology and Manager of Sciences at the South Australian Museum.

Denise Imwold is a writer and editor from Sydney, Australia, who has also worked for many years as a bookseller. She studied literature and anthropology at Macquarie University, where she received a Bachelor of Arts, as well as a Postgraduate Diploma in Editing and Publishing. Denise has contributed to a wide range of publications in fields such as travel, literature, sport, gardening, health, and spirituality. Currently she is working on her first novel, which draws inspiration from Irish mythology and history. Her interests include reading, walking, animals, and traveling, and she finds special joy in visiting sacred places.

Dr. Deanna Paniataaq Kingston is half King Island Inupiaq Eskimo and an Associate Professor of Anthropology at Oregon State University, U.S.A. She conducts research with the King Island Native Community and teaches about Native North Americans, natural resources, and oral traditions. Her primary interests are in folklore, songs, dances, oral traditions, ethnohistory, and visual anthropology. Dr. Kingston earned her Ph.D. in Anthropology from the University of Alaska Fairbanks in 1999. Her dissertation is entitled "Returning: Twentieth Century Performances of the King Island Wolf Dance." She currently lives in Corvallis, Oregon, U.S.A., with her son and husband.

Dr. 'Okusitino Mahina holds a Ph.D. in Pacific history from the Australian National University located in Canberra, Australia. His doctoral thesis examined the formal and functional relationships between oral and written history. Dr. Mahina has taught at both 'Atenisi University in Tonga and Massey University, Albany Campus, Auckland, New Zealand. He currently teaches Pacific political economy and Pacific arts in the Department of Anthropology at the University of Auckland, New Zealand, and has been published in each of these fascinating fields. Dr. Mahina has also published poetry, mainly in the Tongan language. His areas of research interests include time and space, culture and history, language and art, and political economy and development.

Dr. Alice Mills is an associate professor of literature and children's literature at the University of Ballarat located in the Australian state of Victoria. One of the many interesting subjects that she teaches is Myth and Mythmaking. She began learning Latin when she was just 11 years old, then classical Greek when she was 12, and has had a lifelong interest in the mythical stories and characters that underlie contemporary Western culture. Dr. Mills has published many scholarly articles on the topics of children's literature and fantasy, and has edited several anthologies of children's literature including the Random House *Treasury of Children's Literature*. She is also a Jungian psychotherapist, and she brings Jung's ideas about the human psyche to bear on her understanding of the ancient myths of Greece and Rome.

Mark Anthony Rolo is a member of the Bad River Band of Ojibwe in Wisconsin, U.S.A. He holds a bachelor's degree from the University of Minnesota-Twin Cities. He has reported on Native American affairs and arts for numerous publications, and is the former Washington D.C. correspondent for *Indian Country Today*. Mark also served as executive director of the Native American Journalists Association. He edited *The American Indian and the Media—Second Edition*, which is a resource guide for journalists covering Native American issues. Mark has also written and produced work for the theatrical stage. He continues to write plays and articles about Native American communities.

Rawiri Taonui is of Maori descent from the tribes of Nga Puhinuitonu, Ngati Maniapoto, Te Aupouri, and Te Rarawa. He has lectured at the Department of History, University of Auckland, Aotearoa–New Zealand, in the areas of Maori Oral Tradition, the Treaty of Waitangi, Indigenous Issues, and Human Rights. He has also taught Maori Studies and Pacific Studies. Rawiri's research covers oral tradition; the politics of treaties and settlements with indigenous peoples in Aotearoa–New Zealand, Canada, and Australia; and human rights. He has written extensively for magazines and newspapers including *The New Zealand Herald*. In 2001 he received the internationally recognized Qantas Media Award for the "Best New Zealand Columnist on the Human Condition." He wrote and co-produced the documentary series *Hawaiki*, which traces the origins of the Maori and Polynesian peoples.

CONTENTS

MYTHOLOGY OF OCEANIA

OCEANIC MYTHOLOGY

Right **Tortoise shell spirit carving.** The sea spirit or *adaro* appears in many Polynesian and Melanesian myths and legends. Sharks, fish, and turtles merge in a sea spirit, which appears as a humanlike figure.

Oceania, according to the well-known Tongan anthropologist Epeli Hau'ofa, can be considered a sea of islands. The peoples and the cultures of Oceania have been conveniently divided into three main culture areas: Melanesia, Micronesia, and Polynesia. This classification, while problematic in many ways, is made mainly on the basis of a number of things, such as geography, race, art, mythology, religion, and language. Oceania, contrary to stereotypical portrayal, is far from static and uniform—it is quite complex and made up of different elements. While there are cultural and historical variations within and across Oceanic societies, these cultures share a lot in common, respectively exhibiting both differ-ences and similarities. The same applies to particular mythologies found in Oceania.

Numerous differences are mingled with similarities of the gods and within storylines. Sometimes, in the different islands of an archipelago, in the different districts of an island, or even in a single tribe, and according to different individuals, the same god is endowed with different attributes, or unites in himself, or herself, the attributes which belong to different gods in other places within Oceania. This can also work the other way around, where different gods in different populations have the same, or at least very similar attributes.

As in all cultures, mythology in Oceania is seen as a system of knowledge where people organize themselves in relation to nature and the environment. Obviously, as in the case of Oceania, mythology functions as an instrument of both investigation and explanation, as it symbolically explains how things work in reality, but mythology also works as an excellent means of communication, or oral tradition. This brings nature, mind, and society, as is evident in the retelling of a number of Oceanic myths, into conflict as different themes are stronger than others within mythological stories. The form and content of these many Oceanic mythologies vary from one place to another, and all have common narrative threads running through the stories and linking all cultures.

In Oceania, myths differ in both structure and subject matter, and from one locale to another. Generally, myths reflect the individual and society, as well as major events taking place in nature, and feature volcanic eruptions, landmarks, exploits of great ingenuity, war and peace among the gods, and romance between famous lovers. There are also variations between the local and the regional, where local versions happen to express themes relevant to the specific region. For example, some regional myths—such as the Maui, Tawhaki, and Tangaloa hero cycles—occur in Polynesia, but there are different versions of the stories throughout the whole Oceanic region. New myths, such as the Origin of Kava, Tonga's Lament for his Daughter, and the Fight with Oroi, are seen as being specific to Tonga, Mangareva, and Rapanui. These myths may

Below right **Symbols of fishing and the sea.** The sea is an important element throughout Oceanic mythology. Some existence myths attempt to explain the beginnings of the sea as coming from the sweat of the god of the oceans, Tangaroa, as he works at creation.

Below **Marakihau, a sea monster.** Marakihau are female sea monsters, and often turn into human women to marry men. When their husbands discover their true nature, the Marakihau are forced to return to the sea.

WHAT IS IN A NAME?

The traditional Polynesian name for Oceania is Moana. The original inhabitants were mainly long-distant navigators and deep-sea fishermen, and were called "warriors of the sea." Polynesia is divided into western and eastern Polynesia, with Pulotu and Havaiki as their respective ancestral homelands and afterworlds.

dreams, both as worlds without logical consequence, and where anything, and almost everything is possible.

These myths can be viewed as a work of art, especially the way in which their form and content are specifically organized. As seen in most highly developed myths, the elements of the myths are formally organized in sequences, and are made up of closely related episodes, which then combine to create the central plots and themes of the myths.

All myths tend to have investigative approaches, or they aim to change the way people look at a story or at history and its meaning. These myths provide an important source of knowledge for future generations.

represent an older social order, which diversified as people moved to new islands and adjusted to a new life. This shift is reflected in the substantial change in the form and content of new myths.

MYTHS AND HISTORY

Myths are a social institution, and they exist within and across all human cultures. The following general descriptions are specifically true of all Oceania. Being a hallmark of mainly verbal cultures, myths are transmitted through generations by word of mouth. Generally, myths can be considered as an aid to human memory in recording major historical events of extreme natural, mental, and social significance. Specifically, however, myths record in magical ways the major historical occurrences that concern, and influence, types of social activity, and characterize the relationships between people and their environment. In this respect, myths can be said to be storage boxes of human knowledge about nature, mind, and society. Similarly, material artifacts and languages can be effective sources of history, capable of holding vital information about the past of a group of people.

Oceanic myths are symbolic accounts of actual historical events. Conversely, actual events taking place in time and space are retold using symbols to represent ideas, the meanings of which are widely shared by members of a particular culture.

This is clear in the Oceanic myths retold here, where a number of symbols are used as pointers, or markers, to real occurrences taking place. This leads to myths having no connection to cause and effect, and creates a world of pure possibilities. Some Oceanic examples include Tanematua's pushing of the sky upward, the mortal woman Fataimoeloa being impregnated by the Sun, and Maui's fishing-up of lands, among many others. In this respect, myth tends to share a lot in common with

Below **Protective figure from the prow of a war canoe, Solomon Islands.** It was believed that the figure represented an ancestor that watched over the warriors while they were at sea, and the bird kept the boat on the right course.

13

MAUI AND TAWHAKI HERO CYCLES

In Oceania, the Maui and Tawhaki hero cycles exist on both the regional and local levels. Maui and Tawhaki represent actual powerful individuals or dominant ideologies. As individual protagonists, who are featured either as gods or demigods in many myths throughout the region, they have been described as nonconformist and aristocratic culture heroes. In terms of ideologies, Maui and Tawhaki represent the liberal and conservative tendencies as permanent aspects of the human context. As is always the case, these opposing points of view exist in the form of a constant struggle between social groups over the control of both human and material resources.

These competing ideologies generally reflect the two main social divisions in Polynesia, made up of commoner and "chiefly," or higher social classes. There were also "in-between" professional classes that actively engaged in different forms of social activity such as art, cultivation, navigation, religion, and housebuilding, among other things. These were very highly organized professions that were handed down from father to son. The conflicting relationships between these social relations of domination and oppression, and manifested in the Maui and Tawhaki cycles, highlight the resistance against social norms, and were the main driving force behind the expansive movement of Oceanic peoples.

Ranginui and Papatuanuku

This conflict of social class is evident in the Maori myth of Ranginui and Papatuanuku, gods of the sky and earth, symbolic of the combination of the priestly class and the landed aristocracy, highlighting this relationship as exploitation and oppression. In this myth, there exists an intermingling of the competing Maui and Tawhaki tendencies. Ranginui (Rangi), the Sky Father, and Papatuanuku (Papa), the Earth Mother, were inseparably embraced, with their children living between them in the dark. The children of the gods, Tanemahuta (Tane), Tawhirimatea, Rongomatane (Rongo), Haumiatiketike (Haumia), and Tangaroa—the gods of the forests, winds, kumara, plants, and oceans—had enough of living in darkness, and were eager to see the light of day.

One day, they had a meeting where they decided that the only way for them to realize their long-standing wish was to separate their parents by force. None of the children were eager to follow through with this plan. Some of the gods' children simply feared the consequences of their actions, while others were being respectful of their parents. However, Tanemahuta took on the challenge of separating the parents. He did this by kicking Ranginui skyward and placing Papatuanuku on earth permanently. The children of the gods saw light for the first time. Enraged by Tanemahuta's action against their parents, Tawhirimatea chose to be with Ranginui, his father. To punish his brothers, Tawhirimatea angrily sent his children, who were hurricanes and tornadoes, to ravage the forests, kumara, plants, and the oceans. Fearing the terrifying wrath of Tawhirimatea and his tempestuous children, the brothers all hid, clinging to the breast of their mother, Papatuanuku, for protection.

*Like Maui,
you are a deceiver.*
MAORI PROVERB

Munimatamahae and Sisimataela'a

Like many of the Oceanic islands, the Maui and Tawhaki hero cycles, as opposed heroic entities, are more clearly found in Tonga. As local variants, they are expressed in the myths of Munimatamahae and Sisimataela'a, who were nonconformist and aristocratic heroes. Munimatamahae, literally "Muni-the-shredded-eye," was born to commoner parents, who deserted him at birth, after throwing him into the sea. He was eventually washed ashore on one of the islands, and as he lay abandoned, a seabird viciously pecked out one of his eyes.

A commoner couple found and adopted him. Munimatamahae grew up to be a solidly built, handsome young man of extreme power and exceptional athleticism, and became greatly feared, even by his adoptive parents. If the chiefs on this island assigned a task, the people had to attend to it immediately, with all their might, as failing to do so meant severe punishment. Whenever a task was set, no matter how big or how hard, Munimatamahae would single-handedly and secretly complete any task in less than no time.

Sisimataela'a, literally "Sisi-the-eye-of-the sun," was born as a result of the union between a beautiful woman of noble birth, Fataimoeloa, and her aristocratic husband, the Sun. Fataimoeloa always bathed in a pool near the beach. She would then dry herself, bending forward, and exposing her buttocks to the burning Sun. Over time, she fell pregnant to the Sun, and gave birth to Sisimataela'a. Sisimataela'a was considered to be extremely handsome, and had all the physical attributes of being a chief of high standing. He was also equipped with all the necessary social knowledge of etiquette and protocol.

It happened that one day, the Tu'i Tonga (the King of Tonga) sent a party of high-status people on a voyage to the outlying islands, in search of an appropriate husband for his daughter. They came across the islet of Felemea in the Ha'apai group, where they found Sisimataela'a. All of them were struck by his physical attractiveness and aristocratic manners. He was ordered to come to

Above **Ivory Tiki figure.**
In some regions of Oceania, Tiki is believed to be a creator, while other regions use the symbol of Tiki to represent their ancestors. Tiki pendants were carved with care and presented to others as a gift of respect and acknowledgment.

Left **Ranginui and Papatuanuku.** The myth of the Sky Father and the Earth Mother describes how their tight, loving embrace kept light away from their children. Yearning for a break from the darkness, the children separated the couple and brought light into the world.

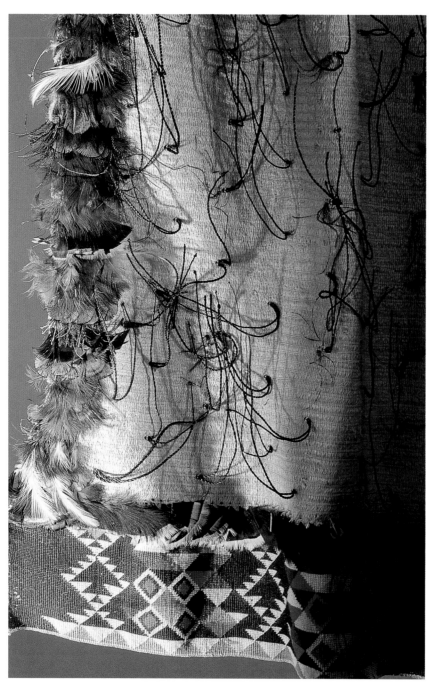

Left **A Maori chief's feather cloak.** A feathered cloak is another symbol for Oceanic kings and the aristocracy. Legendary stories of kings and their exploits give an insight into the social history of the period of time that these stories are set in.

The First Tu'i Tonga

The myth of the origin of the first Tu'i Tonga, 'Aho'eitu, is another variant of the Tawhaki hero cycle. It symbolically records the historical rise of the most ancient Tongan dynasty around the tenth century A.D. In historical terms, the myth is a metaphorical account of the dynastic connection between the Samoan and Tongan elite families, and is generally symbolized by the casuarina tree.

The myth relates how 'Eitumatupu'a, one of the Tangaloa sky gods, regularly descended to earth by climbing down a casuarina tree. On one of his earth visits, 'Eitumatupu'a impregnated 'Ilaheva, an earthly woman of noble birth. Her name was later changed to Va'epopua, after knowing 'Eitumatupu'a. She was the daughter of Seketo'a, an aristocrat of high status from one of the northernmost Tongan islands of Niuatoputapu. The physical union between the heavenly 'Eitumatupu'a and earthly Va'epopua (which signifies the historical links between Samoa and Tonga) resulted in the birth of 'Aho'eitu, who inherited the sky and earth, and both divine (spiritual) and secular (material) position on earth.

MAUI THE FREEDOM-FIGHTER

As a nonconformist culture hero, Maui is renowned for his many heroic exploits. He has been described as a trickster, commonly as "Maui-of-a-thousand-tricks," a characterization of the ingenuity in the conduct of his great deeds. His multiple heroic exploits are allegorical references to his permanent struggle against, and constant opposition to, actual forms of political oppression in the particular society of his time. The Maui gods, or demigods, existed as one of the competing ideologies,

Tonga-tapu to marry the king's daughter, so his father, the burning Sun, and his mother gave him two magical packages, one of fortune and the other of misfortune, instructing him carefully on how to always use them to his advantage or disadvantage.

Right **A bonito fish carving from the Solomon Islands.** When turned upside down, this bonito fish becomes a shark. Annual fishing expeditions were a major ritual event in Oceania. Carrying this type of carving in a canoe served to lure the bonito, while repelling the predatory sharks.

several centuries before the rise of the first Tu'i Tonga, 'Aho'eitu. This was witnessed in the manner of Maui's life and, indeed, in the manner of his death. Maui's exploits were always done for, and in the name of, freedom for the people of the earth. Maui's heroic deeds, among many others, see him as a fire-bearer, a sky-raiser, a sun-snarer, and a land-fisher, all of which are symbolic of a real life of protest against tyranny, in place of autonomy. This becomes more obvious in Maui also being a god of the underworld, which is a symbol for people who are downtrodden.

In Oceania, fire is symbolic of freedom, the driving force behind all forms of creative and innovative works of intellectual, artistic, and technological significance. The concept that freedom is not something given, but rather a form of constant struggle, is the prevailing theme in the story of Maui. He was opposed to the oppression brought about by the sky and earth separating, which was symbolic of the aristocratic classes, as well as people bending their backs under the burden of their social obligations. Similarly, the sun is a symbol of power manifested in the person of either a monarch or an aristocrat. Maui's snaring of the sun, which allowed more time for working people, symbolizes the act of asserting one's self against the powerful, and agitating for more personal power for the underclass. As a land-fisher, Maui symbolizes the liberation of the people, metaphorically represented by the land; these stories also illustrate social transformation, and the changes in the way of life for people from working and fishing the sea for a living, to eventually farming the land. These stories can vary from place to place, but Maui's basic purpose always remains the same.

THE KAVA MYTH

One day the tenth Tu'i Tonga, Momo, King of Tonga, who lived on the easternmost part of the main island of Tongatapu, was game fishing. On this particular fishing trip, he and his royal party couldn't catch any fish. Exhausted and hungry, they landed on the islet of 'Eueki. Living on the island was a man of common status named Fevanga and his wife, Fefafa, and their only daughter, Kava'onau.

Having heard of the arrival of royalty, the couple had to make an offering. They decided to harvest their giant taro plant, but found the king leaning against it. This meant that the taro plant could not be used as it had become taboo, because the king had touched it. Instead, they killed their daughter and baked her in an 'umu (earth oven).

The king told them not to uncover the 'umu, but make it their daughter's grave. From this grave grew kava and sugarcane, which the couple harvested, and then used for a formal kava ceremony. Today this ceremony is performed as a dance.

Below *The Kava Ceremony* by Louis Auguste de Sainson (1801–1887). This ceremony is performed as a traditional sign of welcome for visitors and dignitaries.

MAUI THE FIRE-BEARER

Maui's grandfather, the old Maui, lived in the underworld, where he guarded the only source of fire—a huge log of burning wood. One day, Maui left earth to visit the old man, entering through the secret gate to the underworld. Maui found his grandfather jealously guarding the single fire source. He told the old man that he wanted to take some fire back with him to earth, so that people could use it for cooking, as a change from eating their food raw. The old Maui refused his grandson's request, prompting Maui to work out a plot to smuggle the fire away so he could take it back to earth.

Maui took a piece of burning charcoal, and carefully wrapped it up in a leaf. As he was leaving, his grandfather could smell the fire on him, and challenged the young man to a wrestling match.

Depending on who won, the fire would either stay in the underworld, or be taken to earth. The old Maui grabbed his grandson, and tried to throw him into the sky. Maui was flung upward, and reached the top of the trees. He then fell back down, landing safely on the ground. When it came to Maui's turn,

Left **Kings and dynasties.** A Polynesian statue of a kingly figure has an almost godlike appearance, complete with powerful arms and legs. This figure looks reverently toward the sky as a mark of respect for the ancestors.

Above *Maui Snaring the Sun* by Wilhelm Dittmer (1866–1909). Maui conceived a plan to capture the sun, when the days on earth became shorter and the nights became longer. The sun was captured with a net, which then slowed its progress through the sky. As a result, the daylight hours were extended.

Right Jade *hei matau* or fishhook. The islands of Oceania were said to have been fished up by the hero, Maui. With deceit and trickery, he managed to find a magical fishhook, learn its secrets, and pull up land from the depths of the ocean.

he took hold of his grandfather with one hand, sent him up beyond the clouds, and watched him disappear into the heavens.

The young Maui took off with his hidden treasure, with his grandfather, who had landed, in pursuit. Just as Maui was about to enter the secret gate, the old Maui caught him. As the gate opened, young Maui threw the wrapped-up fire out to earth, instructing it to enter every tree. Old Maui was completely powerless to stop the fire from spreading. This was the origin of how fire appeared on earth, and how it is now used for cooking by its people.

MAUI THE SKY-RAISER

At one time, Maui descended from the earth above to the underworld below. As usual, people on earth went about their daily routine—men, women, and children were busy with their various day-to-day activities, such as fetching water and firewood, and getting food to cook. On his return to earth, Maui discovered a strange thing happening. He noticed that the sky and the earth had moved closer together. To his great dismay, Maui also saw that his fellow earth dwellers were walking around with their backs bent forward, unable to walk upright, and their movements were cramped and restricted.

Immediately, Maui began working out ways to deal with this troubling problem. He decided the best solution was to raise the sky by pushing it upward with all his might away from the earth, and put them into their proper positions. As a consequence of his wilful action, it was said that the people of the earth immediately regained their normal posture, and began walking about, and doing their work with greater ease.

MAUI THE SUN-SNARER

The earth inhabitants were used to a normal day, with the usual division of night and day, and their activities were based around this daily division. However, people could see that the days were strangely getting shorter and shorter. During the day, the sun would rise and set very quickly across the sky, giving people less time and space to carry out their normal tasks such as fishing and the tilling of the land. This meant that they were never able to finish their work. People became alarmed, and then started to complain loudly to the gods.

The people's concerns soon reached Maui and his brothers, Maui 'Atalanga, Maui Loa, and Maui Puku, who then held a meeting to discuss the matter, as it seriously affected life on earth. They decided that one way of alleviating this problem was to slow down the sun, giving the people enough time to do their work. Maui suggested that they make a huge net, which could be used to snare the sun, and anchor it firmly to earth. His brothers were fiercely opposed to the idea, as they feared both the enormity of the task and the fierce intensity of the sun's heat. Maui was unmoved by their concerns, and eventually won over the complete support of his brothers. They successfully managed to capture the sun. This limited the sun's rate of motion, and restored the pattern of normal daily life back to the people.

MAUI THE LAND-FISHER

The god of the sky, the old Tangaloa, and his children lived in the heavens above earth. One of his children, young Tangaloa, the artisan and god of the material arts, was responsible for the creation of many of the Oceanic islands. He would tip the wood chips from his workshop in the sky, down onto the earth, and these chips formed many of the islands. This is how Tangaloa the artisan became Tangaloa, the creator of lands. The word sky, *langi* or *rangi,* is, in Oceania, a symbolic name for Samoa. The creation of land is probably a metaphor for the secret knowledge involving the organization of people of this time. It may mean that Tangaloa was either an

SYMBOLS

Some common examples of symbols as actual markers to history in Oceanic mythology include the bending forward of backs for oppression; sun for power, monarchy, or aristocracy; sky for the priestly class; underworld for the down-trodden; fire-bearing for innovation; sky-raising for opposition; sun-snaring for contestation; and land-fishing for liberation.

influential person or a kind of social norm held up as an example to others in society.

The rest of the islands in Oceania were said to have been fished up by Maui from the depths of the ocean. The fishhook that Maui used for fishing up lands, including many of the Tongan, Fijian, and Samoan archipelagos, is said to have come from Manu'a, the easternmost group of islands in Samoa.

Maui desperately wanted the old, rusty, worn-looking fishhook for its magical qualities, specifically for fishing up lands. Tongafusifonua (literally "Tonga, the Fisher of the Lands") was the owner of the fishhook, and extremely protective of it. Maui set about working out a way to deceive Tongafusifonua so that he could steal the fishhook away. He decided to seduce Tongafusi-fonua's wife, Tonga.

While they were making love, Tonga was said to have romantically whispered the mysterious secrets of the fishhook to Maui, giving him all the information he needed to find it, as well as the details on how to use it.

This story cleverly illustrates that sex is not only a union of physical and social benefit, but it can also be used as an instrument of political manipulation.

Above *Pirogue, Vitu Islands* from *Voyage de la Corvette* by J.S.C. Dumont d'Urville (1790–1842). Canoes are important symbols within the myths of the islands of Oceania, signifying movement and survival. On many of the islands throughout Polynesia, Micronesia, and Melanesia, ancient canoes have been found beside rock paintings, and represent the travel and migration of ancestors.

AUSTRALIAN ABORIGINAL MYTHOLOGY

Right **Map of Australia's mainland.** Australian Aboriginal mythology is extensive and wide ranging. All the myths retold here relate to specific places and landscapes that are found on the Australian mainland.

Below **Clan ancestral mythology, Arnhem Land.** This bark painting represents an episode in an ancestral story. Aboriginal myth is considered as "living." Events relate to ancestral stories, and explain natural and social events. The stories are often recorded in artwork distinctive to each indigenous region.

Australian Aboriginal people see the social and physical aspects of their world as very closely interwoven. They believe that during a creation period, known in English as the "Dreaming," their spiritual Ancestors performed heroic deeds, and in doing so molded a relatively featureless landscape into the present form. These ancestral beings had human traits such as virtues, pleasures, and vices, and were also capable of dying and being transformed. The Ancestors often took the form of particular animals and birds, but were also diseases, plants, and atmospheric and cosmological phenomena. The Ancestors created the world as Aboriginal people experienced it, and laid down the rules and cultural practices that their descendants continued to follow. Although they were active in the past, the Ancestors are still considered to influence Aboriginal Australia today.

The Dreaming mythology comprises an Aboriginal system of beliefs that provides answers to the great universal religious questions of humankind, concerning the origin, meaning, purpose, and destiny of life. Aboriginal people can, through their participation in ceremonies and rituals, connect directly with the Dreaming. The Ancestors are generally seen as the totems for their clans, thereby providing a link to present-day people. Aboriginal people acknowledge the Ancestors' role in creating landscape features such as wetlands, hills, forests, and water holes. Some Aboriginal people have, through actual dreams, gained deeper insights into their past, and have had revealed to them the significance of particular places in their landscape. Nevertheless, the Dreaming and Dreaming Ancestors are not the direct products of dreams. To Aboriginal people, the power of the Dreaming is present everywhere, just waiting to be discovered. The "Dreaming" can loosely be described as the entire body of mythology that provides Aboriginal people with insight into their religious traditions. It therefore relates to the Ancestors, the customs, and sacred objects they introduced, and the

sacred places that they left in the landscape. Although chiefly concerned with past events, the Dreaming is still of primary importance to many Aboriginal people for making sense of their modern world.

THE DREAMING AS HISTORY

Across Australia the "Dreaming" was known by a number of language terms: for example, Ngarranggarni (Gooniyandi people, southeastern Kimberley), Djang (Kunwinjku people, western Arnhem Land), Wongar (Yolngu people, northeastern Arnhem Land), Tjukurpa (Western Desert region), Altyjerre (Arrernte people, MacDonnell Ranges, Central Australia), Muramura (desert groups, east of Lake Eyre, Central Australia), Bulurru (Djabugay people, northeastern Queensland), and Yemurraki (Wemba Wemba people, northwestern Victoria). A related word in Aboriginal English is "Law," which refers to the body of religious and cultural knowledge that is used to inform and direct Aboriginal society. A "law man" or "law woman" is a person who has been through the relevant initiation ceremonies where they have received important religious knowledge. In some northern areas, Aboriginal people refer to the Dreaming knowledge that they possess as their "history."

Dreaming Ancestors are central to Aboriginal religion and the sharing of beliefs and customs, helping to bind together Aboriginal people from a wide-ranging area. For example, in northeastern Arnhem Land, Yolngu people celebrate, in ceremony, the arrival of two sisters and a brother, collectively known as the Djanggau, during the Dreaming creation period. They came to the region by paddling a bark canoe from the Land of the Dead in the east. They traveled across Yolngu country, transforming the landscape, and after many deeds departed to the west where the sun goes. The first people were the children of the two sisters, who gave them territorial boundaries. Another sister pair in Yolngu mythology was the Wawalag sisters, who traveled north across Arnhem Land to Roper River. They arrived at a water hole, which was the home of Yulunggul, the Ancestral Python. After giving birth to children, they were all swallowed by Yulunggul, but later regurgitated. The Djungguwan ritual celebrates the Wawalag Dreaming, with young initiates being symbolically regurgitated. Both the Djanggau and Wawalag myths are ritually important, and form the basis of the Yolngu religious system. It is impossible to speak of Yolngu culture without making reference to these particular mythologies.

Before the arrival of Europeans in Australia, all the different Aboriginal groups possessed religious beliefs that explained how people, the land, plants and animals, and their customs came into being. In south-eastern Australia, many of the main creation Ancestors were male figures, whereas elsewhere there was, typically, a much greater range of Dreaming identities. It is thought that this may have been a post-European development. These "high gods" had names such as Korna, Kulda, Ngurunderi, Nureli, Bunjil, Baiame, and Daramulun. Whether such male Ancestors were so dominant in southeastern Australian cultures before Aboriginal experience with non-Aboriginal people will never be known for certain. Nevertheless, there is a possibility that the rapid demise of the Aboriginal population on the frontier significantly enhanced the importance of their beliefs, in particular, Ancestors, especially those associated with death and living in the Skyworld.

Above **Three-masted European ship with trailing anchor.** After the arrival of non-Aboriginal people, the importance and strength of Aboriginal beliefs grew as the indigenous population started to diminish. Although based on the past, these beliefs are still very important today.

Left **Carved stone disk.** In some Aboriginal cultures it is believed that the Ancestors of the Dreaming and their weapons became disks. They represent each Ancestor's immortal spirit, and show the specific area that they came from.

NGURUNDERI, A LOWER MURRAY DREAMING

In the Ngarrindjeri Dreaming, known as the Kulhal, Ngurunderi was the first Ancestor to wake. Three or four other Ancestors woke later, some complaining that they were cold and hungry. Ngurunderi told one Ancestor to make a fish, and then he taught the other Ancestors how to cook it. He then ordered the Ancestors to collect firewood and water. These Ancestors lived somewhere in the inland region of southeastern Australia, so Ngurunderi sent other Ancestors away to lands he was creating, while he and his sons drove an enormous Murray cod, Pondi, down the Darling and Murray Rivers. These rivers were just small streams, but as the giant fish pushed its way through the mud, it created the deep channels of the rivers, and with a flip of its tail it made lagoons. Ngurunderi was losing Pondi, so with smoke signals he managed to get the help of his brother-in-law, Nepeli, who was camped

downstream on the southern shore of Lake Alexandrina. They finally caught Pondi near Raukkan. Ngurunderi tore the large fish into small pieces, throwing each of the fragments back into the water, creating the different species of fish that live in the waters today.

Ngurunderi stayed in the Lower Murray region for a while. He was a large and very powerful man with two wives, who were sisters, and four children. Ngurunderi was a renowned hunter, along with Nepeli, and Nepeli's brother-in-law, Waiyungari. As evidence of their hunting prowess, Nepeli and Waiyungari were credited with having created numerous salt lagoons by pegging out fresh kangaroo skins, and denuding these places of grass. (The kangaroos back then were much larger than today.) One day, two of Ngurunderi's children strayed into the bush, and were lost. To escape the wrath of their husband, the wives ran away. The two sisters had also broken a food taboo by eating bony bream, which was forbidden to young women. Ngurunderi chased them

Right *The Murray, 1836* **by Thomas Mitchell (1792–1855).** After Europeans moved through the Australian landscape, different representations of the scenery appeared. According to the Lower Murray Dreaming, an Ancestor created these lands when he followed a huge Murray cod.

across the land, and, in doing so, created many geographic features. He made fresh water soaks by digging between sand dunes, and his brush shelters became hills. While he was desperately searching for his children, Ngurunderi quarreled with Parampari, a sorcerer at Salt Creek. Ngurunderi killed him and then burnt his body, the remains of which formed a large granite outcrop on the ocean beach near Kingston. After finding his children, Ngurunderi finally caught his wives and beat them, but they escaped again. He was tired of chasing the women, so he commanded the sea to flow and drown them. The bodies of the wives became The Pages islands, which can be seen in the Backstairs Passage near Kangaroo Island.

Ngurunderi had family connections to other Ancestral creators. The Barkindji people who lived along the Darling River knew that Ngurunderi's two wives had earlier been in their country, when married to Tulu, the Kingfisher Ancestor. Here, it was believed that Waku, the Crow Ancestor, had chased the women. Two warriors from Ngurunderi's group returned to the Upper Murray-Darling area, where their Dreaming adventures had begun, but were never heard of again by the Ngarrindjeri.

One of Ngurunderi's sons traveled further south, and was attacked and chased by a "big devil" named Mirka, who emerged from the Blue Lake at Mount Gambier. The son fled north, crossing the Mount Lofty Ranges to arrive at Willunga, near the present city of Adelaide. Here, Ngurunderi joined the fight and wounded Mirka. The congealing blood of the "big devil" formed a rich red ochre deposit at this place, which is now known as Red Ochre Cove.

After leaving Ngarrindjeri territory, Ngurunderi went on to create other lands to the west. Before leaving, he foretold the coming of Europeans and their destruction of the environment, saying "Beware of *puruki* (ants)." Leaving the Lower Murray, Ngurunderi swam to Kangaroo Island. One of his sons was accidentally left behind, but found his way by grabbing at the cord thrown toward him, the end of which was attached to Ngurunderi's testicles.

Ngurunderi and his family went to the western end of the island. From this point of land, he threw his spears out into the water, and they became rocky islets. The creation of new rivers, hills, and other features in the Lower Murray ceased after Ngurunderi left, and he went to live in the Skyworld, Waieruwar, which was a place where life was extremely comfortable, and there were many kangaroos and emus for him to hunt.

The legacy of Ngurunderi was tangible to Ngarrindjeri people. The present major landforms were shaped by his powerful actions. Another illustration

of Ngurunderi's creative power was to give numerous fine bones to the bony bream fish. Thunder was regarded as his voice, while rainbows showed him urinating. Customs attributed to Ngurunderi's law include the prohibition of young male initiates eating certain types of fish. He and his son, Matamai, are also credited with introducing mortuary rites, which involve smoking the dead, to Ngarrindjeri people.

Above **Aboriginal bark painting of two fish.** A number of Aboriginal Dreamings tell how enormous fish moved through small, muddy streams, creating rivers and lagoons with their gigantic fins and tails.

THE DREAMING LANDSCAPE

The landscape was an artifact that Dreaming Ancestors left behind for Aboriginal people. Through their actions Ancestors created the landscape, forming hills by killing a large kangaroo, making a quartzite rock formation with the fat of a cooked snake, or forming a water hole with their tears. After the main creation period was over, these places were thought to retain some of their Dreaming character, as well as part of the essence of the particular creator Ancestor. These sacred memorials, or "sacred sites," may be such things as a mountain, water body, plant formation, rock outcrop, or another environmental or geographical feature. They form part of the trails that knowledgeable Aboriginal people recognize, and are seen as evidence that the Dreaming actually happened. The sacred memorials are central places that provide connections that link present-day Aboriginal people with the Dreaming. The number of sacred places linked together through the webs of Dreaming traditions is enormous.

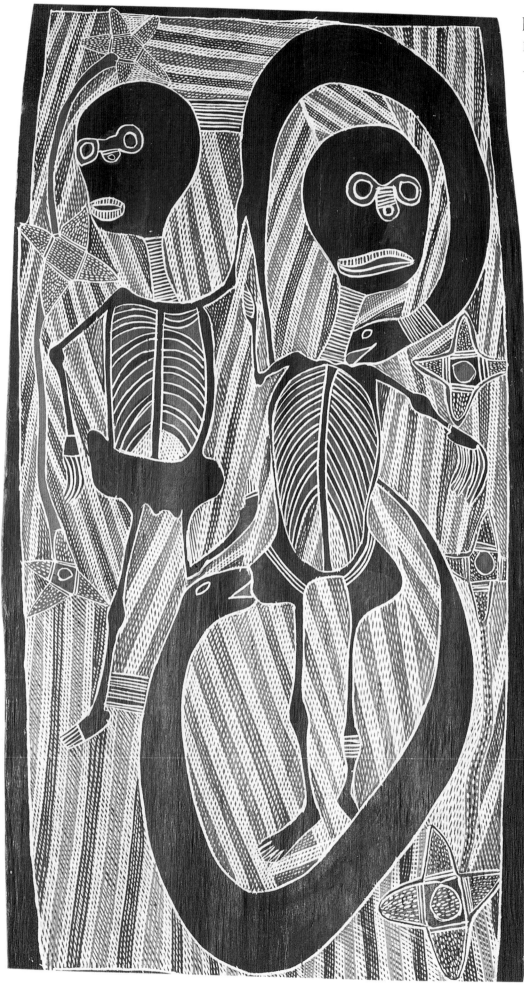

BUNYIPS, WATER SPIRITS FROM SOUTHEASTERN AUSTRALIA

Throughout southeastern Australia there are recorded accounts from Aboriginal people of water spirits, now commonly known as "bunyips." The early European settlers were convinced that bunyips existed. Although Europeans generally referred to them as "bunyips," there was much variation in how they were described; some looked like large and ferocious emus, seals, crocodiles, and serpents, while others were more like hairy humans. In the case of the latter, they appear to be related to the "yowie" spirits—apelike monsters from southeastern Australia. The term "bunyip" is from the Wergaia language in northwestern Victoria, where it was originally recorded as *banib*. The word "yowie" was derived from *yuwi*, from the Yuwaalaraay language of northeastern New South Wales. The European colonists recorded from Aboriginal groups in the Hunter River region of eastern New South Wales, the term "wowee" used for bunyips.

The variable descriptions of bunyips are not solely accounted for by the cultural differences between Aboriginal groups, as variation occurred even within the same region. For example, in the 1840s along the Murray River in South Australia, it was noted that local Aboriginal people had difficulty in describing the water spirit being, some thinking that it was like an enormous starfish, whereas others described a spirit with more humanlike features. Given that many Aboriginal

Left **Mythical figures surrounded by a sacred python.** Among the thousands of mythic paths that crisscross the Australian mainland are tracks commemorating the journeys of giant snakes.

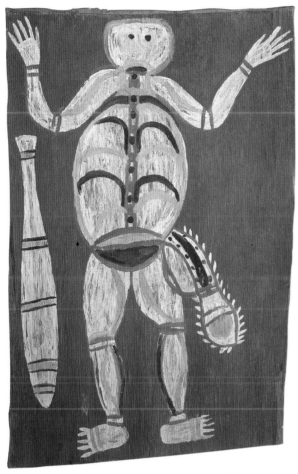

SKYWORLD

The belief in the existence of the Heavens or Skyworld as a region much like the world we live in was widespread across Aboriginal Australia. Various star constellations and planets were considered to be Dreaming Ancestors, while large features, for example, the Milky Way, were seen as celestial rivers or large canoes.

The association between the human spirit and the Skyworld is broad, involving both ends of a person's life. In many Aboriginal cultures it was believed that the spirits of babies fell down from the sky and that secret knowledge could be gained through visits to the Skyworld, usually using special ropes. Aboriginal people considered that the spirits of their dead followed the Ancestor's path into the Heavens. The Skyworld was considered to begin at the height of a large tree or small hill, and was therefore part of the landscape, which meant that it was not beyond the physical reach of Aboriginal people.

spirits had the ability to change shape and use sorcery, it is not surprising that the bunyip beliefs have a myth-like quality. Due to the wide-ranging descriptions, it is best not to treat the bunyip as a single entity, but as a class of spirit beings based around permanent inland water bodies.

Aboriginal people living in the extreme south of Victoria, near where the city of Melbourne now stands, believed that an amphibious "bunyip" spirit was the size of a full-grown calf, and had dusky gray feathers. The bunyip here was considered to have a magical power over humans, causing them considerable misfortune. Places where there were many eels tended to be where bunyips lived, as this was their food. On one occasion, Aboriginal people claimed that a bunyip lured a woman to her death by distracting her with a large catch of eels. It was considered extremely bad luck to kill or injure a bunyip.

The best-recorded traditions concerning the bunyip are from the Lower Murray region of South Australia. Here, the bunyip, known by Ngarrindjeri people as the *mulgyewonk,* had some humanlike features. It was said to have a body resembling a seal, a bearded face like a man, and very long, trailing hair that looked like waterweed. This water spirit was generally thought to be a threat to people. The bunyip could hurt people with sorcery, and the booming noises it made were thought to cause

rheumatism. The booming noises were also linked to the broken up gum trees that often floated down the Murray River into the lakes, particularly during the heavy seasonal floods.

In the Lower Murray, bunyips would lie submerged in the shallow waters near the edge of the lakes waiting for human victims. When children washed their hands in lake water after eating, the smell of grease from fish and duck meat was said to attract the bunyip. Ngarrindjeri people claimed that a man was able to rescue a child abducted by the bunyip, by rubbing a magical substance over his body and descending, by a rope, to the bottom of the lake. He could then drag the child out from among the sleeping bunyips, and get back safely. If he was unsuccessful, it was thought that the child would eventually be transformed into a bunyip. Ngurunderi, the main Dreaming creator of the Lower Murray region, also suffered from the actions of these water spirits. A bunyip tore holes in his nets, which prevented him from fishing for his family.

Certain spots along the Murray River, often at the base of cliffs, were considered to be the main refuges for bunyips. Understandably, Aboriginal people did not swim at these places, and avoided passing by on reed rafts and in bark canoes at night. Bunyips were said to produce the bubbles that were sometimes seen in the lake water, and when they were swimming they made the unexplained ripples often seen in the river. Ngarrindjeri people claimed that whirlpools were bunyips cleaning out their homes.

One Ngarrindjeri man believed that a particular hole he found along the edge of a lake was another bunyip lair. This water hole had a foul stench, along with a strange whooshing noise.

Left **Warrior spirit from Croker Island.** These spirits in the landscape are sometimes threatening. This makes certain areas, such as deep water holes, very dangerous to venture near at particular times.

Below **Horned spirit figures.** Depending on the place of Dreaming, spirits can either live within part of the landscape, such as in rocks or caves, or their bodies might create significant landforms, such as mountain ranges.

Above **An incised hair ornament.** As part of various rituals and ceremonies, certain body decorations and headgear are worn.

PURRUKUPARLI, WHO BROUGHT DEATH TO THE TIWI

The Tiwi people live on Melville and Bathurst Islands, north of Darwin in the Northern Territory. Before European settlement, they were largely isolated from the Aboriginal cultures on the Australian mainland, due to the large breadth of Clarence Strait, and to the roughness of the seas for canoe travel. The Tiwi believe that during the Parlinari creation period, an elderly blind woman named Mudunungkarla rose out of the ground at Murupianga, in the southeast of Melville Island. She had three infants—two girls, Wuriupranala and Murupiangkarla, and a boy, Purrukuparli. Mudunungkarla crawled northward, carrying her children from her breasts, and while doing this she created many of the major landforms, and finally separated the islands from the mainland. Before leaving the islands, she also made the numerous freshwater wells, and left behind plants and animals for her children to survive on.

In order to start creating families, Purrukuparli visited the homes of the various spirit children, to bring some of them back to become people. He lived at a place called Impanari on Melville Island with his family—a wife, Pima; his much-loved baby son, Tjinini; and his unmarried "brother," Thaparra. Purrukuparli, like his mother, was a major creation Ancestor. On one occasion, Jurumu, the Wedge-tail Eagle, and Mudati, the Fork-tailed Kite, accidentally made fire when they rubbed two sticks together. They decided to approach Purrukuparli, and wanted him to put it out. However, he recognized the value of the fire in keeping them warm and for cooking

We are all visitors to this time, this place...Our purpose here is to observe, to learn, to grow, to love...and then we return home.

AUSTRALIAN ABORIGINAL PROVERB

their food. Purrukuparli lit a large bark torch and gave it to his sister, Wuriupranala, the Sun Woman. He gave a smaller torch to his "brother," Thaparra, the Moon Man. Today, because of the differences in torch size, the light from the sun is stronger than the light from the moon. Purrukuparli made the first large painted poles for the Tiwi people, and created songs and dances, and established the Kurlama initiation ceremonies.

As was typical of most Aboriginal families, Purrukuparli and Pima were apart during the day. Pima would go into the bush each morning to gather food, carrying the infant Tjinini, while Purrukuparli went away hunting. She would return to camp with Tjinini and the food in the late afternoon. It became an illicit practice of Thaparra's to meet up with Pima

PERFORMANCE

Aboriginal people hold ceremonies that may be both sacred and heavily ritualized, or on other occasions, secular and less formal events. They often involve widely dispersed groups coming together at a single place, which may be an area of sacred Dreaming significance. In sacred ceremonies, the dancers will act out events associated with particular Dreaming Ancestors, while secular ceremonies usually relate to everyday incidents or historic events. Aboriginal people hold ceremonies associated with births, initiations, and mourning, which might last many days. They may involve singing, playing musical instruments, and performance. The participants typically wear special decorations, headgear, and feathers, and have totemic designs painted with ochre on their bodies. At larger events, occurring over several days, there are opportunities for people to arrange marriages, settle disputes, and to trade. Some ceremonies are formally passed on to neighboring groups, establishing good relations between potential enemies.

Above **Ritual dance ceremony.** Ceremonies and performances serve as living records of the past, as well as being vital in ensuring that the stories of the Dreaming are passed down to younger generations.

during the day. They would leave Tjinini in the shade, while they went off together to be lovers. This had been going on for some time when, on one particularly hot day, Pima was late getting back. As the sun shifted, Tjinini was exposed to the sun and died.

Purrukuparli was enraged and stricken with grief when he returned to find his son dead, and his wife was no-where to be seen. When he found Pima, and discovered what had happened, she was severely beaten with a club. Pima was remorseful, chanting a song that means, "Evil woman am I to have caused the death of my son." Purru-kuparli refused to allow Thaparra the three days it would take to bring Tjinini back to life. The two male Ancestors then fought with forked clubs, from one end of Melville Island to the other. Both were injured about the face and body. When the fight was over, Purrukuparli picked up his son's body, which was wrapped in paperbark, and walked backward into the sea. As he did this he uttered, "As my son has died, and will never return, so shall all men." The creation period was coming to a close. At the place where Purruku-parli drowned a whirlpool appeared, and his footprints

remained visible on the ground nearby. Before Purru-kuparli died, he stabbed Thaparra in the eye and killed him. Thaparra became the moon, and although he died, he is able to come back to life, as the new moon, after three days of darkness. The dark spots on the moon's surface are the wounds he received from fighting with his angry "brother," Purrukuparli.

Pima was left alone in the bush, and became a stone curlew. This bird has a wailing call, which, when heard by the Tiwi people at night, is said to be Pima calling out for her dead son. The curlew

as a dark mark on its head where Purrukuparli's club had violently struck Pima.

The Tiwi people also have a song that they say was sung by Pima in mourning, after Purrukuparli had killed her lover, Thaparra. In more recent times, a woman would sing this when goading her husband to take action, in response to her illicit affairs be-coming more widely known within the community. Tokampini, the Honeyeater Bird Man, established the first Pukumani mourning ceremony, as a mark of respect after the death of Purrukuparli.

Above **A distorted female figure.** Images like this were thought to be used in magical processes to inflict harm, or gain re-venge. Some Dreaming stories tell of dangerous women feared by men because they are drawn to them, similar to the Sirens of Greek and Roman mythology.

Right **A rock painting of mimih spirits.** Mimih and men come together in many Aboriginal stories from Arnhem Land. Although sometimes shy, the mimih spirits did make themselves known to Aboriginal people, teaching humans the arts of painting, water divining, and cooking.

Below **A male spirit painting.** Mimih spirits are often painted on bark. These spirits generally do things that humans do, but they live in a special landscape behind rocks. Mimih spirits are usually portrayed as very fragile and delicate.

MIMIH SPIRITS OF THE ARNHEM LAND ESCARPMENT

The mimih spirits are important to the Kunwinjku people of western Arnhem Land, although they are not Dreaming Ancestors. They are similar to humans in form, but very long and thin, and so delicate that out in the open, a slight breeze causes them to face into it and brace themselves, and a very strong wind would break their slender necks. The mimih spirits have excellent vision and hearing, and are able to avoid contact with people they detect coming their way by disappearing into rock faces, which they open like a door by speaking to the rocks or by blowing onto them. They have pets, which may be possums, rock wallabies, geckos, rock pythons, or echidnas. If these are killed, the mimih spirits are believed to feel grief, and to want retribution. The mimih are considered to lead separate lives to humans, with a culture of their own. They live inside a landscape embedded in escarpment rocks, and this landscape has its own plants and a sun.

Unlike many other spirit beings, Aboriginal people generally regarded the mimih as harmless to people. Some Kunwinjku hunters have claimed to have met mimih, and also talked to them. The mimih are believed to have painted their images in the rock art galleries of the escarpment. The Kunwinjku also believe that their Ancestors were taught how to paint by the mimih spirits, who showed them by painting on rock. The mimih also instructed them on how to find water when it was dry, as well as how to cut up animals and cook them for food.

Mimih spirits and people both fear Namarrgon, the Lightning Man, who is shown in paintings as having stone axes, which make lightning, that stick out from his head, elbows, and knees. The mimih spirits bury their own axes when he is about, so as to avoid his anger. When visiting the "stone country" (western Arnhem Land escarpment), Aboriginal people typically call out to the mimih spirits, announcing who they are and why they are there. Aboriginal people were warned not to follow the mimih to their homes in the rocks, as they might never return. In one myth, a young man followed a mimih spirit into his cave so he could sleep with the mimih's sisters. The young man was trapped there until his father, who had special powers, was able to break into the cave to kill the mimih.

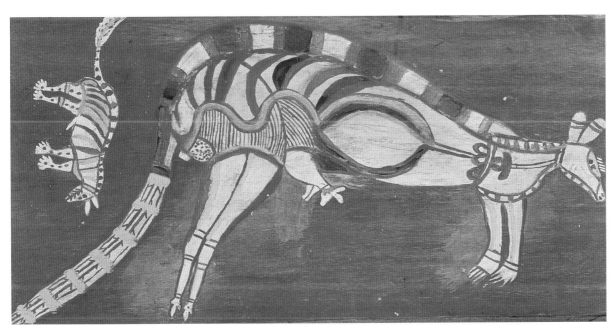

Left **The kangaroo and dog.** These animals are enemies because the kangaroo promised to paint the dog to make it look beautiful. The kangaroo made the dog look ugly, so, for revenge, the dog will always chase the kangaroo.

The red paintings commonly found in the rock art caves on the western edge of the escarpment, which archaeologists refer to as the "dynamic figure style," are considered by the Kunwinjku to be mimih spirits. They believe that some of them are painted in blood. The mimih spirits are often painted on bark, where they are seen hunting, giving birth, and participating in ceremonies that regenerate kangaroos and people. Aboriginal people believe that these spirits were able to magically bring down a vertical rock wall to a horizontal level, paint on it, and return it to its original position. Strange things that present-day Aboriginal people see in the rock art are said to have been painted by the mimih. Today the bark paintings of the spirits are important for teaching younger generations about the Dreaming, especially those who no longer have the opportunities to visit rock galleries.

The Kunwinjku have a myth about two mimih spirits, Ngurdyawok and Nawalabik. The following account shows that their lives were parallel with humans, having all the pleasures and vices normally associated with people. Ngurdyawok was attracted to Nawalabik's two wives, despite them being his sisters. One day, when Ngurdyawok and Nawalabik were out collecting sugarbag (native bee nests), Nawalabik cut off Ngurdyawok's head with a stone ax. Back at camp, Nawalabik told his wives that Ngurdyawok had gone hunting. Then, Nawalabik went away with his dog to hunt echidna.

The birds eventually told the women what had happened, and they got their father's relatives together to punish their husband. Nawalabik was confronted, and for three days managed to dodge spears that were thrown at him by the relatives of his wives to resolve the dispute. When it was over, he slept at his wives' camp, but his father-in-law killed him with a club.

Nawalabik's dog saw all this happening, and after snapping the rope that had him tied to a tree, he covered himself with his owner's blood and fled to the camp of Nawalabik's brother. A large number of warriors, Nawalabik's relatives, gathered and followed the dog back to the body of Nawalabik, and respectfully buried him. They then went to the camp of Ngurdyawok's people, who were holding a ceremonial dance. They hid in the shadows, and as soon as they got their chance, the relatives of Nawalabik revenged his death by rushing the people of the camp and killing them all.

PUKUMANI MOURNING CEREMONY

The Tiwi people of Melville and Bathurst Islands in northern Australia hold Pukumani ceremonies in honor of the deceased, and in celebration of their Dreaming Ancestors. These ceremonies are held as a series of mortuary rituals that release the spirit of a recently deceased person. To those outside their culture, the distinctively carved burial poles, which are erected vertically near the grave, have become widely recognized symbols of Tiwi culture, and are often made today for sale to art galleries and museums. The poles are cut from the trunks of ironwood trees, and may be up to 10 ft (3 m) in length. They are decorated with designs that relate to the mythology and the land. Heavily decorated spears and bark containers are also made for ceremonies. The mythology behind the Pukumani ceremony is based on the Purrukuparli Ancestor who, in Tiwi Dreaming, first brought them death.

Right **Aboriginal bark painting of a funeral ceremony.** Funeral rituals vary. Some rites involve smoking, which clears away unwanted spirits.

WANDJINA, SPIRITS FROM THE KIMBERLEY

The wandjina spirits are important, as they control the monsoon clouds that bear rain. Aboriginal people consider them to have both humanlike and cloudlike forms. In one sense, the wandjina represent the monsoon clouds. In the Kimberley, Aboriginal people sing to these spirits to keep them calm during the monsoon. In some areas, the wandjina are also considered to be major creators of the child spirits that enter the bodies of women to become babies. Similarly, the wandjina control the child spirits of animals, such as kangaroos and emus. Like people, they have been involved in many adventures, which are illustrated in Kimberley rock art. The wandjina have, at various times, fought with people. They have also had fights among themselves, over such things as the stealing of wives. Each wandjina spirit had at least one personal name. The mythology behind them is extensive, with their intersecting paths spread throughout much of the Kimberley region.

The wandjina spirits are featured in some of the most spectacular examples of rock art surviving in the world today. The wandjina figures are often very large, some measuring over 20 ft (6 m) in height, and typically painted in black, red, or yellow lines over a white background. Their figures may be represented in full, with arms or legs, or as just the head and halo, or reduced to the extreme as eyes peering through the halo. Their headdress can be described as their hair, but can also be seen as cloud. The strands of material coming from the hair may be feather decoration, or the lightning under the control of the wandjina.

Protocol demands that caves of wandjina paintings be approached properly, with the names of visitors announced, and by telling the spirits that they have upheld their religious obligations since the last

ROCK ART

Rock art sites occur widely, but unevenly, across Australia, and are part of traditions that stretch back over 40,000 years. The techniques are rock painting, stenciling, and engraving. It is estimated that there are presently over 100,000 examples of surviving rock art in Australia, representing a small part of all the rock art ever produced here. The use of "rock art" to describe these traditions presents a problem, as it is generally not known why individual pieces were produced. In general, from the few accounts received directly from Aboriginal artists, it is known that rock art sites collectively contain images of people, Dreaming Ancestors, spirit beings, animals, plants, artifacts, and cosmic phenomena, and are often linked to particular cultural sites. Some rock art contains images of extinct animals, such as Thylacines. Aboriginal rock art painting traditions continue today, particularly in central and northern Australia, where they are strongly connected to Aboriginal ceremonial life.

Left **Aboriginal rock paintings near Alice Springs, Northern Territory.** These particular paintings mark the place where women of the Dreaming watched the performance of a sacred ceremony by men of the tribe. In the Dreaming women shared the knowledge of important tribal rites.

visit. At some sites, visitors burn tobacco for the spirits. As with many important painting sites across Australia that have mythological significance, there must be no unruly behavior or any physical damage done to the paintings. Tradition demands that the wandjina paintings are regularly repainted to conserve them, which apart from maintaining their galleries, helps to maintain the fertility of the region. Nevertheless, most Aboriginal people believe that people did not do the original wandjina rock paintings, but that they represent the image of each spirit as they died. If the above practices are not kept, and the wandjina become angry, it is believed that they will strike down people with lightning, cause a flood, or bring on a cyclone. The wandjina art has also appeared on carved boab nuts, and on artifacts such as bark containers.

The following account of a wandjina named Wodjin is from the Ngarinyin, Worora, and Wunambul people, but is also widely known across the Kimberley region, with many variations.

Two boys were playing with a bird named Tumbi, which they thought was a honeyeater, but it was actually an owl, and the son of a wandjina. They mistreated Tumbi very badly, plucking his feathers, flicking him with speargrass, and throwing him naked through the air. When the bird spirit eventually escaped, he flew into the sky to complain to the wandjina spirits. In revenge, a wandjina known as Wodjin brought together his fellow spirits. Although he sent out animals to find out where the people of the boys were, they were not initially found, as the animals did not want to reveal them. Eventually, Wodjin created a bicycle lizard from his penis, and the people were finally located at a spring near Tunbai. The wandjina spirits came together on top of a nearby hill, and held ceremonies in secret. Although

Wodjin had become too ill to fight, the other spirits formed themselves into two groups and attacked the people. Afterward, the tracks of the wandjina remained as two scars running down the hill. A great flood was called, and most of the remaining people were drowned.

The two boys who had caused the conflict through their mistreatment of Tumbi managed to escape. Some people say that they hid from the wandjina spirits in the pouch of a kangaroo, and were later able to start their whole tribe again. Others assert that they eventually crawled inside a split boab tree to hide from the rain and lightning. Unfortunately for them, the tree was a wandjina, and once they were inside they were crushed to death. After the massacre, the wandjina spirits split up and went their separate ways.

Most traveled westwards, some to as far north as Kalumburu, others south to Fitzroy River. Wodjin hurt his foot in a cave known as Wanalirri, and decided to stay there.

Today, this site is a major rock art gallery containing powerful images, among which local Aboriginal people identify Tumbi the owl and the bicycle lizard. It is at this site that the image of the powerful Wodjin is particularly large and imposing.

Left **Spirits on a hill.** This abstract bark painting is said to represent the gathering of Wandjina spirits before they decide to fight with the people who have offended them. Wandjinas call on the help of animal spirits when they are trying to find people.

Opposite page **The "Lightning Man" of northern Australia.** This bark painting depicts the legendary Wala-Undayna spirit with axes growing out of his knees. He moves across the land terrifying humans and other spirits.

BARK PAINTINGS

The bark painting art styles of Arnhem Land are directly related to the extensive rock art galleries found elsewhere in the region. Many of the early bark paintings collected from this region were on bark slabs that had been used in making the roof of wet-season shelters. Bark paintings convey information about the landscape, and are often based on local myths, containing images of major Dreaming Ancestors such as the Djanggau and the Wawalag Sisters, or of spirit beings such as the mimih. Food animals, such as kangaroos, turtles, and barramundi fish also appear in bark paintings, as do images of past contact with strangers, like the Macassans and European buffalo hunters. From the early twentieth century, European interest in bark paintings has placed them in the international indigenous art market. Since then, this art style has spread to many Aboriginal groups that formerly did not produce bark paintings.

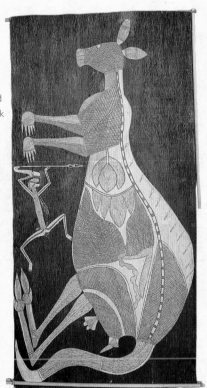

Right **Bark painting in an x-ray style.** The cross-hatching relates to a specific tribe.

FIRE DREAMINGS

Fire is important to Aboriginal
people as it provides warmth,
protection against darkness and
spirits, and is a means to cook
food and make artifacts.
Aboriginal people practiced
"fire-stick farming"—burning
bush to help with hunting,
to make traveling easier, and
to produce food plants for
the animals they hunted. Fire

Dreamings are widespread throughout Australia,
and typically have one Ancestor who knows how
to make fire, but who selfishly keeps it secret from
other Ancestors. Eventually, this knowledge of fire
is discovered and stolen, and becomes widely known
to people. As a result of this, fire escapes and is now
present as bushfires.

Aboriginal people living near Katherine, in the
Northern Territory, have a myth where only the
Crocodile Ancestor possessed fire. The Rainbow Bird
kept asking him to share it, but he was repeatedly
denied. The Rainbow Bird had to camp without fire
to cook his meals. This made him angry, so one day
he swooped down from a tree to try to snatch the
fire-sticks. He missed the first time, but he later
managed to steal the fire-sticks when the Crocodile
Ancestor had turned the other way. The Rainbow
Bird Ancestor flew into the trees, telling the Crocodile that he would give fire to all men. The Rainbow
Bird placed the fire-sticks in his rump. From that
time onward, rainbow birds live in dry country, and
crocodiles are restricted to living in water.

The Western Desert people of central Western Australia have a Dreaming myth where Tjilpi, meaning

"old man," remained in camp while his son,
Yilgadidi, went hunting with other young men. The
hunters returned with kangaroo and possum meat,
which was cooked and eaten, but none was given to
Tjilpi. The old man was both hungry and angry, so
when the young men left again to hunt, he put out
all the fires by covering them with sand. He then took
the fire-stick with him on a long trip east, camping
first at Walangara. On returning to the campsite, the
young men were unable to start their fires, and they
became very cold during the night. Alone, Yilgadidi
tracked his father to Walangara, but discovered that
his father had already left, and his campfire was cold.

Tjilpi continued on his journey, finally heading
south toward the Southern Ocean. He entered the
sea near Eucla. Yilgadidi caught up with Tjilpi when
the water was up to his neck, with the fire-stick held
above his head. Tjilpi was dragged from behind,
back to land. Yilgadidi saved the fire-stick, and then
camped with his father nearby, where they eventually
turned into rocks. In a related account, it was the
Turkey Bustard Ancestor who had fire and fled to the
coast near Eucla. Here, he intended to hide the fire

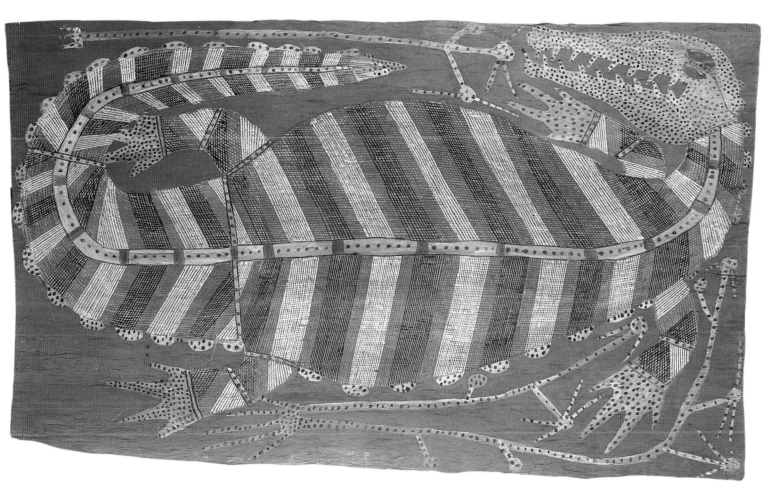

in the flint nodules under the sea. In this account, it was the Hawk Ancestors who rescued the flints, which are still accessible today, but only at low tide on extremely calm, windless days.

The Booandik people in the southeast region of South Australia believed that the Ancestor Mar was the one who solely owned fire in the Dreaming period, and that this was hidden inside an ornament on his head. Other Ancestors met to discuss how they could discover the secret of fire. Several of them tried to spy on Mar, and the Ancestor Tatkanna had his chest singed red from the heat of Mar's fire. When fire was at last caught in a dead grasstree flower spike, it accidentally spread to dry grass and shrubs, where it quickly grew into a bushfire.

When he realized that the fire was stolen, Mar rushed to where the other Ancestors were camped, and started a fight. One of the Ancestors, a large man named Kounterbull, received a deep spear wound in the back of his neck. He rushed into the sea where he became a whale and was later seen spouting "steam" from his wound. Mar flew up into a tree and became the sulfur-crested cockatoo, which has yellow feathers ("fire") on the top of its head that are only visible when the crest is extended. Tatkanna turned into the scarlet robin, which has a red breast.

Ever since this happened, Aboriginal people have been able to continue to make fire, using the fire-sticks made from dried grasstree flower spikes and dry shrubs that dot the landscape.

In western Victoria, Aboriginal people believed that during their Dreaming period, fire had been the property of the Waa, Raven Ancestors, living in the Grampian Mountains. The Ravens enjoyed the ability to make fire, and would not let any of the other Ancestors get a light. An Ancestor named Yuuloin Keear, described as a Fire-tail Wren Ancestor (probably the Beautiful Fire-tail), saw a group of Ravens throwing fire-sticks about as they played. He picked one up and flew away. Tarrakukk, the Hawk, robbed Yuuloin Keear of his fire-stick, but in the process he started wildfires that raged across the country. Since that time, Aboriginal people have been able to start fires.

Above **Ancient crocodile.** Stories from Aboriginal people living near Katherine, in the Northern Territory, tell of the great Crocodile Ancestor who possessed fire, but did not want to share it with anyone else. The wily Rainbow Bird tricked the crocodile into sending out the fire to all men.

WESTERN DESERT ART

The Western Desert is a large region where Aboriginal people speak one of dozens of related dialects, and share many of the same Dreaming traditions and cultural practices. Here, Aboriginal art appears on artifacts, rock paintings, on bodies, and directly on the ground. In the case of ground paintings, these were often associated with ceremonial activities, such as dancing. Western Desert art is distinctive in its predominant use of dots and concentric circles.

On less formal occasions, people draw in the sand when telling stories. Here, the sand acts as a slate on which pictures related to the myth or event are illustrated, and then erased. All these art forms are still widely practiced today, with canvas and acrylic paints being the preferred media to produce art for sale. Several painters may collaborate to produce an individual piece, particularly if it is large and is associated with a special ceremony.

Right **Rainbow Serpent with a lizard.** Rainbow Serpents are powerful Ancestors. A young man was once forced to ride on the back of one, holding onto the stingray nails behind its head. When he was returned to his family, the Serpent forbade him to wash. The man ignored this advice, and died.

WATER SERPENTS

Across Australia Aboriginal people associated large snakes with water and rain. Often called Rainbow Serpents, these Ancestors are generally thought to live in bodies of fresh water. They are associated with rainmaking, and are considered very dangerous to people. In Arnhem Land, rock art featuring serpents has been dated at more 8,000 years old. The Dreaming Tracks of the Water Snake Ancestors crisscross the whole of the Western Desert, and are generally associated with water holes. Aboriginal people believed that certain men were rainmakers, having the ability to bring on a change of weather. In some regions, rainmakers wear shell ornaments that are symbolically linked to the Rainbow Serpent.

Although the mythology connecting snakes with water is large and varied, the common themes are control of water and danger to people.

In western Arnhem Land, the main Rainbow Serpents are Yingarna and her son Ngalyod, who are believed to live in the deep water holes. These Serpents represent the monsoon weather, which fills the inland waterways when the heavy rain comes. In particular, the rainbow that appears after the rain is identified as Ngalyod. This Rainbow Serpent is still, in a sense, a creator, as he increases plants and animals with the change of the season. The Rainbow Serpent is also believed to possess the power to send spirit children to water holes, to wait before becoming human. Ngalyod is like a Supreme Being to all Ancestors, and because of this is connected to most mythological sites in the western Arnhem Land region. In myth, Ngalyod swallows people for their failure to observe the sacred Law. The Rainbow Serpent can also cause floods, storms, and even drought. The Rainbow Serpent is part of the major rituals of western Arnhem Land, including the Wubarr, Marrayin, and Kunapipi.

The Western Desert people living on the northern edge of the Great Victoria Desert have a Dreaming account involving a large number of Geniga, Spotted Native Cat Ancestors, camped at Beril-beril water hole near a lake where two Wanampi, Snake Ancestors, lived. Minma Murulu, Marsupial Rat Woman, came down from the north looking for water. She found that the Geniga Ancestors were away hunting and gathering, apart from an old Geniga woman still in camp. Minma Murulu offered to delouse the elderly woman, who accepted and then fell asleep. Going to the lake, Minma Murulu dipped her wooden container, which was extremely large, into the water. By filling her container, she completely drained the lake and everything that lived in it.

Minma Murulu then headed back north toward the Kimberley, managing to escape the Geniga men who were tracking her. Once she got back home, she went hunting, and carelessly put her wooden container with the water still in it on top of a spinifex grass tussock. The dish tipped over, and all the water poured out and formed the Fitzroy River in the southern Kimberley. The Wanampi came out of the wooden container, and one of them swallowed Minma Murulu. The large serpents then traveled toward the sea, making the rivers and the streams, with their meandering courses.

The Kaurna people of the Adelaide Plains believed that the dark spots seen in the Milky Way were water lagoons, where a large serpent named Yura lived. These dark areas in the sky were known as Yurakauwe, which translates as "monster-water." The Milky Way was considered to be a large river with reeds growing along the banks. Aboriginal people feared Yura would swallow them if they did not hide. When he appeared on earth, an abundance of water was created. Yura gave the Kaurna people some of their initiation rituals, and would severely punish those who neglected these practices.

The Akurra spirits of the Adnyamathanha people of the Flinders Ranges are considered to be very large, with scales, beards and manes, and fangs. On the back of the Akurra's neck are ticks that cannot be removed by the spirit. In some accounts there are two Akurra spirits—a smaller male and a large female. The eggs, feces, and vomit of the Akurra became landforms in the Flinders Ranges. A large ring of mountains, known as Wilpena Pound, represents the bodies of a pair of Akurra. The male forms the northeastern wall of the Pound, while the body of the female makes up the southwestern side.

Adnyamathanha people believed that the Akurra moving underground caused earthquakes and rock falls. They are creators and guardians of the large permanent water holes in the region.

When camping near these water holes, people must always remember not to cook meat near the water, as this could bring the local Akurra spirit out, and encourage it to attack them. Swimming at such places is also very dangerous. It is also believed that at the water holes that have dried up, the Akurra spirits are considered to be dead.

Above **Pearl shell ornament.** In some regions, these ornaments are linked to the Rainbow Serpent and are used by rainmakers. A story of a man who came from the clouds relates how he used the lightning that he carried to create rain. Areas where he rested are called "soaks."

Left **Totemic stone.** Totemic patterns carved on stone relate stories of the Dreaming Ancestors. Sometimes these stories are told through aerial drawings of the mythical landscape. These carvings are used in ceremonies and rituals.

SKYWORLD OMENS

Above **Female ancestral figure.** These painted figures are said to represent sacred beings described in tribal mythology. The designs depict seasonal changes.

Aboriginal people were keen observers of the movements of celestial bodies in the night sky. Changes in the Skyworld signaled the timing of events on earth. For example, the halo of the moon was considered by some Kimberley groups to signify the time for the initiation of boys. In the MacDonnell Ranges of Central Australia, the lunar halo was believed to be string being made by the Moon Ancestor from possum fur, which is spun by running a flat hand along the upper leg. Such string is used in the making of ceremonial ornaments. Across many regions in Australia, the arrival in the Skyworld of the Pleiades constellation, which was often seen as a group of sisters, and perhaps one younger brother, was taken as a cue for commencing major ceremonial activities such as initiations.

Many of the planets and constellations were considered by Aboriginal people to be their Ancestors, linked together through kinship and Dreaming events. For instance, the Kaurna people who lived on the Adelaide Plains of South Australia believed that Tindo Yerle, or Sun Father, had a pair of sisters who were "long," and probably comets. Aboriginal people here considered most of the strange events they saw in the sky to be bad omens. In March 1843, a comet seen by Aboriginal groups along the Murray River in South Australia was believed to have been created by powerful sorcerers in the north. Aboriginal people considered it had arrived to punish Europeans who had taken away land from Aboriginal people. The same comet seen in the Port Lincoln area of the Eyre Peninsula in

South Australia caused Aboriginal people to hide in caves. In Central Australia, comets were sometimes believed by desert Aboriginal people to be spears thrown by particular male Ancestors.

In the Adelaide region of South Australia, the exceptions were meteoric lights (a "shooting star" or "falling star"), which the Kaurna people described as "orphans." The rarity of their appearance, and their random pathways across the Skyworld, would have contributed to their status as outsiders. Across Australia, meteors were generally treated as bad omens. In the Lower Murray region of South Australia, an Ancestor named Kulda was believed to be a meteor, who had came out of the Southern Cross. Kulda foretold the coming of a disease epidemic. Whenever a falling star was seen, the Lower Murray people reportedly said *Peika baki*, meaning "Death is coming." Similarly, to the Gundidjmara people of southwestern Victoria, a meteor represented "deformity." The Southern Lights (Aurora Australis) and the eclipse of the moon were also widely treated as bad omens across Aboriginal Australia.

Left *Fishing by Torchlight* by Joseph Lycett (1775–1828). Aboriginal people looked to the sky and stars for signs of change in the Skyworld. These changes indicated the time for special ceremonies, events, or movements of the tribe.

Opposite page **Hunter with spear surrounded by spirits.** Hunting was dictated by the seasons. Aboriginal people used the constellations to predict the change of seasons, as each season influenced the types of animals they could hunt.

MAORI MYTHOLOGY

Right **Sky Father and Earth Mother.** From Te Po, or the great Unknown Darkness, came a series of varying periods of darkness. This creation couple was born from the darkness before knowledge. From their union came the gods of the Maori pantheon.

Below *Volcanic Regions of Pumice Hills Toward Tongariro and Ruapahu* by G.F. Angas (1789–1879). There is a close connection between the physical and the spiritual world in Maori mythology.

The main body of Maori mythology contains three great complexes. The first is the traditions of creation, concerning the genesis of the universe, the heavens and earth, gods, humans, and all animate and inanimate forms. Many of these myths derive from the Polynesian pantheons of creation, and were adapted and localized in Aotearoa-New Zealand. The Maori mythologies of creation are a blend of allegorical explanations, moral codes and prescriptions for behavior, precedents for the existence of social institutions, deep-seated beliefs about the nature of being and non-being, the relationship between the known and the unknown, and the origins of all things seen and unseen. They are a template of deep philosophies and important religious, cultural, and social beliefs.

The second complex involves the demigod cycles, headed by Maui and Tawhaki, and follow on from the creation cycle. Many of the figures in these myths also come from the wider Polynesian body of oral lore. They make an important connection between the gods of creation and humans in the terrestrial world. Gods are the source of all things. Demigods, such as Maui and Tawhaki, therefore act as intermediaries between the gods and humans, fetching knowledge from the deities and transmitting it to humans. This adds order and sense to the world. Demigods also test the parameters of creation by revisiting the threshold laid down in the genesis traditions. Typically one demigod will test the darkness of creation and death by attempting to gain immortality. In the Polynesian pantheons this figure is Maui. Another demigod will characteristically revisit the origins of creation by attempting to ascend into the heavens. In the structure of the numerous Polynesian pantheons, this

Left *The Birth of Tawhaki* by Wilhelm Dittmer (1866–1909). The Maui and Tawhaki cycles illustrate the lives of these demigods, who were able to travel between the world of the gods and the world of the humans. Their adventures also serve as moral instruction.

Te Po-uriuri, represented different shades and depths of the darkness; and Te Po-te-kitea was the darkness within which nothing was known or seen. The descriptions of Te Po sometimes culminated in a numerical sequence of darkness, from Te Po-tuatahi (the First Darkness) to Te Po-tuangahuru (the Tenth Darkness), and on to the hundredth and thousandth darkness, which implied a progression rather than a static state. This great period of darkness is also a metaphor for the mind. Without light there was no knowledge. The abyss of darkness prevailed.

Te Ao (Light) followed and represented the birth of the world and life, the emerging understanding of increasing knowledge, and awareness. Te Kore (Primal Potential, Primeval Source) represented a state of unformed phenomenology or chaos within which lay the latent potential for all things to exist. Te Kore was the source from which all animate and inanimate things took their substance and form. Like Te Po, Te Kore was also characterized by divisions, each with its own descriptive terminology. Te Kore-te-whiwhia (the Source of all Things), Te Kore-te-rawea (the Source of all Forms), and Te Kore-te-matua (the Parental Source) were typical characterizations.

Other versions likened the evolution of the universe to a tree, with its base, tap roots, rootlets, and branching roots reaching out to form a forest. Another theme characterizing evolution was one that connected the emergence of thought to consciousness. Some, or all, of these concepts appear in the same genealogy.

figure is Tawhaki. A second layer of culture hero myths underpins the Maui and Tawhaki cycles. These lay down particular rules, and include the traditions relating to Tinirau, Rata, and Whaka-taupotiki, among many others.

A third body of myths relates to the natural world and includes tales involving Maori astronomy. These traditions reflect a deep-seated intimacy and understanding of the natural world, presenting sophisticated knowledge in poetic form.

CREATION TRADITIONS, DARKNESS AND LIGHT

Maori beliefs about the evolution of the universe are embodied in genealogical form. There are many types of these genealogies, with quite a number of recurring themes. Creation was likened to a series of periods of unknown darkness, light, and primal source or primeval potentiality, each qualified by some descriptive term and/or quantitative sequence. These distinctive periods of time corresponded to eons of cosmological time, when the seeds of the universe scattered throughout the vast emptiness of space came together to form the Sky Father and Earth Mother.

Many creation narratives began with Te Po (Unknown Darkness) which likens creation to the darkness of the womb, an absence of knowledge, and the unknowable nature of ultimate origin. Te Po was timeless with internal divisions: Te Po-nui was the great unknown darkness; Te Po-roa was the extensive darkness; Te Po-kerekere, Te Po-tangotango, and

MAORI GENESIS TABLE

CREATION AS THE GENESIS OF A GREAT FOREST

TE PU	THE ROOT CAUSE
TE WEU	THE EMERGING ROOTLETS
TE MORE	THE FIRM TAPROOT
TE AKA	THE SPREADING VINE
TE TIPURANGA	THE MATURING GROWTH
TE WAONUI-A-TANE	THE GREAT FOREST OF TANE
RANGINUI = PAPATUANUKU	SKY FATHER AND EARTH MOTHER

CREATION AS THE GENESIS OF KNOWLEDGE

TE RAPUNGA	THE SEEKING
TE KUKUNE	THE INCEPTION
TE PUPUKE	THE SWELLING
TE HIHIRI	THE PSYCHIC ENERGY AND DESIRE
TE MAHARA	THE THOUGHT AND REMEMBRANCE
TE HINENGARO	THE CONSCIOUSNESS
TE MANAKO	THE LONGING
KA HUA TE WANANGA	THE FRUITFULNESS OF KNOWLEDGE
RANGINUI = PAPATUANUKU	SKY FATHER AND EARTH MOTHER

THE GODS

After the darkness the creation of the gods began, along with a complex tradition of oral history that provides the background for Maori beliefs.

Sky Father and Earth Mother

Most versions of the cosmogonic genealogy culmi-nated in the two names Rangi (Sky Father), and Papa (Earth Mother). Their marriage produced the gods and, ultimately, all life on earth.

Below **Maori gods, Rangi and Papa.** This heavenly couple were separated by their children, so that the world could have light. Tane (God of the Forests) forced them apart, and soon Rangi became the sky and Papa became the earth.

One traditional chant refers to Rangi as the Great Sky Father (Ranginui), the Encompassing Sky Father (Rangiroa), the Heavenly Winds (Tawhirirangi), the Life-Giving Winds (Te Hauwhakaora), and finally the Winds that Caress the Skin of all People (Te Hau-e-pangia-te-kiri-o-te-tangata). Papa is referred to as the Earth Mother Trampled by the Ancestors (Te Papa-i-taka-takahia-e-nga-matua-tupuna), the Earth Mother Left in Remembrance by the Ancestors (Te Papa-i-wai-hotia-e-ratou-ma), the Earth Mother Stretching unto the Sunrise (Te-Papa-e-maroro-ki-te-itinga), the Earth Mother Stretching unto the Sunset (Te Papa-e-maroro-ki-te-opunga), the Embrac-ing Earth Mother that Comforts all People (Te Papa-awhiawhi-e-awhi-ana-i-a-tatou), the Earth Mother Over Land (Papa-tuanuku), and finally, the Earth Mother Under the Heavens (Papa-tuarangi).

The concept of the Sky Father and Earth Mother is found deep within Polynesian philosophical thought and religion. In Samoa, Tangaloa-lagi was the God of the Heavens, Papatu was the Mountain Father, and Papa'ele was the Earth Mother. In Hawai'i, Rarotonga, and Tahiti, Atea (Wakea in Hawai'i) represented the Sky Father. In Hawai'i Papa was the Earth Mother; in Tahiti she was Papa-tu'oi and Papa-raharaha, the Life-Giving Earth; in Rarotonga she was Papa-i-te-itinga and Papa-i-te-opunga, the Earth Mother at the Sunrise and the Sunset.

The Separation

The most comprehensive account of the Sky Father and Earth Mother comes from the Te Arawa tribes of the central North Island of Aotearoa-New Zealand. This tradition says that the primeval Sky Father and Earth Mother caused darkness because of the close coupling of their bodies in the act of procreation. Their children longed for light to enter the world so that they and all of their descendants could flourish. Some of the children plotted to kill their parents, but one of the sons, Tawhirimatea (God of Wind and Storm), felt pity for his parents and argued that they should not be killed, only separated. One by one, Rongo (God of Cultivated Foods), Haumia (God of Uncultivated Foods), Tangaroa (God of the Oceans), and Tu (God of Human Martial Consciousness) tried to separate their parents. They all failed. Then, Tane (God of the Forests) lay on his back, pressed up-ward with his feet, with all his might, and gradually forced them apart, until one was far above and the other was far below. Tane's separation of the Earth Mother and Sky Father ushered in Te Ao-marama (the World of Light).

The Wars of the Gods

Tawhirimatea was angered by his brothers' treatment of their mother and father, and flew off to join the Sky Father. He carefully gathered together his many offspring, who included the hurricane, storm clouds, hail, rain, and sleet, and sent them to all corners of the heavens. Once they were in place, Tawhirimatea attacked his brothers. The great forest trees of Tane broke under the attack and fell to the ground, becoming food for decay. Having defeated Tane, Tawhirimatea then turned his wrath on the oceanic domain of Tangaroa. Tangaroa fled into the waters of the earth where he became the progenitor of all fish species, reptiles, and sea birds. Next, Tawhirimatea attacked Rongo and Haumia, who were in great fear. However, as they were being attacked the Earth Mother reached out and drew them to the safety of her breast, leaving only their hair above ground. The storms raised by Tawhirimatea passed harmlessly overhead. As a consequence, Rongo and Haumia remained condemned to a lower estate. Rongo became the god of the kumara (the Maori word for sweet potato), agriculture, and peaceful arts. Haumia became the god of the fernroot and wild plants. Tawhirimatea finally turned his rage against Tu, and violently attacked with all his force, but Tu was able to stand against Tawhirimatea when all others failed. When Tawhirimatea's anger finally abated, it

was then Tu's turn to become angry, and he attacked his brothers for failing to support him. He attacked Tane of the forests, felling the rest of his trees and trapping, spearing, and eating his birds; then he wove nets from forest plants, and cast them right out into the sea, so that the children of Tangaroa soon lay in stranded heaps upon the shore; he found Rongo and Haumia's hiding place, and dragged them by their long hair, that was exposed, from the earth, and then ate them.

The war of Tawhirimatea highlights the notion that all life is subject to the tempests of storms, winds, and rain. Tu's assertion of dominance over the natural domains of his brothers reflects the natural order. It also introduced the fundamental dichotomy between *tapu* (sacred) and *noa* (human use).

The world's resources emanated from the realm of gods. This made them sacred. Tu's subordination of the descendants of Tane, Tangaroa, Rongo, and Haumia resulted in their transformation from the sacred estate of gods to the profane level of human use as artifacts and food. Tu made these gods available for human use in the world of light, a task that could be repeated through use of the appropriate incantations and the act of mediating between the gods and their human progeny. Tu represents human consciousness, and the ability to command the resources of nature.

Below **Carving of Rangi and Papa on a war canoe prow.** The carved spirals represent the light and the knowledge that entered the world when Rangi and Papa were separated. The figure also serves as a reminder of the anger of the God of Wind and Storms, Tawhirimatea. The prow is a protective measure against turbulent seas.

Above **Gods and
ancestors.** This carving
illustrates the bond be-
tween ancestors and the
gods. All of nature and the
land was created by the
gods, and the ancestors
protect this legacy.

Opposite page *Tane, God
of the Forests* by Wilhelm
Dittmer (1866–1909).
This god is responsible
for bringing light into the
world. He also adorned his
naked father, Rangi, with
stars, and created the
constellations of the skies.

Tangaroa, the Father of the Seas

Tangaroa (God of the Oceans)—known as Tagaloa-
lagi in Samoa, Takaroa in Hawai'i, Tanaoa in the
Marquesas, Ta'aroa in Tahiti, and Tangaroa in Rarotonga—is the oldest of the Polynesian first order
anthropomorphic gods. One of the better known
West Polynesian accounts is that Tagaloa-lagi dwelt
in the heavens from where he sent a bird named Tuli
to soar across the seas. Tuli returned, and reported
that there was only water, and no land. So Tagaloa-
lagi decided to throw down stones, which became
the islands of Manono, 'Upolu, Savai'I, Manu'a, and
'Olosega, creating the Samoan archipelago.

In East Polynesia, the god Tangaroa is usually
associated with the oceans. To the Maori, Tangaroa
was the progenitor of all life associated with the sea,
and was also considered the great guardian of
canoes. Whenever the people in canoes ventured
out on the ocean to make long journeys, or to catch
Tanga-roa's children, they were careful to perform
the appropriate rituals and make offerings to
Tangaroa, both on departure and arrival.

His numerous offspring included Hine-moana
(the Ocean Maid), Hine-wai (the Water Maiden),
and Hine-awaawa (the Maiden of the Rivers) who
was responsible for the many tidal streams, inland
lakes, and rivers of the region. Tangaroa-whai-ariki
(Tangaroa the Lordly Chief) is one of Tangaroa's
many expansive titles. He was also known as
Tangaroa-whakamau-tai (Tangaroa, the Controller
of Tides), whose breathing was said to control the
ebb and flow of tides.

Tane, God of the Forests

The god Tane originated in East Polynesia, where he was a deity of creation, light, and life. He was known in Rarotonga, Tahiti, Tuamotu, and Hawai'i as Kane, and is identified as a son of Atea, Watea, or Wakea (the Space of Heavens). These names are remembered in one of the Maori titles for Tane's father Rangi-atea, meaning the Great Expanse of the Heavens.

In Maori tradition, it was Tane who separated the Sky Father and Earth Mother. When Tane separated the two, he placed props between them to hold them apart. The event is marked by the name Tane-te-toko-o-te-rangi (Tane with the Posts Upholding all the Heavens). Tane has other extended names that recall how he slowly stretched out his legs while raising his father; these include Tane-tuturi (Tane with Bent up Knees), and Tane-uatika (Tane with a Straight Backbone). It is said that these props can still be seen as the mighty kauri, rimu, kahikatea, and totara trees

TANGAROA AND THE ORIGIN OF MAORI CARVING

In some traditions, as well as being the father of all life in the oceans, Tangaroa also had human offspring. In one East Coast tradition, one of these human children, Rua-te-pupuke, is said to have discovered the art of carving. Tangaroa kidnapped Rua-te-pupuke's son, Te Manu, took him to his home in the sea, and placed him on top of his carved house as a *tekoteko* (gable figure). Rua-te-pupuke found the house and burnt it down after retrieving the carved posts from the porch. These posts became the models for carvers. In a more general way Rua-te-pupuke represents forms of knowledge, the desire for knowledge, and its acquisition. Rua-te-pupuke conveys the idea of the welling up of knowledge. Sometimes the personifications of Rua-te-pupuke are male, and sometimes female.

of Te Waonui-a-Tane (the Great Forests of Tane), or Tanemahuta (God of the Forests).

Tane is credited with giving form, and creating much life after the separation of the Sky Father and Earth Mother, through marriages to feminine aspects of creation. Tane married Hine-tumaunga (Mountain Woman). From this union came all mountains, hills, rocks, pebbles, and sand. He married Hine-parauri (Woman of Autumn Browness), whose children included all the great trees. From his marriage to Hine-waoriki (Woman of Small Foliage) came the small trees, shrubs, vines, and other plants. Tane also married Punga and their children were the reptiles and insects. His marriage to Kahu-parauri (Brown Cloak of Autumn) gave rise to the birds of the forests. The bird song of the *tui* (parsons bird), and *kokako* (bellbird) at the dawn of each day was called Te Putangitangi-a-Tane (The Songs of Tane).

The title Tanenui-a-Rangi (Great Tane of the Heavens) celebrates two mythological events. The Ngati Awa tribe of the Bay of Plenty say that he obtained the stars, the moon, and the sun from Tangotango (Blackness of Heavens), while the Ngati Kahungunu of the East Coast say the stars came from a cloak named Wehinui-a-mamao, with which he adorned the Sky Father. In other traditions, Tane is believed to have retrieved three *kete* (baskets) from the heavens that contained knowledge for humankind. One basket, Te Kete-tuauri (Darkness) contained the unknown; the next, Te Kete-tuatea (Light) contained the things we know, and Te Kete-aronui (Pursuit) contained the knowledge humans currently pursue through study.

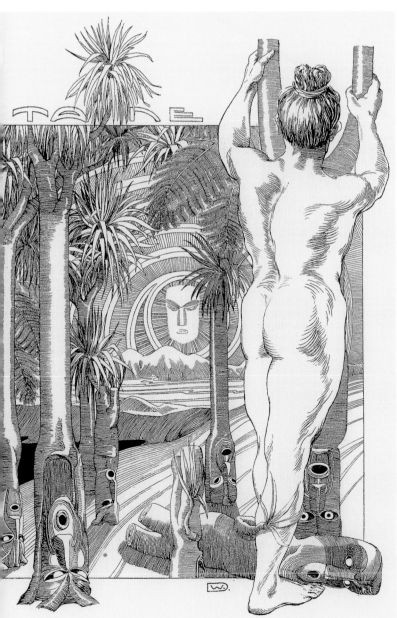

Below **A *tekoteko* or gable figure.** According to Maori legends, Tangaroa (God of the Oceans) accidentally revealed the secrets of carving to Rua-te-pupuke when he rescued his son from the top of the god's carved house. From that day, carving became central to Maori culture.

Above *Taumata atua*, the resting place of Rongo, the God of Cultivated Foods. These stones were placed beside sweet potato crops. Using the correct rituals, Rongo is asked to enter the stone to watch over these crops.

Right **Tu, the God of Warfare.** This carving is believed to be a place where the spirit of the god lives. The *haka* (a dance) used to be performed in honor of Tu, before the warriors headed off for battle.

Rongo, the Origin of the Kumara

Rongo is another well-known East Polynesian deity. In Rarotonga, Rongo was one of the five sons of Atea and Paparoa. In Maori traditions Rongo was the deity of all cultivated plants. Rongo became the progenitor of the kumara at the separation of the heavens and the earth. In the East Coast Ngati Porou traditions, Rongo-maraeroa (Rongo of the Long Marae) is the father of the kumara, while a secondary figure, Rongo-i-amo (Rongo of the Ceremonies), actually conveyed the kumara to human beings in Aotearoa-New Zealand. The Ngati Awa tribe say that Rongo is a son of Tane, and father of the kumara. Rongo's association with cultivation meant that he also represented peace.

Kumara, the main source of carbohydrate, was the most vital crop in Maori society. It was the equivalent of the potato to the Irish, the taro to the Polynesians, and rice in Asia. Kumara was also difficult to grow, as it needed to be specially propagated and prepared for cropping to be successful.

Precise planning was required to ensure success, therefore the association between the kumara and the stars was very strong. The mid-June rising of Matariki (the Pleiades) signaled the time when the earth was turned in preparation for planting. The rising of Poutu-te-rangi (Altair) and Whanui (Vega) in late summer signaled the optimum time for harvesting and storing the kumara. Each tribe had their own account of the first human ancestors to bring the kumara to Aotearoa-New Zealand. Taranaki tribes say it was Turi and his wife, Rongorongo. Bay of Plenty tribes say the canoe Te Aratawhao fetched the kumara from Hawaiki. The Ngati Awa tribe say that Rongo-maui acquired the kumara from the star Whanui (Vega). East Coast tribes say Kahukura went to get the kumara on the canoe, Horouta. South Island traditions say Rongo-i-tua brought the kumara from Hawaiki.

Tu, the Origin of Human Martial Consciousness

Tu is known in Tahiti, Tuamotu, and Rarotonga, and is known as Ku in Hawai'i. In Maoridom he is best known for the tradition of turning on his brothers—the terrestrial gods Tane, Tangaroa, Haumia, and Rongo—consuming them and their offspring. In this way, Tu set the pattern for the future, as he represents human beings, and the brothers he killed and ate are the creatures and plants upon which humans depend for their survival. The martial nature of Tu also means that he is the god of warfare. Humans make war now because Tu did so in the beginning. Warriors were dedicated to Tu as were the chants or *haka* (war dance) they performed when warriors girded themselves for battle. The body of the first enemy warrior killed was often offered to Tu. Even though Tu was primarily the originator of warfare, every tribe also possessed other powerful gods such as Kahukura, Uenuku, or Maru, whom they sought assistance from in times of war. The name Tu is a personification associated with assertive, aggressive action, since the word "tu" literally means to "stand upright." He was honored with many titles, among them Tu-mata-uenga (Tu of the Fierce Countenance), Tu-ka-riri (Tu who Fights), Tu-kai-taua (Tu the Consumer of War Parties), and Tu-mata-kura (Tu with a Flushed Face).

THE FIRST HUMANS

According to various traditions, the gods are responsible for creating humans that combine a human principle with the elements of the divine.

Hine-ahu-one and Hine-titama, The Woman Shaped from Sand

Tane and his brothers embodied *ira atua* (the divine principle). In the most well-known traditions Tane searched for the female element in nature to create *ira tangata* (the human principle). Many traditions say that when Tane was unable to find a suitable female to bear human children, he decided he would create a female for himself.

He went to a beach, Te Oneone-o-Kura-waka (the Sands upon the Vulva) which was on the *mons veneris* of his mother, Papa. Here he modeled from the earth a woman that suited him. This woman was the first human, and was named

Hine-ahu-one (Earth-Formed Maid) or Hine-mata-one (Maid with Earth-Formed Face). Finally, Tane breathed his *mauri*, and now there is a duality of *ira atua* and *ira tangata* in human beings. But humans, unlike gods, are not immortal. When the *mauri* leaves the body death occurs. Only *the wairua*, the spiritual remnant, and *ira atua,* survive death to return to Te Po, back to the beginning from where all things came.

Tane cohabited with Hine-ahu-one, and from his merging with different parts of her body he created human sweat from her head, human pupils from her eyeballs, and mucus and saliva from her nose. In the final act, Tane produced a daughter named Hine-titama (Dawn Maid), also known as Hine-i-tauira (Patterned Maid) and Hine-manuhiri (Newly Arrived Maid). Tane then slept with his daughter to beget more children. On finding out that Tane was her father, Hine-titama fled to the portal of the under-world, Raro-henga. Tane pursued Hine-titama, but she commanded him not to follow as he was to re-main on earth to care for their children in the world of light. Hine-titama promised to wait, and receive them into the world of night in the form of Hine-nui-te-po (Goddess Guardian of Death). Hine-titama's flight from Tane encapsulates the belief that humans came from an original incestuous relationship, as well as dramatizing the serious nature of incest, and sets a social prohibition against its continuation.

This myth also adds further continuity to creation. Creation began from Te Po, and culminated in the for-mation of the Sky Father and the Earth Mother. The food that springs from the bosom of Papa sustains life in this world. It is for this reason that the earth is loved and cherished as a mother. Tane then created humans out of the earth. The creation of human life also predetermined that death would eventually come into the world. Physical death and decay is therefore conceptualized as a return beneath Papa, the portal of Rarohenga, where Hine-nui-te-po awaits as a ben-evolent mother figure to receive the dead, before freeing their *wairua* (spirits) to return through the heavens of the Sky Father, back to Te Po, the origin of all existence. Rarohenga was not to be feared, as it was thought of as a pathway through which the dead would be reunited with their ancestors.

Tiki, the Origin of Sexuality

In other traditions, particularly on the West Coast and in the South Island, the first human made by Tane was a man named Tiki. In some traditions Tane

Right *Kuwaha pataka.* This is a symbol of the gateway to the under-world, or Rarohenga. The figure represents Papa, the Earth Mother, awaiting the arrival of the dead.

47

makes a wife for Tiki. In other accounts, it is Tiki himself who creates the first person. And some traditional accounts bring these ideas together by saying that Tiki is Tane's penis. When Tiki makes the first human he is sometimes regarded as a son of Rangi and Papa. In one account, Tiki's wife was formed from earth by the echo and the quivering heat of the sun.

Another story is that Tiki took red clay and kneaded it with his own blood, forming eyes and limbs, and gave the image breath. Tiki's main symbolism seems to be as the initiator of sexuality and human reproduction. Even when Tane was believed to have made the first woman, or slept with her, lovemaking was Tiki's specialty. In songs, Te Mahi-a-Tiki (Tiki's Work)

Right *Maui Fishing up the Land* by Wilhelm Dittmer (1866–1909). Using a magical fishhook, and some of his blood and hair as bait, Maui casts out to sea. With his mighty strength, he hauled up all of the islands of Aotearoa-New Zealand. Maui is a popular demi-god of Maori mythology.

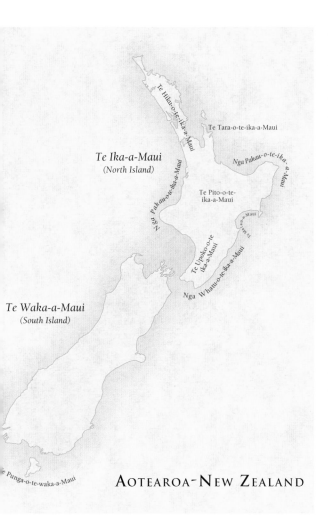

Te Hihi-o-te-ika-a-Maui

Te Tara-o-te-ika-a-Maui

Te Ika-a-Maui
(North Island)

Nga Pakau-o-te-ika-a-Maui

Pukau-o-te-ika-a-Maui

Te Pito-o-te-
ika-a-Maui

Nga N...

...Maui

Te Upoko-o-te
ika-a-Maui

Nga Whatu-o-te-ika-a-Maui

Te Waka-a-Maui
(South Island)

...e Punga-o-te-waka-a-Maui

AOTEAROA-NEW ZEALAND

are caused by the cycles of the sun. Another of the main themes encapsulated in the Maui myth cycles is that he is a precocious youngster, an archetypal culture hero who overcomes the disadvantage of being the last born to gain fame and adulation as a benefactor of humankind. He also stands as a model to all *teina* (juniors) that they can succeed, provided they have the required personal qualities and traits exemplified by Maui—such as intelligence, cunning, initiative, boldness, and determination.

Maui and his Family

Maori oral traditions say that the human offspring of the gods increased and multiplied, and did not know of death, until the generation of Maui. They also say that Maui was abandoned at birth. The most well-known tradition from Te Arawa in the central North Island is that he was aborted by his mother, and cast into the sea, wrapped in her loin cloth, or in a basket made from her hair. Washed ashore, entangled in seaweed and swarmed over by gulls and flies, Rangi is said to have rescued him and nursed him back to life.

On reaching adulthood, Maui's first exploit was to find his family. This dramatized the pivotal nature of identity because, in the Maori world, talent without identity is insufficient to succeed. On finding his kin, Maui legitimized his ancestral credentials. With his place in the world secured, Maui set about acquiring knowledge from his ancestors, because talent and identity are most effective when they are balanced with knowledge.

Maui and Knowledge

From his grandparent, Muri-rangawhenua, Maui acquired a jawbone symbolizing knowledge. From this, he was immediately able to manufacture hooks and weapons, and began his journey as a benefactor for humankind. Maui also used a hook, fashioned from the jawbone, to fish up the North Island of Aotearoa-New Zealand.

Maui's fishing up of the North Island of Aotearoa-New Zealand is celebrated in the name Te Ika-a-Maui (the Fish of Maui—the North Island), and the South Island is called Te Waka-a-Maui (the Canoe

was the act of coitus rather than procreation. The stories of Tiki and Hine-mata-one come from ancient accounts in the Marquesas, and Tuamotu and Tahiti archipelagoes.

THE MAUI CYCLE

This is one of the key demigod cycles that follow on from the creation cycle.

Maui in the Pacific

Maui is the most ancient figure in the pantheons of mythology carried by the ancestors of the Maori to Aotearoa-New Zealand. Maui is also widely known throughout the islands of Polynesia, Melanesia, and Micronesia. The full geographic extent of these traditions range from the island of Yap in Micronesia to the west, to Mangareva in the east, and north from Hawai'i to Aotearoa-New Zealand in the south. The distribution of these traditions suggests a pre-Polynesian origin, meaning that they have been told for 3,500 years or more.

Across the Pacific, the Maui cycles explain how the things necessary to sustain life were obtained, including the acquisition of knowledge, the finding of land, the origin of fire, and the seasonal cycles that of Maui—from which he fished up the North Island). Stewart Island is called Te Punga-o-te-waka-a-Maui (the Anchor Stone of the Canoe of Maui). Te Hiku-o-te-ika-a-Maui (the Tail of the Fish of Maui) refers to the narrow stretch of land in the far north of the North Island. The thin stretch of the Coromandel Peninsula is Te Tara-o-te-ika-a-Maui (the Barb of the Fish of Maui), with the barb coming from the belief that the fish of Maui was a stingray. The coastal abutments north of Gisborne on the East Coast of the North Island and around New Plymouth and Mount Taranaki on the West Coast form Nga Pakau-o-te-ika-a-Maui (the Wings of the Stingray of Maui). Te Pito-o-te-ika-a-Maui (the Navel of the Fish of Maui) is Lake Taupo in the middle of the North Island. Te Matau-a-Maui (the Hook of Maui) is the curve of Hawke Bay. Te Upoko-o-te-ika-a-Maui (the Head of the Fish of Maui) is the Wellington area. The waters of Wellington Harbour and Lake Wairarapa form Nga Karu-o-te-ika-a-Maui, or Nga Whatu-o-te-ika-a-Maui (the Eyes of the Fish of Maui).

Maui also slowed the sun's passage across the sky, putting in place the customs for the working day, according to seasonal agricultural cycles. He also provided human beings with a valuable companion,

when he turned his brother-in-law Irawaru into a dog for beating him at fishing. The kuri (Polynesian dog) served as a valuable resource. Its flesh was eaten, the skin used to make cloaks, and its delicate bones crafted into ornaments and small tools. The event dramatized the uneasy nature of the relationship between the brothers-in-law.

Maui wrested the secret of fire from the fingers of another grandparent, Mahuika. He did this by extinguishing all the fires in the village, and asked for the fingers of his grandparent one at a time, until only one was left. Mahuika, realizing that Maui was tricking them, hurled the last finger at him, causing the world to catch on fire. Maui escaped by taking the form of a pigeon, and calling on Tawhirimatea to extinguish the fires with rain.

The fire then became embedded in the trees of the forest, and it was from these trees that the ancestors of the Maori were able to make fire to keep warm, and cook food.

Maui's adventures brought him closer and closer to the parameters of primeval forces. This adventure nearly caused his death, and is a lesson that the fullest extent of human ability cannot overcome the primeval forces of nature.

Below **Jade pendants.** These pendants are a symbolic reminder of the fishhook that Maui fashioned out of a jawbone to create the islands of Aotearoa-New Zealand. Fishhook replicas were worn by chiefs and priests, and were seen as a mark of great knowledge.

asleep with her legs apart. Maui was determined to enter Hine-nui-te-po's body, consume her heart, and then aimed to reappear from her mouth, reversing birth, so that people would be able to live forever.

As Maui started on his task, the feathered cheeks of the watching birds puckered with suppressed laughter. When his head and arms disappeared, the fantail burst out laughing. Hine-nui-te-po awoke, clapped her legs together, and cut Maui in two. Maui was the first being to die, and because he failed in his self-appointed task, all humans are born mortal.

The adventures of Maui reflect the human reality that great things can be accomplished through a combination of talent, secure identity, and the acquisition of knowledge, but only within the boundaries of life and death as laid down in creation.

Left *Hine-nui-te-po, the Goddess Guardian of Death* by Wilhelm Dittmer (1866–1909). Maui bravely braced himself to face this terrifying goddess, but he was fatally defeated by her. As a result, death became part of the life cycle of humankind.

THE TAWHAKI CYCLE

The Whaitiri-Kai-tangata, Hema, and Tawhaki cycle is the most enduring genealogical sequence in the East Polynesian pantheon of demigod traditions. This bespeaks the power of Whaitiri, and the regard in which she was held. Whaitiri was called Hina-hana-ia-ka-malama in Hawai'i and 'Ina-ma-nguru-nugru in Rarotonga. Hema was also known in Hawai'i, Tahiti, and the Tuamotu archipelago, and as

Maui and Death

Maui prepared himself for one last adventure. His parents told him that Hine-nui-te-po (the Goddess Guardian of Death) lay on the horizon. Her body was like that of a human being, but her eyes were greenstone, her hair sea-kelp, her mouth was like that of a barracuda, and sharp flints of obsidian and greenstone were set between her thighs. Maui took with him the smallest birds of the forest—the tomtit, the robin, the gray warbler, and the fantail—and set off toward the horizon. There he found Hine-nui-te-po

HEITIKI

Heitiki are traditional ornaments made out of *pounamu* (greenstone), or whalebone, and worn around the neck as items of adornment. In traditional Maori society Heitiki represented fertility, birth, and life. They were often associated with formal betrothals, marriage celebrations, and important births. The first Heitiki was said to have been worn by Hine-te-iwaiwa (Woman of Subtle Light). Hine-te-iwaiwa appears in many myths. She is often associated with the origins of female action songs, and is one of several female personifications of moonlight, linking the cycle of the waxing and waning moon with that of female menstruation. Heitiki also represented ancient genealogies, and were therefore highly prized as gifts of honor and

respect. In modern times, Heitiki continue to be presented as gifts to respected elders, visitors, or dignitaries. Older, and much more valuable, Heitiki presentations from Maori people never become absolute personal property as it is expected that the Heitiki will be eventually returned to the presenter's tribe.

Right **Heitiki pendant.** Prized as personal ornaments, some heitiki became clan heirlooms passed down for many generations. They are believed to embody *mana*, or the spirit of the tribe.

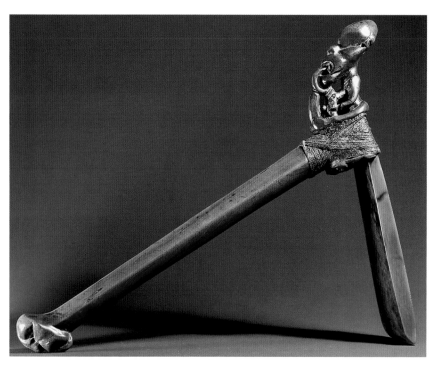

Above *Tokipoutangata,* **ceremonial adze.** This is a ritual tool used to invoke the gods when the first chips of a canoe are carved.

actions made certain that her grandson, Tawhaki, would become a great leader. After his birth, Whaitiri set in place a sequence of events leading Tawhaki on a series of adventures that culminated in his ascent into the heavens where he was finally reunited with her at the point of creation.

'Ema in Rarotonga. Tawhaki was known as Kaha'i in Hawai'i, Tafa'i in Tahiti, Tahaki in Tuamotu, and as Ta'aki in Rarotonga.

Whaitiri, Kaitangata, and Hema

Whaitiri or Whatatiri (Thunder), a cannibal, is the most potent female demigod figure in Maori oral traditions. Some Maori accounts hold that it was she who performed the *karakia* (ritual chants) that allowed Tane to separate the Sky Father and the Earth Mother. Other myths say that she came down from the sky, and married the man Kai-tangata (Man-eater), thinking that he shared her taste for human flesh because of his name. Disappointed at finding that this was not so, she left him to look after their son, Hema. Whaitiri guided Hema toward marrying a woman of high status so that the genealogical lines of her descendants would increase. Her

Many stars cannot be concealed by a small cloud.
MAORI PROVERB

Tawhaki

Hema had two sons, Tawhaki and Karihi. As guided and predicted by Whaitiri, Tawhaki became a great leader. Where Maui tested the parameters of life and death by exploring the pathway to Te Po guarded by Hine-nui-te-po, Tawhaki retested the parameters of creation by ascending to the heavens. Each significant event in Tawhaki's life represents a step toward this goal and reunification with Whaitiri. Tawhaki overcame the many challenges that faced him through the assistance of a number of benevolent female figures, such as a sister, mother, or aunt who, as representations of Whaitiri, his grandmother, increased in potency from one adventure to the next, only revealing their true identity when Tawhaki was considered ready to know.

Maori myths say the first significant event occurred when Tawhaki was attacked, injured, and, in some of these myths, killed by his relations who were jealous of his high status. In some accounts Tawhaki was revived by his wife Hine-piri-piri, in others it was his mother, sister, aunts, or other women who rescued him. In another adventure Tawhaki is said to have married Tangotango, the Blackness of the Heavens found in the very boundaries of Te Po. On returning to the heavens she indicated that Tawhaki should follow. Eventually, Tawhaki and his younger brother, Karihi, started to climb into the heavens. Traditions say that at the beginning of their journey they found an old blind

Above **Lizard from a storehouse roof.** The lizard is a symbol of life and death for the Maori people. It also represents the combination of *mana* (spiritual power) and *tapu* (sacred creation), a strong spiritual force that influences the specific way the mediating rituals between the gods and the humans must be conducted.

woman named Matuku-mata-kamo-kamo. She sat counting sweet potatoes, her only food. The brothers tormented her by snatching the food away, upsetting her tally. Eventually, they made themselves known to her, and Tawhaki restored her sight. In return, the old woman gave them advice about the ascent to the sky. Karihi tried first, but made the mistake of climbing up the *aka taepa* (hanging vine). He was blown about by the winds of heaven, and was killed. Tawhaki climbed up the *aka matua* (parent vine), reciting the appropriate chants, and entered the heavens. Here, he was reunited with Whaitiri, who rewarded him with chants from Tama-i-waho, and with remarriage to Tangotango. Some traditional accounts say he was imbued with supernatural powers in warfare, and that lightning emanated from his armpits. The tenet of the Tawhaki cycle is one where humans cannot defeat death, but they are able to, and can, attain extraordinary heights in life through their respect for its gifts, which ultimately came from the heavens through the Sky Father.

OTHER CULTURE HEROES

There are a number of demigods that play a role in Maori traditions. Here are some key heroes, and their influence on the importance of rituals for humans when negotiating with the gods.

Rata

After Maui, Rata is the mostly widely known demi-god in the Pacific. The Tongans speak of him as Lasa, the Samoans as Lata, the Hawai'ians as Laka, and the Rarotongans as Raka. Rata's most famous adventure is the construction of a canoe to be used to avenge his father's death, which happened at the hands of ancestral enemies. By forgetting to follow the appropriate rituals, his first attempt to fell a tree for the hull of the canoe failed. When this omission was fixed, the guardians of the forest stopped obstructing the work, and helped Rata complete his canoe. Rata sailed off and defeated his enemies. Rata reinforced the sanctity of nature, and reminded the Maori that the resources of nature came from the gods, and permission of the gods must be sought before they could be used. This also clarified the idea of *mana* (mandated spiritual power) and *tapu* (sacredness of creation). Rata was highborn, and had a just cause to build the canoe; this gave him *mana*. However, *mana* could not be exercised without negotiating the *tapu,* the power of creation through mediating rituals.

Tinirau

Tinirau is another important Polynesian culture hero known in Rarotonga and Tahiti; he is also known in

Above **Ritual war canoe.** Used by both gods and demi-gods, the war canoe was considered a prized possession. The spirits of the ancestors were consulted before the building and carving began.

Above *Ta Moko,* or Maori tattoo. The distinctive patterns of these facial tattoos represent specific ancestors. They are also a sign of great courage, and are regarded as the key to revealing a person's true spiritual identity.

performed amorous dances to make Kae laugh, they put him into a trance, and then carried him off to be killed by Tinirau. Kae's teeth are remembered in the carving pattern Te Kata-a-Kae (the Laughter of Kae) where the edges of the traditional spiral patterns are indented to represent his crooked teeth. This pattern also represents the wealth of the whale, which was an important commodity in pre-European Maori society, as it was a source of bone for tools and weapons, and provided meat for food.

Whakataupotiki

Whakataupotiki is another important figure whose adventures laid down the dictates of warfare. In one of his main adventures Whakataupotiki adopted a disguise to enter the camp of his enemies. There, he kidnapped one of them for interrogation to gain intelligence about his enemies. Having done that, he organized his men into attacking columns and ambushed his foes while they slept at dawn. In another campaign, Whakataupotiki defeated 10 men in successive single-handed combat.

For the commander of warriors, the dictates of Whakataupotiki included careful selection of personnel; military drills, practicing orders of battle; the disposition of warriors into assault, supporting, and reserve columns; disguise; spying and reconnaissance to gain intelligence on the enemy; interrogation of prisoners; denial of intelligence to the enemy; and other exploits. Maori war parties were called Te Hokowhitu-a-Tu (the 140 of Tu—the God of War), after the tenets of Whakataupotiki. These tenets of war were followed, and explain the successes of Maori leaders in the colonial period against the British army that outnumbered and outgunned them. Maori war strategies were subtler than the European traditions of bombardment and the wasteful expenditure of human life by frontal assault.

ASTRONOMICAL KNOWLEDGE

This is an essential knowledge that explains and gives expression to the change of season, traditional farming practices, and respect for natural cycles.

Tamanui-te-Ra, the Sun

Traditions say that the sun (Tamanui-te-Ra) was placed in the sky by Tane after he had separated the heavens and earth. Some traditions claim there is a bird in the sun, but others say that Te Manu-i-te-Ra (The Bird in the Sun) is the sun itself. Sunrise was associated with life and well-being, and the sunset with waning health and death. The east was a propitious direction. At divination ceremonies, it was a

Bellona (a remote Polynesian region) as Tinipau, in Samoa as Tigilau, in Tonga as Sinilau, and as Kinilau in Hawai'i. He is associated with traditions about the origin of performing arts.

Maori traditions say that Tinirau married Hinauri, a sister of Maui. When her child was born, a priest named Kae performed the ritual birth ceremony. After this was done, Tinirau lent Kae his pet whale, Tutunui, to take him home. In spite of strict instructions to the contrary, Kae foundered the whale in shallow water, where it died, and was eaten by Kae and his people. Tinirau sent his sisters to capture Kae, telling them that they could find him by getting him to reveal his overlapping front teeth. To make sure they had found the right man, the sisters

THE ORIGIN OF *TA MOKO* (MAORI TATTOO)

One day, the chief Mataora (Face of the Living) was visited by young people from Rarohenga (the underworld). With them was the daughter of Hine-nui-te-po (Goddes Guardian of Death) and her husband, Uetonga. Her name was Niwareka, and Mataora fell in love with her. They married, and were happy together until one day Mataora became jealous of Niwareka, and hit her. She returned home to Rarohenga. Grieving, Mataora followed her to Uetonga's house. Uetonga agreed to tattoo Mataora, using the technique of deep puncturing. During the tattooing, Mataora sang of his sorrow and his search for Niwareka. Niwareka heard him, and returned.

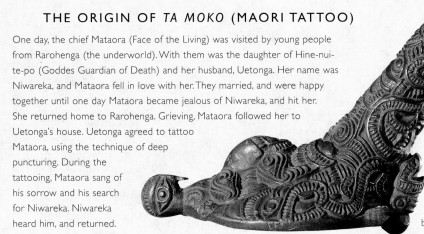

Permission was granted for Mataora's return to his world. However, he forgot to leave an appropriate offering for Kuwatawata, the guardian of the portal between Rarohenga and the human world, so a decree was set that living humans should no longer enter the underworld. *Ta Moko* reminds Maori people of the boundaries between life and death, the ancestors who have already departed, and the guardians that await them. The honor of being tattooed requires wearers to treat others with respect.

Left ***Ta Moko* funnel.** A feeding funnel was used to prevent food from touching the tattooed person's lips. Any contact with food before the tattoo work had healed would remove spiritual power.

good omen if the ceremonial rods fell toward the east, a bad one if they fell toward the west. One tradition from the Ngati Awa tribe of the Bay of Plenty demonstrates the awareness the Maori had about the movement of heavenly bodies. Te Manu-i-te-Ra was married to two sisters, Hine-takurua (Winterwoman) and Hine-raumati (Summerwoman). During summer he lived with Hine-raumati, whose house was on land in the south. During autumn he would venture northward, having affairs with several female stars, before living with Hine-takurua, whose house lay in the sea to the north. This tradition is a clear allegorical depiction of the summer and winter solstice.

From the Bay of Plenty, where this tradition is told, the sun rises over the hills from the land during summer, and from the ocean to the north during winter.

Hine-raumati bore Te Manu-i-te-Ra a son named Tane-rore (Shimmering Tane), who composed the first *haka* (action dance) celebrating the fine weather and the bounty of summer. The quivering movements of his dance are still seen in the shimmering heat of summer days.

Te Manu-i-te-Ra sent Auahi-tu-roa (Long Current of Smoke) to earth as a comet, where he married a beautiful woman named Mahuika, and gave her the gift of fire. Mahuika held the gift from her husband in her fingers, before implanting the fire in a number of softwood and hardwood trees. The rubbing of a hardwood stick against a flat piece of softwood was used to make fire. This myth explained the origins of a form of dance, the heat of summer, the existence of comets, and the gift of fire.

Left *Battle of Gate Pah* by Orlando Norie (1832–1901). Whakataupotiki is a Maori hero who developed specific approaches and strategies toward war. These principles saw the success of Maori leaders in battles against the Europeans.

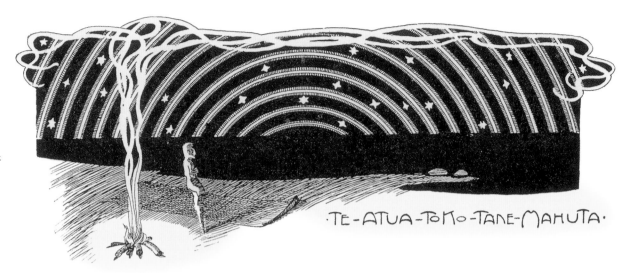

·TE-ATUA-TOKO-TANE-MAHUTA·

Te Marama, the Moon

All living beings beneath the moon will die, while those above it will live forever. The fate of Te Marama (the Moon) is different, because every month the moon dies, then lives again. The moon was also associated with the menstrual cycle of women, and often referred to as Hina (Maiden), hence the saying, "Na Hina te po, na Hina te ao" (By Hina is the day and the night).

Traditions from the far north of the North Island say that Rona, a woman, set out one night carrying her gourd to go and draw water. When the Moon passed behind a cloud, she stumbled among the bushes and cursed the Moon for not giving light. This enraged the Moon, who came down and seized her. Rona clung to a nearby tree, but this tree was suddenly pulled from the ground, roots and all. When the Moon is full, Rona can be seen with her tree and her gourd. The insults she shouted at the Moon were sometimes regarded as the origin of curses and vilification in this world, and a saying warned "Ka mahara ki te he o Rona" (Remember Rona's mistake). Rona was thought to regulate the tides, so another of her names was Rona-whakamau-tai (Rona, the Controller of the Tides). The tribes along the West Coast of the North Island tell a similar story, except that Rona is a man, a *rangatira* (high chief) who is annoyed that he has to draw water in his wife's absence. In the southern Bay of Plenty and the Urewera region, Rona went searching for water with her sister Tangaroa-a-roto, and when Rona cursed, both women were carried up to become the Moon's wives. In the Hawke Bay region, and some parts of the South Island, the phases of the Moon, along with eclipses, were thought to be due to the constant struggles between the Moon and Rona.

Kopu (Venus) and Pare-a-rau (Jupiter)

Kopu (Venus—the Bowl) and Pare-a-rau (Jupiter—the Headband of a Hundred Lovers) are the two brightest bodies in the heavens after the sun and the moon. Kopu and Pare-a-rau were said to be husband and wife. Their house was on the horizon. Traditions say that Pare-a-rau would sometimes leave her husband, and embark on numerous affairs with other stars. Maori beliefs about these stars reflect an appreciation of planetary motion. The path of Venus is closer to the sun than that of the Earth, therefore it is only seen on the eastern horizon before dawn, and on the western horizon after sunset when the sun is absent from the sky. Jupiter, whose path around the sun is wider than that of Venus and the Earth, is seen tracking across the sky for much of the year. When Pare-a-rau is on the horizon with Venus she is at home with her husband, but when tracking through the heavens alone she is thought to be embarking on her amorous affairs. Venus was also called Tawera (Burnt Up) when seen on the eastern horizon, because the rising sun soon obliterated its appearance. Venus was called Meremere-tu-ahiahi (the

Evening Display) when on the western horizon, because he was able to show his entire luster once the sun had set.

THE NEW YEAR STARS

The Maori New Year is in the middle of June, when a line of stars including Atutahi or Atuatahi (Canopus), Takurua (Sirius), Puanga (Rigel), Tautoru (Orion), and Matariki (the Pleiades) rise in the morning on the eastern horizon.

Atutahi or Atuatahi is one of the brightest stars in the southern sky and stands out, so its name means to "stand alone." This was often the main New Year star for tribes in the South Island. Takurua is the brightest body seen in the heavens after the sun, the moon, Venus, and Jupiter, and its appearance signals the coming of winter. Puanga was said to be a daughter of Rehua (Antares), the chief of all stars. This star

was held to be of particular significance by northern tribes and was their marker of the New Year. Tautoru, meaning Three Abreast, referred to the belt of Orion.

The small cluster of seven stars known as the Pleiades has the Maori name, Matariki, which means Little Eyes. Matariki is often thought to be a woman, with her six daughters making up the seven star configuration. For many tribes, the appearance of Matariki at dawn (or sometimes the first new moon after their appearance) marks the end of the old year and the beginning of the new. When Matariki first reappeared, she and her daughters were greeted with laments remembering the loss of those who had died in the previous year.

Matariki also brought food supplies to human beings, marking the times to till the earth and signaling when the birds and other game, grown fat on berries and other foods in season, were able to be caught, collected, and preserved.

Above **Maori rock drawing.** Early records of these paintings show the hunting and gathering during the seasons. The birdlike ancestor figures are pictured with their arms outstretched as they try to trap a shark.

57

MYTHOLOGY OF
THE AMERICAS

NORTH AMERICAN MYTHOLOGY

Before European ships reached the shores of North America, life among the tribal communities was never marked by a fragmented existence. Tribal communities embraced a worldview in which all aspects of life were connected (language, teachings, ceremonies, food gathering). This, of course, is not to suggest that indigenous peoples lived in paradise. The ways of harmony included acceptance of social disruption, even unforeseen tragedy. And myth played a vital role in explaining the ways of the world, and the individual's place in it. In our modern world we note a conspicuous reality of detachment from the natural and spiritual world around us, and it is with this contextual understanding of historical tribal communities that we approach the role of myth among native North Americans—both yesterday and today.

Myth was once at the core of maintaining this harmonious balance in tribal life. Stories offered indigenous peoples an understanding of many different things: their origins; their relationship to land, water, and animals; and their connection to the spirit world. Myths also provided guidance for finding an individual's place within the village community. All of the above served to shape an expansive tribal worldview that informed tribal communities of collective values, and of a complex body of knowledge that served to direct tribes for a number of generations.

Storytellers (often elders) held a special place within the community, for they were the teachers, the bearers of these ancient stories. It was their duty to impart this knowledge to the villagers, especially the young ones—"indoctrinating" them into the fold with the

ultimate goal of perpetuating the tribal way of life. Often infused with sacred ceremonies or celebrations, tribal myths were the foundation of tribal existence, purpose, and identity.

The season of storytelling in tribal communities was held in high regard among tribal members. In these tribal worlds, context was critical to storytelling. How these tribal myths were presented was just as important as the message. In fact, one can observe that the true power of tribal myths rested on proper setting. Myth was delivered orally to tribal members. Parents and children reverently listened as their storyteller told great tales of how the Creator formed the world, or how evil was overcome with the help of kind spirits. From this intimate setting villagers would depart, deeply impressed.

THE INFLUENCE OF EUROPEANS

One of the most severe disruptions forced upon tribal communities by the presence of Europeans was the end of traditional tribal life as it was known. The dismantling of tribal village systems resulted in a massive rupture of social order. Traditions were lost at a rapid pace as the colonization spread. As Native Americans were displaced or dispersed (a number of tribes were wiped out entirely), so too were their ancient ways. The end of traditional tribal community life was evidenced not only by the loss of land, but also by the demise of culture, language, traditional knowledge, and vital ceremonies. Nearly every tribe on the continent faced a harsh measure of loss.

For those tribes that have survived it has been and will continue to be a different world. Though there are native communities living on partitioned land, the infiltration of European life (the institution of a nuclear family; modern technology; as well as political, social, and religious worldviews) have prevented nearly all native communities from returning in entirety to the tribal-centered world of the past. Today's tribal forms of government no longer function like ancient tribal governments. As "wards of the state," native communities have been forced to accept from the Federal Government systems of governance that are in direct contradiction to traditional tribal systems. And many would argue that these forced-upon forms of government have been, and are still today, aimed at

Right **Shield, Plains culture.** Important symbols were often painted on shields to enlist the help of spirits in protecting the shield's owner. In this case a bear is bravely coming out of its hole to face a barrage of bullets—giving the owner the strength of the bear spirit to face his enemies.

Left **Alaskan Eskimo mask.** Native North Americans celebrate their connection to the spiritual world. This Eskimoan mask represents the flight of a shaman's spirit, with the face in the center of the mask symbolizing the shaman's soul.

subverting or perhaps blocking any attempts by tribal people to rule over themselves in the original ways their ancestors once ruled.

But in this postcolonial world tribes are seeking to reclaim those old ways as much as possible, despite the change in landscape. Tribes are trying to recover that which was taken from them. And while many myths were scattered, or have been lost through the years, many stories remain alive—saved by memory and recorded in oral libraries hidden deep within the hearts, minds, and souls of tribal elders. These are the amazing stories that continue to be passed down from generation to generation.

THE IMPORTANCE OF CONTEXT

While native people across North America have held on to many of their greatest and most powerful myths, it is evident that the destruction of the traditional way of life has robbed these tribal myths of their full authority over the descendants of those who were first affected by European colonization. For if we recognize that the power of tribal myths is contingent upon a proper setting for storytelling, then we must wonder

what role tribal myths play in these modern times for native North Americans, given this loss of traditional tribal communities?

This important issue of contextual loss begs the question: have tribal myths forever lost their highest influence, that of informing one's purpose, place, and direction in the world because there no longer remains traditional tribal villages? If the answer is yes, then is the retelling of tribal myths, at best, a glimpse into how indigenous North Americans once lived a life of balance with their world? Or, at worst, is the retelling of tribal myths merely an entertaining act of theater intended to humor the audience, to tickle the imaginations of children and adults alike?

And perhaps an equally important question to address is this: what role do indigenous North American myths play in the lives and belief systems of the rest of the world's populations? Of course, this and all such questions about traditional tribal knowledge are best left to those who study history, race, anthropology, and other related disciplines, but one must certainly wonder how it would be a different world if it were informed with a base of indigenous North American knowledge.

Above **Bentwood serving dish, Yup'ik culture, south-western Alaska.** A male caribou is linked to his spiritual counterpart, which is shown with three strange legs. Native North Americans believe that all animals have a soul, and that hunters need to treat their prey with respect if they are to ensure continued success with their hunting.

Right **Sinister spirit figure, Eskimo culture, Alaska.** Many spirits—both benevolent and malevolent—inhabit the Eskimo world. Evil spirits of the sky would create devastating storms, while diabolical earth spirits could make unwary travelers disappear into thin air.

But for the purposes of this chapter we should consider what is to be gained in learning some of the many rich tribal myths of the native North Americans. Tribal myths are finding a place in the popular culture of modern North America. Not too many years ago a Native American playwright was commissioned by a theater company to write a special play for children based on a tribal myth of her choosing. Once the play had been written she stopped in to see how the rehearsals were going. She burst into tears when she realized just how the theater company had coopted her script, how they turned that myth into nothing more than a fairy tale aimed at amusing children. This tribal myth that was once greatly revered as vital knowledge was now, in fact, nothing more than shallow entertainment for the audience.

An editor and/or writer should have a sense of trepidation if committed to retelling indigenous North American myths in published form. Certainly publishers should be fully aware of the fact that these stories lose so much of their power when removed from their original, traditional setting. Despite these concerns, it is apparent that if the reader pays close attention to these tribal myths, they will make a wonderful discovery. The reader will find that tribal myths still feature a wealth of ancient knowledge and wisdom—that not even the printed page could rob them of their secrets. If read carefully and thoughtfully, tribal myths still reveal age-old truths, no matter how removed they are from proper context.

A DIVERSE ARRAY OF MYTHS

The fascinating myths included in this chapter represent the tribal diversity of North American indigenous communities. There are well over 500 Native American tribes within the borders of the contiguous U.S.A., and more than 250 Inuit tribes in the North American Arctic, which includes Alaska, Canada, and Greenland. (Note that the definition of "tribe" is different in Native American and Inuit cultures—Native American tribes can be an amalgamation of several groups or "bands," while Inuit tribes usually only encompass a single village.)

Included in this anthology are myths from nearly every region of North America. From Greenland, Canada, and Alaska, to the northwest, down the Pacific Coast and to the southwest, through the mountains, across the Great Plains, around the Great Lakes, trailing the northeast and eastern region, then throughout the south the reader will find myths that are as similar as they are different. What these tribes share is a worldview that is based on their relationship to land. The stories of land-based "religions" instruct us on how to live in balance with our world. Tribal myths emerge from our knowledge of the land.

Many of the major themes found in native North American myths are covered in this chapter—there are stories about creation, hero journeys, tricksters, spirits, animals, love, humans, Mother Earth, the sky, and life's passages. Myths from various tribal regions are presented, and the panoramic retelling of the myths should give the reader a taste of the diversity and commonalities among tribal nations. Given that myth is a spiritual language, if it is accurately decoded

Below **Shell gorget (throat pendant), Mississippian Southern Cult.** Flourishing between A.D. 1000 and 1500 in the southeastern woodlands of the U.S.A., the people of this culture decorated much of their art with woodpeckers, their symbol for war.

it can open up the universe to any and all with an ear to hear. One might be surprised to learn that North American tribal myths trace themes similar to those of other ancient myth-making cultures, such as the good and evil of the spirit world, and how the earth was formed. As an example, there are many tribal creation stories that tell of a great flood that covered the earth, similar to the flood in the biblical story of Noah. One can also find an indigenous version of some of the myths told by the Greeks, such as the story of Pandora's box. The universality of these myths is fascinating, but upon closer reading of the stories one will find an entirely different world and worldview that is clearly from a tribal perspective.

These myths come from a wide range of sources, and are retold with noticeable differences to the stories that readers may have heard or read before. This is due to the fluid nature of the myths, which allows the story-teller to alter the stories based on his or her own knowledge and ex-perience. It should be pointed out that even before the arrival of the Europeans, tribal myths were quite fluid. Stories evolved almost with each retelling, and storytellers often introduced new characters and plot lines, changing the myths over a period of years. And throughout native North American communi-ties today, these myths continue to evolve. But their central truths remain and the ancient knowledge has stayed intact, despite the many changes during retellings.

Finally, it should be understood that traditional storytellers never told their myths in the manner in which modern Western readers are accustomed. Western structures of plot development—introducing conflict and gaining resolution—were not the indigenous ways of conveying knowledge. It was more common for a tribal storyteller to embrace a circular style of telling, which kept the myths fresh. This style allowed the storyteller to reveal knowledge when they felt it was

most important, or would have the most impact. How-ever, the myths in this chapter are presented in a mostly conventional, Western form of storytelling. Though they have been reshaped, it is believed that the ancient knowledge still lingers within these pages.

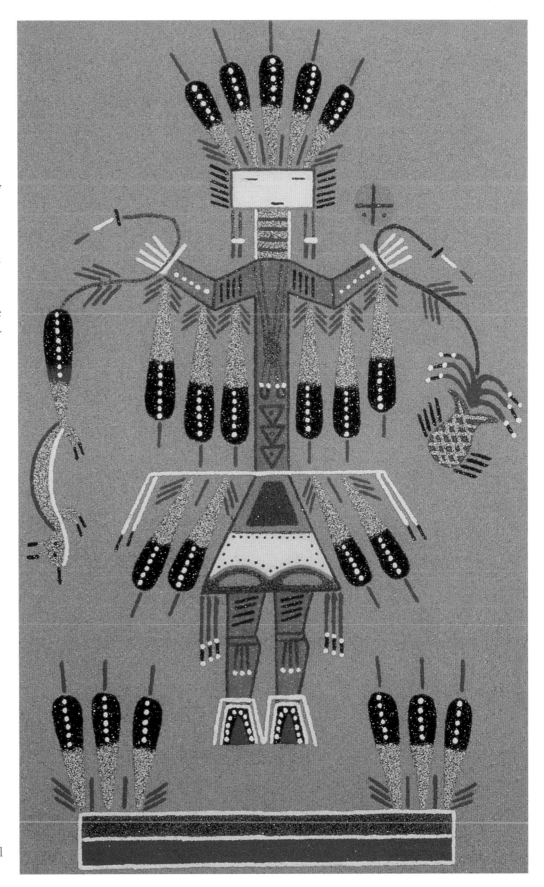

Below **Sand drawing, Pueblo culture.** Sand drawings were created by many different southwest-ern U.S. cultures as part of a shaman's healing ritual.

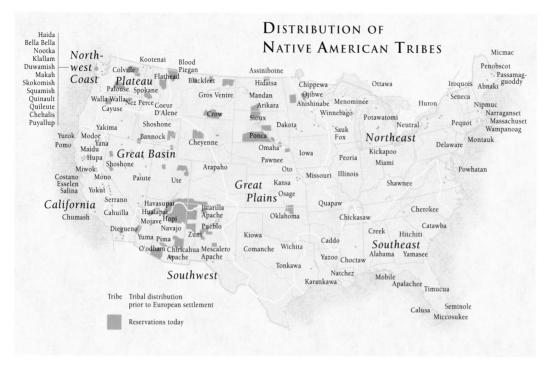

DISTRIBUTION OF NATIVE AMERICAN TRIBES

Haida
Bella Bella
Nootka
Klallam
Duwamish
Makah
Skokomish
Squamish
Quinault
Quileute
Chehalis
Puyallup

North-west Coast

Kootenai
Colville
Flathead
Palouse Spokane
Walla Walla
Nez Perce
Cayuse
Coeur D'Alene
Yakima
Shoshone
Bannock

Plateau

Blood
Piegan
Blackfeet

Assiniboine

Hidatsa
Mandan
Arikara
Sioux
Dakota
Ponca
Omaha
Pawnee
Oto

Gros Ventre

Crow

Chippewa
Ojibwe
Anishinabe
Winnebago
Sauk
Fox
Iowa
Missouri

Ottawa

Menominee
Potawatomi

Micmac
Penobscot
Passamag-guoddy
Iroquois Abnaki
Seneca
Huron
Nipmuc
Neutral
Pequot
Delaware
Montauk

Narraganset
Massachuset
Wampanoag

Northeast

Kickapoo
Peoria
Miami

Powhatan

Shawnee

Yurok Modoc
Pomo Yana
Maidu
Hupa
Miwok
Costano Mono
Esselen
Salina Yokut

California
Chumash

Shoshone

Great Basin

Paiute Ute

Serrano
Cahuilla
Diegueno
Yuma Pima
O'odham Chiricahua Mescalero
Apache Apache

Havasupai
Hualapai Hopi
Mojave
Navajo
Zuni

Jicarilla
Apache
Pueblo

Kiowa
Comanche

Great Plains
Kansa
Osage

Quapaw

Chickasaw

Caddo
Wichita
Tonkawa
Yazoo Choctaw

Creek Hitchiti
Catawba

Cherokee

Southeast
Alabama Yamasee

Karankawa
Natchez
Mobile
Apalachee
Timucua

Calusa
Seminole
Miccosukee

Southwest

Tribe — Tribal distribution prior to European settlement

Reservations today

NATIVE AMERICAN MYTHOLOGY

Originating as oral stories, the engaging myths of the Native American peoples were first written down in the nineteenth century. And although taken out of their tribal context, these fascinating stories continue to be powerful legacies of a proud cultural heritage, with themes and lessons that are as valid today as they were centuries ago.

CREATION DREAMS: THE BIRTH OF PEOPLES AND THE EARTH

Tribal myths that reveal how the natural world came into existence can be found within every Native American community in the U.S.A. They are some of the most ancient of all stories, and explain the origins of the sun, stars, and moon, as well as the land, water, and the indigenous peoples. These rich stories are the very foundation of all other tribal myths, for they speak directly to a unique sense of place and identity. Though these tales vary greatly in structure and the use of imagery from tribe to tribe, they share the common theme of teaching tribespeople the importance of living in balance and harmony with their world.

Right **Mask, Bella Coola people.** Featuring a human-like face with an eagle's beak for a nose, this mask represents a revered ancestor. In Bella Coola mythology, the Creator sent four carpenters to earth from the sky to form the first human beings.

Father Sun, Mother Moon
OSAGE PEOPLE

Long ago in the land where the sky and earth met, in a time when the ancient peoples used to live in both worlds, there was a pair of brothers who grew up never knowing their father. Their mother often told them he died in a great battle while she was pregnant. But as the brothers grew older they heard rumors from among the other ancient peoples—rumors that their father had not died in battle. In fact, the ancient ones said their father was not even a warrior—that he was a stranger who wandered into their world one evening. But even more astonishing was one rumor that implied the sun, who sees all, was the only one who could tell the brothers the truth. And the boys were determined to find out that truth.

The day the brothers planned to embark on their great journey to meet the sun, some of the ancient ones warned them that it was too dangerous. They knew that no other ancient one had ever journeyed to see the sun. However, the warnings did not even make the brothers think twice. They started out on the long journey across the sky.

It was a long journey indeed. The brothers grew low on food. And as they considered that they had at least another week of travel, the younger brother wondered if they should turn back. The older brother, worried that the ancient ones would mock them on their early return from their quest, and gossip even more about their father, convinced the younger that they should continue toward the sun.

The brothers were nearly starving by the time they reached the sun. The sun got right to the point. He told them that he was their father. But that was not all he revealed.

"The woman who raised you both as her own children is not your real mother," he said. "The moon is your real mother. If you don't believe me then ask her yourself. She will be passing by tonight."

And so the two brothers approached the moon as night fell. Sure enough, the moon confirmed to them that she and the sun were their parents. The younger brother was very upset—he knew that the brothers could not return to the ancient ones, as they were not the brothers' people.

The moon lowered her eyes in silence. Then she pointed to the earth and told the brothers to live among the animals.

The brothers nodded and began the new journey to the earth. But as they neared the surface they realized that the earth was covered with water. The water lapped up against their feet, pulling them down. Suddenly they were surrounded by a herd of elk. The brothers begged the elk for help as they splashed in the water.

The leader of the herd turned to the brothers. In an instant the entire herd reached down and began to drink the water. It was not long before the waters were nearly consumed by the herd. The brothers soon found themselves standing on solid ground.

The brothers heartily thanked the elk leader for the animals' help, and invited the herd to live with them on earth. The elk agreed. In time the brothers would learn to grow corn and beans that they would share with the elk. But of course, the brothers politely turned down the herd's offer to share the grass.

Left **Shield, Cree people.** The central figures of this warrior's shield are Pisim the sun and Tipiskawipisim the moon, which are a brother and sister in Cree mythology. The design idea was probably received in a dream or trance.

Below **Nineteenth-century blanket, Navajo people.** One of the Navajo creation myths tells of the "Holy People," gods who were responsible for creating the four original Navajo clans. The first clan, Kiiyaa aanii ("Tall House People"), was produced from maize.

Above **Woven basket, Modoc people.** The Modoc culture is known for its baskets featuring simple geometric designs. The baskets were used to carry and store food and other items, and were traditionally woven by women from tule reeds and porcupine quills.

Basket of Bones
MODOC PEOPLE

There was a time when only an old man and his daughter roamed the hills and valleys of the west. One day the old man decided there needed to be more peoples living in the upper world, and told his daughter that they should go down to the spirit world and see if they could find a way to bring some of them back into their world.

The old man led his daughter down a dangerously steep hill into the lower world. The daughter was amazed at how many spirits lived below. "It's like looking at the stars," she said.

Indeed, at night, the spirits danced and sang—glittering like the stars in the sky. During the day they returned to their homes within the rocks. The old man and daughter noticed that the spirits turned to bones once they entered the rocks, and decided to gather some of the bones in a basket.

When the basket was full they began to climb up the steep hill. But the old man slipped and he lost his basket. The basket tumbled against the rocks, spilling the bones. Immediately the bones turned back into spirits. The spirits quickly raced back into the rocks, before turning back into bones.

Once again the old man and his daughter gathered up some of the bones into their basket. This time though the daughter carried the basket, but she too slipped and lost the bones. Again the bones turned back into spirits, fleeing to the safety of the rocks.

The old man decided they would try one more time to bring the bones to the surface. As they picked up the bones, the old man scolded the spirits. "You don't know how wonderful my world is for you. When you see the land, the sun, and the sky you will never want to return to this dreary spirit world again."

Right **Warrior's cloak, Apache people.** Painted with representations of Apache gods or spirits, who lived in a world where death and disease were unknown, this cloak served to invoke the power of the otherworld to protect the wearer from harm during battle.

The old man told his daughter that they should carry the basket between them up the slippery slope. Finally they reached the upper world. The old man scattered the bones on the ground. With great care he picked out certain bones, and threw them in each direction of his world to create more peoples.

And so it was that the world became filled with other peoples—in the mountains, the valleys, and along the water's shores. In order to help the peoples survive, the old man spoke the names of fish, animals, and plants. As he mentioned each name they appeared as if by magic. Then the old man instructed all the peoples to hunt and gather food to sustain them. The daughter marveled at how all the peoples heeded the old man's words.

The old man looked over his peoples and saw that his work was done. So he and his daughter traveled to the eastern sky to a place near the sun where they could see over the entire land below. Even today the old man and his daughter still watch over the peoples from the sky above.

The Great Chief
YAKIMA PEOPLE

One day the Great Chief decided he was tired of living in the sky, all alone. Even the world below held no life, as it was covered with water.

So the Great Chief came to the water below and began to make big fists of mud. He threw the mud across the waters, creating huge piles of land. Some of the piles grew so high that the tops became frozen

with ice. In only a short amount of time trees and grass began to grow on the large piles of land.

Then the Great Chief rolled a smaller ball of mud, shaping it into human form. Like the trees and grass, the human form came to life. The Great Chief told the man to fish and to gather food from the forest.

But before long, the man told the Great Chief that he was lonely. Taking pity on the man, the Great Chief created a woman for him. While the man hunted, the Great Chief showed the woman how to gather berries, how to sew, and how to cook fish.

One evening the woman had a dream that left her with the burning desire to please her husband even more. She prayed to the Great Chief. The Great Chief answered her prayer by blowing his special breath on her, giving her an invisible gift—the ability to have children. In the years to come, the woman found she could show her daughters and granddaughters all the wonderful home-making skills the Great Chief had taught her.

But as the people grew in number they began to quarrel among themselves. Jealousy and greed overcame many. Harmony among the people was entirely lost. Mother Earth became so tired and angry at all the constant fighting she savagely shook the mountains. Large rocks rolled down the mountains, crushing many of the people and burying them.

The remaining people knew that they had brought on the wrath of Mother Earth because of their fighting. Many raced to the bottom of the mountain hoping to find their loved ones alive. But alas, none of them had survived. Great mourning came over the people.

The people mourned for many days. When the season of grief had passed they returned to their lives—hunting, gathering, and preparing food. Some of the people would return to the mountain graves and they would report hearing the lost spirits of those buried call out sadly.

Many sought the Great Chief, looking to see if he would remove the rocks and allow the spirits to return to their remains. But he would not give them an answer. Instead, the people were instructed to keep the ways that they learned from their grandparents and to pass them on to their own children. It is only by keeping the old ways alive that the Great Chief will one day open up the graves and allow the spirits of the dead to return.

GODS OF THE NATIVE AMERICANS

Although they often have different names from tribe to tribe, certain gods and goddesses of the Native Americans are similar in function. The Great Spirit, Creator, or Master Spirit—known by a variety of names such as Awonawilona (Pueblo people), Isakakate (Crow people), and Tirawa-atius (Pawnee people)—is the omnipotent and omniscient deity responsible for the creation of the universe, and is sometimes represented by the sun. Mother Earth—known as Atira by the Pawnee people, Eithinoha by the Iroquois people, and Isanaklesh by the Mescalero Apache people, just three of her names—is associated with agriculture and fertility, and thanks are offered to her in times of bounty.

Other gods represent the elements, or facets of human life, and can be prayed to for help in times of great need or for relief in times of hardship.

Thunder—Heng (Huron), Hino (Iroquois)
Rain—Sio Humis (Hopi), To'nenile (Navajo)
Wind—Gaoh (Iroquois), Hotoru (Pawnee), Master of Winds (Iroquois)
Love—Ca-the-ña (Mojave)
Sex—Tunkan Ingan (Dakota)
Childbirth—Chakwaina Okya (Zuni)

Below *Sioux Myth of Ictinike* by James Jack. Son of the sun god, Ictinike was infamous for his lying, trickery, and love of war. In one particular myth, Rabbit has his revenge on the deceitful Ictinike by magically compelling him to leap higher and higher into the air with every drum beat—eventually breaking every bone in Ictinike's body.

HONORING WARRIORS: THE POWER OF BRAVERY AND SKILL

The journey of the Native American hero is, for the most part, not unlike that of hero journeys found in other mythologies. Along his quest, a young man must acquire the wisdom and skills he will need when he faces his most challenging test—usually slaying a formidable foe or waging a victorious battle. In many cultural myths the hero's journey is that of overcoming some inner, personal demons that are manifested in outer forms and threaten harm. But in almost every tribal myth the hero's journey is not merely a search for self-improvement. It is a journey on behalf of the community— one that seeks to improve the welfare of the tribal whole.

Bear and Boy

PAWNEE PEOPLE

There once was a boy who never knew just how poor he was until he visited the home of the village chief. The boy was invited to the home by his best friend, the chief's son. From that day forward the boy grew increasingly sad because of his family's poverty. Overcome with this deep sadness, the boy decided to

Right **Rock art, Plains culture.** Depicting an important warrior with a feathered headdress, this ancient rock engraving reveals the value placed on the warrior and his skills. Storytellers would often regale the tribe with tales of heroic deeds and great battles.

leave the village and journey into the woods, hoping to be killed by a pack of ferocious animals.

On the second day of his journey he came upon a cave. Thinking he was alone, the boy curled up on the cold ground to sleep.

"Who are you?" a voice said in the darkness.

The boy jumped up to flee but he was grabbed by a large furry paw. Immediately the boy realized he had entered a bear's cave. The boy begged not to be eaten, and the bear told him to keep his voice down, or he would wake the bear's cub.

Suddenly the boy realized that the mother bear had no interest in eating him. In fact, the bear offered to let him spend the night. But she warned him that her husband would eat him when he returned, unless the boy wrapped his arms around the cub.

And so it happened that the father bear returned. When he saw the boy he flashed his great teeth at the sight. But the boy did as the mother bear instructed. He grabbed the cub and stared straight at the father bear who quickly calmed down.

"I will now call you my son," the bear said. He told the boy that he would give him special powers that would make him a great warrior, and that he would take his cub's life and give the boy the cub's skin to protect him in battle.

In the months that followed this meeting the boy returned to the village and joined the war party. He performed many great feats in battle and was praised by the tribe's chief.

Over time the boy's affection for the chief's daughter grew, and he longed to make her his wife. But during the night the bear came to him in a dream and told him he could not marry her until he performed one more grand deed in battle. The boy heeded the bear's words. He led his war party into one final great battle and was successful.

But when he returned from war he found that the chief's son—his best friend—was deathly ill. The boy carried the chief's son to the edge of a cliff and left him alone to feed the birds with buffalo meat. After a few days the boy returned to find that the chief's son was well and that he had acquired particular powers from each of the birds.

The chief was so grateful to the boy for helping his son recover from sickness, he offered his daughter's hand in marriage to the boy.

For many years the boy, now a man, ruled over the village alongside the chief's son. When the time came for him to pass on to the next world, he held his young child in his arms and gave him a special gift—his remarkable bear powers.

Return of the Horses

BLACKFEET PEOPLE

One day an old chief watched as a young orphaned boy was being cruelly teased by a group of others his age. The old man had heard that the boy was deaf, and he knew that the tribespeople all perceived the boy to be stupid as well.

The old chief waited until the children grew bored with teasing the boy and went away. Once the boy was alone the chief approached the boy and offered him some dried meat. The boy knew by the gentle look in the old chief's eyes that he was welcome to live with him.

One day while the old chief and the young boy were walking along the shoreline of a nearby pond, the boy pointed to a herd of horses grazing in the distance. Knowing the boy could not hear his words, the old chief took a stick and drew pictures in the sand. He drew pictures of the tribesmen riding the horses, and then he drew a picture of the horses roaming the plains without the men.

Left **Bear claw necklace, Sac and Fox people.** Necklaces such as this could only be worn by men who had shown their bravery by making contact with the Bear Spirit. This is a deeply religious culture, with the belief that each person and animal in the world has its own guardian spirit.

Below **Horse effigy, Blackfeet people.** Effigies such as this were strapped to the back of Blackfeet warriors who sought visions of power, protection, and success during horse-raiding expeditions. Horses were seen as symbols of great honor and respect by the Blackfeet people, and were either stolen from their neighbors or obtained through trade.

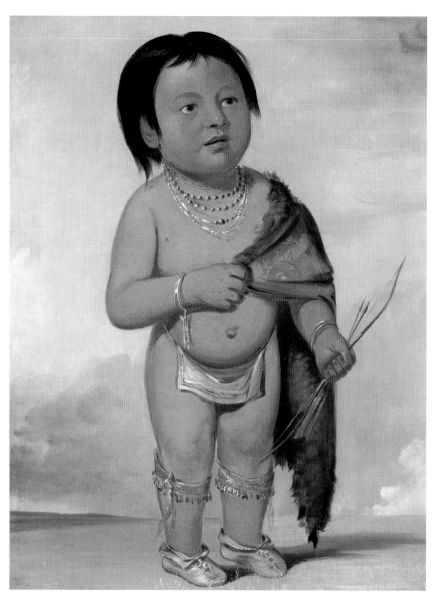

the young man to the bottom of the pond where he was introduced to the man's grandfather.

The grandfather sat the boy down and told him he would help the boy bring the horses back to his people. He took off his belt and his robe and gave them to the boy, telling him that the belt and robe held magical powers that would allow the boy to charm the horses.

As the boy was putting on the robe and belt, he saw that the grandfather's feet were actually horse's hooves. Suddenly the young man put his hand on the boy's shoulder, telling him that he needed to return to the surface of the pond.

When he returned the old chief was gone and the boy knew that he needed to set out on his journey to capture the horses. When the horses saw the boy they were stunned and awed at the beauty of his robe and belt. The boy easily befriended the horses, who told the boy that they would only return to the tribe if he learned how to ride properly.

For many days the boy rode the horses across the prairies, gaining their trust and confidence. Finally the horses agreed that it was time to go back to the tribe.

When they returned the boy discovered the sad news that the old chief had died. But the tribe was so grateful to the boy they threw a large celebration to honor his great feat.

The Strong Infant
SENECA PEOPLE

The little boy watched his father grieve at the side of his dead mother. She had passed on while giving birth

Above *Grandson of Buffalo Bull's Back Fat* by George Catlin (1796–1872). Tcha-aés-ka-ding, the grandson and heir of the Blackfeet chief Buffalo Bull's Back Fat, is shown by Catlin in a robe of raccoon skin and grasping his bow and arrows. In Catlin's words he "stood forth like a tried warrior." Native American boys were encouraged from an early age to emulate the strength, bravery, and skill of the warriors.

The boy realized that the old chief was explaining how the horses decided to leave the tribe. Then the boy took the old man's stick and he drew in the sand a picture of a little boy riding a horse. The old chief knew that the boy wanted to do something great for the tribe. He knew the boy wanted to bring the horses back, something that no warrior had been able to accomplish.

The old chief led the boy a few feet into the pond. The boy lowered his head and stared into the waters. Beneath the surface he could see a young man bidding him to come into the waters. The boy looked at the old chief and then he plunged into the pond.

To his great surprise the boy found that he could breathe under water, and he found that he could hear all the sounds of life beneath the surface. He followed

Above **Pipe in the form of a frog or toad, Hopewell people.** In Native American mythology frogs were sometimes the demonic guardians of fresh water, or they could represent more positive things such as cleansing, regeneration, and fertility.

to her second child. And though the child lived, the father was distraught at the very sight of him. The child was such a painful reminder of the loss of his wife he decided he would take it to the woods and leave it to die.

The boy secretly followed his father as he carried his younger brother deep into the woods. He watched as his father placed the infant on a tree stump and then turned his back on the child and left. Quickly the boy ran for the child and took him in his arms.

The boy had not even thought of how he was going to keep the child's continued existence from his father. He only hoped his father's grief would fade and that one day he would welcome his child back. But as the boy sat in the woods holding the infant, it jumped from his arms. Before the boy knew it, the infant was walking, even running among the trees.

The boy realized that this was a very special infant with great powers. Suddenly the infant reached for a large branch and began felling trees with powerful swings.

The boy decided to keep the infant hidden in the woods, away from his father, but it was an impossible task. Upon hearing the loud crashes, the father raced to the woods to see what was happening. He saw his young boy and the strong infant standing among the downed trees.

Fearing that the villagers would not accept the unusual infant, the father instructed his son to take the child far away from the village, and to raise him alone. But he warned his son not to go north, as it was too dangerous due to the devilish frogs waiting there to eat unsuspecting travelers.

Right **Cradleboard, Pawnee people.** Featuring the symbol for the deity Morningstar—protector of the people's well-being—this cradleboard was used as a supportive base for a soft, skin baby-carrier. Cradleboards were traditionally cut from the center of a living tree to preserve the "heart of life."

But confident that the infant could overcome the frogs, the boy led the child into the north. And sure enough, the infant engaged the evil frogs in a fierce battle—killing all of them quite easily.

The boy believed that the infant could survive on his own, and decided to leave the infant to journey on alone. And indeed, the infant conquered a vast number of enemies who sought to destroy him. The infant defeated enemies in every direction he went. Whether it was east, west, south, or north there was no enemy that could match his powerful strength. Soon word grew throughout the land about the infant's remarkable strength.

When word of the infant reached a peculiar giant who lived farther north, he decided it would best to trick the child rather than fight him. When the infant entered the giant's territory, he agreed to an eating contest. The giant thought he would lure the infant into a deep sleep after feasting on the big meal. But as soon as the giant could eat no more, as soon as he declared the infant to be the winner, the child ripped the giant into pieces.

It was not long after all of his journeys that the infant grew tired of waging wars with his enemies. One day he came upon some villagers playing ball. Curious at the sight of the infant, the villagers challenged the infant to a game. If the child should win they would give up their land. And, in fact, the child did defeat the villagers. The infant called for his father to come to the village and rule as chief. His father came and ruled for many years.

TRICKSTER TALES: COYOTE AND OTHER TEASING SPIRITS

The impulse for trickery or teasing is very strong within Native Americans. One of the most familiar characters and motifs in tribal myths is that of the trickster. Often showing up in different shapes such as coyote, spider, or beaver, the trickster is always creating havoc, even if his intentions may be good. Depending on his form, the trickster often seeks to deceive the other animals, people, and elements of the sky in order to satisfy his greed. His ever-constant presence in tribal mythology serves to always remind people that there should be a little coyote, spider, or beaver in everyone.

Coyote and the Boxes
HOPI PEOPLE

It had been another long day for Coyote. He had traveled for many miles in his search for food. As his stomach growled in hunger, he felt his luck had run out. He decided he needed to enlist the help of Eagle if he were to survive.

He told Eagle that he had a plan for them to work together in a hunt. With Eagle's eyes in the sky and coyote's nose on the ground he figured that they could catch enough prey to fill both their stomachs. Although Eagle was skeptical, he agreed because he was not having much hunting fortune on his own.

But the hunt did not go well. Coyote complained that Eagle's eyes must be growing old and weak. Eagle answered that he could see perfectly well under ordinary conditions, but there was a lack of good light—there was only so much that he could see in these very trying conditions.

Eagle was preparing to tell Coyote that his nose was failing him when they came upon a village of spirits. The two hunting partners were standing on a hill looking down at the village when Eagle saw that the spirits were gathering around two boxes. Eagle watched as they opened each box; one for more light and the other for less.

KACHINAS

Legend has it that long ago deities known as Kachinas came to earth to live among the tribes of southwestern U.S.A. At first they were honored as both educators and guardians of the people, but as time passed the Kachinas saw that they were being taken for granted and decided to return to their home in the sky. Before they left, however, they taught the tribesmen how to fashion clothing and masks in their images, so that when ceremonies and dances were performed in these costumes the tribesmen would take on the powers of the Kachinas—including the capacity to bring rain for the crops and health to the people.

Kachina dolls, also known as *tithu*, are created by the Hopi people to teach their children about the Kachinas, and are believed to contain some of the power of the particular Kachina they represent. They are carved from cottonwood roots, then brightly painted and decorated with colorful feathers and special religious symbols.

Below **Kachina dolls, Hopi people.** There are hundreds of different Kachinas, from those that represent the sun and clouds to special animal and bird spirits, and no two handmade Kachina dolls are alike. The most prized dolls are carved from a single piece of wood.

Coyote wanted to steal the boxes and keep them, but Eagle only wanted to borrow them for a short time. Coyote consented and it was agreed that Eagle would fly over the village of spirits to get a better look. When Eagle returned he told Coyote that the spirits were careful to not completely open the boxes, fearing that the contents would escape.

Suddenly Coyote's hunger gave way to curiosity. He desperately wanted to know what was in those boxes. It was decided that Eagle was the most qualified to seize the boxes. But they would have to wait until nightfall.

While Eagle went after the boxes, Coyote could think of nothing except the contents of the containers. Eagle returned, carrying a box in each of his two claws. Coyote offered to carry the boxes on the journey back home, saying that Eagle looked tired.

Eagle admitted that he was tired, but he was suspicious of Coyote. He decided to let Coyote carry the boxes only if he promised not to open them. Coyote faithfully promised he would not open the boxes until they returned home.

But as soon as Coyote had the boxes in his grasp he opened them up. In a flash the sun and the moon escaped from the boxes and they fled to the highest parts of the sky, out of reach.

"You fool!" Eagle cried. "Now we shall be at the mercy of the sun and moon. We will only be able to hunt whenever they decide to give us sufficient light!"

But that was not all the trouble that Eagle and Coyote caused. For now that the sun and moon were free to give the world light and darkness whenever they wanted, they also decided to create the cold winter.

Above **Wicker plaque with eagle design, Hopi people.** There are many Hopi myths featuring the eagle, including one where the eagle tricks the coyote into cutting off his own leg, and another where the eagle makes his nocturnal friend the owl hunt during the day, only to see the owl fall asleep and be shot by a human's arrow.

Left **Red argillite pendant in the form of an eagle, Sinagua people.** Living in what is now Arizona between A.D. 500 and 1300, the Sinagua people were influenced in both their artwork and mythology by the bald and golden eagles that soared overhead.

Right **Green quartzite effigy of a buffalo, Plains culture.** Figurines like this would have been used in rituals to honor the buffalo's spirit, ensuring that hunters were not trampled by these mighty beasts and that they came back to the tribe with a bounty of buffalo meat.

Freeing the Buffalo

COMANCHE PEOPLE

There was a time when the buffalo did not always freely roam throughout the land. Long ago an old woman and her young cousin found all the buffalo grazing on a hill. While the buffalo fed they built a large pen, fencing in the animals.

One day Coyote decided he needed to approach the people to complain about the woman and her younger cousin. He convened a council meeting and announced that as long as the buffalo were fenced in, he would starve. But while the council members were sympathetic to Coyote's concerns, they said the buffalo did not want to be freed for they were charmed by their captors.

From Wakan-Tanka, the Great Mystery, comes all power. ... Man knows that all healing plants are given by Wakan-Tanka; therefore they are holy. So too is the buffalo holy, because it is the gift of Wakan-Tanka.

CHIEF FLAT IRON (MAZA BLASKA),
OGLALA SIOUX CHIEF (LATE
NINETEENTH CENTURY)

Coyote would need to trick the woman and her cousin into freeing the buffalo— trick them in the same way she tricked the buffalo into captivity.

Coyote agreed and offered a clever plan to free the buffalo. The people would send a small animal to the watering hole where the young cousin went each morning. He would be so taken with wanting a pet of his very own that he would bring it home and convince the old woman that he should keep it. The buffalo would soon become jealous of the new pet and storm the gate, breaking it down. They would race down the hill, free from the old woman and her cousin.

Coyote convinced a small bird to go along with the plan. So one morning the little bird appeared at the watering hole. As Coyote guessed, the young cousin was completely taken with the bird and he brought it home.

"Take this bird back!" the old woman screamed at him. "Can't you see that Coyote is trying to make our buffalo jealous!"

The young cousin, with much regret, returned the bird. Coyote was furious but not defeated. The next day he convinced a squirrel to try to win the heart of the young cousin. And the squirrel did.

Again the old woman called her cousin foolish, and told him to return the animal to the watering hole or risk losing their buffalo.

And, just like the bird, the squirrel reported to Coyote that he had failed to outsmart the old woman. Upon hearing of the failure of this second attempt, Coyote decided he would send just one more animal—knowing that if this last trick failed then he was unable to beat the old woman and retrieve the herd of buffalo.

For the third attempt Coyote sent a small rodent. The young cousin was so excited at meeting the rodent that he decided that no matter what the old woman said he was going to keep the little rodent as his precious personal pet.

The old woman was so angry she wasted no time yelling at her young cousin. Instead she reached for a large stick and charged at the rodent, trying to kill it. The young cousin screamed as the rodent ran out the door. Desperate to flee from the old woman's wild rage, the small rodent crawled under the fence to hide among the buffalo.

But as soon as the buffalo saw the rodent they were frightened. Chaos broke out among the herd of buffalo, and they charged the front gate, breaking it down easily. The herd roared down the hill, scattering throughout the land. Coyote was pleased with himself.

Fire Thief

NEZ PERCE PEOPLE

It was known for a long time that the pine trees were the only ones who had the secret of fire. And the last thing they ever wanted to do was let any of the animals in on their secret of how to create these great orange flames.

Each winter the animals would growl in anger at the pine trees as they struggled to keep warm. The cold could become so severe that not even the animal with the thickest coat of fur could stay warm.

Attempts to reason with the pine trees over the years were always to no avail. The pine trees were just simply selfish, not at all open to sharing with anyone except their own kind.

During a time of terrible cold air that came upon the land, the animals called a secret meeting to consider ways in which they could get the pine trees to give up their fire secret.

Beaver decided to sneak around on the outskirts of the pine trees the next time they held their council meeting. He knew that the pine trees always prepared a huge fire for their council meetings, and was sure he could snatch a stray coal or two. For once the animals were hopeful that they would learn the secret of fire.

Beaver was extremely patient and careful as he silently made his way around the outskirts of the council gathering. Before the meeting started he watched as the pine trees bathed in the cold waters by the river. He also watched as they dried themselves before one of the largest fires Beaver had ever seen in his life. But Beaver was smart, for he knew that the ancient pine trees were no fools. They had a number of guards posted around the area.

Left **Shell gorget (throat pendant), Mississippian Southern Cult.** The Mississippians worshipped a fire or sun deity, which was represented in their art by a cross. The spider is symbolic of weaving and balance, and was thought to have given the gift of fire to the people.

Below *The Beaver* by **Josiah Wood Whymper (1813–1903).** In Native American mythology, the beaver could be a trickster or a hard-working animal. There are also legends from northeastern tribes that tell of a giant beaver— fossil evidence has shown that a beaver as big as a black bear did once exist in the region.

Above *American Indian Sweat Lodge* by H.E. Sylvester. The sweat lodge ceremony is called *oenikika*, which means "breath of life." In order to reach a higher state of consciousness—and a closer relationship with the spirits—the participants must purify their body by fasting before the ritual, then use the ceremony to dispel negative feelings such as jealousy and hate.

SWEAT LODGES

Sweat lodges are found in most tribal cultures across the U.S.A. Skins or other materials are stretched across a simple wooden frame, and the air inside is heated by burning logs or hot rocks sprayed with water. The sweat lodge combines the four elements of the universe—earth, water, air, and fire—in a sacred structure that is as important to Native American culture today as it was centuries ago.

There are three main purposes for taking part in a sweat lodge ceremony: cleansing the body, purifying the mind, and connecting with the gods. Sweating removes toxins from the body through the pores of the skin, and the beating of drums or chanting during the ceremony focuses the mind. Once the participant has a clean body and mind, they are able to make contact with the spirits.

In the past, shamans (or medicine men) used sweat lodge ceremonies to call upon the most powerful spirits of the universe, and ask for their help in times of adversity.

Below *Blackfeet Shaman* by George Catlin (1796–1872). Many Blackfeet ceremonies—such as the sacred Sun Dance—were preceded by ancient sweat lodge rituals that were performed by the shaman of the tribe.

Beaver sat quietly as the council got under way. And as the fire blazed, a number of small embers burst from the flames and rolled down the bank of the river. Beaver cautiously crawled along the ground and down the bank. While one of the guards was not looking he snatched a handful of hot coals and placed them in a pouch. Beaver dashed toward the dark woods. But as he was fleeing the guards heard his heavy paws crunching the dead leaves beneath him. The council ordered an immediate pursuit.

Beaver tore through the thick woods, leaping over fallen branches and tearing through bushes. But even though he raced as fast as he could, the guards were gaining on him. Beaver decided to risk running along the rugged shores of the river in order to keep ahead. It was a good move. Soon some of the tree guards grew tired of chasing Beaver or fell along the banks, where they remain today.

But just as Beaver breathed a sigh of relief and thought he might be in the clear, a band of guards approached him from the front. Beaver started up the bank only to find another band of guards closing on him. Surrounded, Beaver had no choice but to venture across the river. He held the pouch of coals above his head as he swam across.

When he neared the other side of the river his eyes made out another band of guards waiting for him to arrive on shore. Beaver, though one of the best swimmers among the animals, was growing very tired from running and swimming.

He had only one choice to save the fire. Beaver let the river's current take him downstream. He opened the pouch and, as he floated along, he cast the coals ashore on either side of the river into patches of cedar and birch trees. It was a good move because these trees proved to not be as greedy as the pines. Today you can create fire very easily by rubbing together small sticks of cedar or birch.

SPIRIT WORLD: JOURNEYS TO THE OTHER SIDE

One of the most effective ways to maintain order among tribal villagers was to tell tales of good and evil spirits. Stories told about man-eating spirits that roamed the forest, or about an angry sun that sends a deadly fever to the peoples, proved successful in keeping villagers in line. There was a great belief in and respect for the spirits. Keeping on their good side could also mean help from the spirits as well. Myths about the spirit world were not simple fairy tales for the peoples. They were stories that gave tribal villagers guidance on how to properly conduct themselves while in the community.

Battling Sky Spirits
ANISHINABE PEOPLE

In the days when the land knew only freezing winter, Badger and his friends decided that they were tired of the cold, and they would work together to see if they could change the harsh season to something warmer.

Badger was the first to address the determined group, and told them he had been watching the high place called Skyland for quite some time. He proposed that they make their way up the mountains to Skyland—where it was warm—and bring some of that warmth to earth.

Well, of course, it sounded like a good plan except the other animals were not quite sure of how they were going to bring the warmth back to earth. Otter in particular was certainly not interested in staying in Skyland just to be warm.

Badger told Otter that the journey to Skyland was long, and that they would have plenty of time as they made their way up the mountain to think of a plan to capture some of the warmth and bring it home.

And that appeared to be a good plan for the animals. At once they started up the mountain on their way toward Skyland.

But try as they may, no one could come up with a plan for bringing the warmth back. And yet they had traveled so far that at the very least they were comforted by the fact that they would feel Skyland's warmth, if only for a few days.

Once they reached the place where Skyland met the mountaintop, they were discouraged to learn that they

could not break their way inside. Determined to get into Skyland, the animals took turns banging against the invisible wall. Finally—with one last, mighty effort—they broke through.

Skyland was a warm and beautiful place full of flowers and birds, just as they had expected. And to their joyous wonder they found the warm air of Skyland pouring down to the world below through the hole they had created. The warm air melted the ice and snow from the mountain.

Below *Sacred Otter* by James Jack. In a Blackfeet legend, Sacred Otter dreams of visiting the tipi of Es-tonea-pesta, Lord of the Cold Weather, who gives him special "medicines." Later, he is able to use those "medicines" to ask the Lord to save his people from a blizzard.

Above *Sioux Hare Myth* by James Jack. In this legend, Hare enters the cave of Pahe-Wathahuni and is swallowed by the monster. Hare cuts open the monster's stomach to escape.

But as the animals basked in the warm world of Skyland, a large number of Sky Spirits came upon them. The animals were surrounded by a flurry of arrows. Fearing for their lives, they raced to the hole. But when they reached the hole Badger stopped. He realized that they would have to make the hole bigger or else the Sky Spirits would seal it up again and never let the warmth come to earth.

As the animals hurried to enlarge the hole, one of the Sky Spirits' arrows hit Badger in the side. Badger fell, and as he neared death he told the other animals to go on without him as the hole was big enough.

The animals refused to leave without Badger but they knew they were no match for the Sky Spirits. Badger smiled as he watched the earth below melt away into summer. And then he closed his eyes for the last time. Saddened by his death, the other animals knew they had to flee down the mountainside.

Suddenly the Great Spirit Manitou appeared and took pity on Badger. He waved off the Sky Spirits and knelt at Badger's side. He placed healing medicine on his wound and brought Badger back to life—a different life, in which Badger ascended into the heavens above Skyland.

The inspiring story of Badger's courage is often told when he is spotted in the night sky—some know of Badger as the Big Dipper.

Cave Prophecies
SIOUX PEOPLE

It had been a long day of hunting for the young warrior—a day that yielded no kill. Deciding that he would try again the next day, the warrior started for home. Since it was growing dark he thought he would take a short cut through some hills. And that's when he came across a strange cave that he had never seen before.

Curious, he entered the cave where he found paintings of animals on the walls. And he found many necklaces and bracelets on the ground. He realized that they must have been offerings. Though it was getting darker the warrior wanted to explore the cave in detail. He found many chambers and wall paintings.

Suddenly, the air went black. The man could not even see a glimmer of light in the cave. Chills ran up his arms and he raced to find the cave's entrance.

When he returned to the village he reported what he had seen to the chief. The very next day the chief ordered five of his best warriors to venture to the cave and make their own report about it. Led by the young warrior, the men made their way to the cave.

But once they entered the cave the young warrior noticed that the paintings had changed. The animals were completely different. The young warrior showed the men many of the chambers he had found. Suddenly a sweet odor filled the room they were in. The men traced the delicious smell to a small opening leading to another chamber.

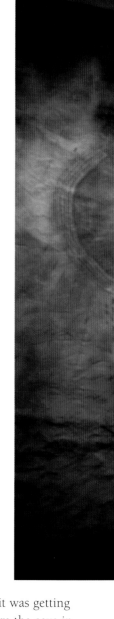

ANCIENT PETROGLYPHS

Native American petroglyphs are ancient forms of rock art found mainly in the present-day southwestern U.S. states of Utah, Arizona, Colorado, New Mexico, and Texas. Symbols and images were either scratched, carved, or pecked into the darkened surfaces of basalt and sandstone canyons, caves, and boulders up to 12,000 years ago, revealing the lighter colored stone underneath.

The specific meanings of many of these images have been lost in time, but it is generally thought that they represent historical events such as the arrival of the Spanish; day-to-day proceedings like hunting and fishing; the relationship between Native American

peoples and nature; religious ceremonies, beliefs, or prayers; elements of warfare; or mythological characters and stories. For Native American tribes of the southwest, petroglyphs have been a vital part of their environment since the time of creation, and are still considered significant symbols revealing their ancient histories, intricate societies, and strong beliefs.

Below **Newspaper Rock petroglyphs, Canyonlands National Park, Utah.** Created by many different peoples—including Navajo, Fremont, Ute, and Anasazi—these symbols are said to record important rituals or events.

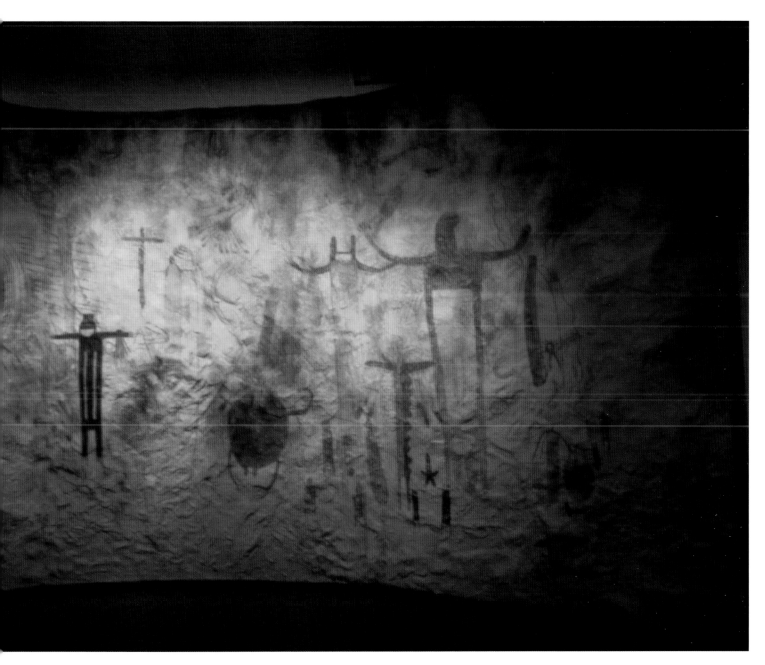

The group's leader decided that instead of exploring this chamber they would return to the camp and report what they had found to the chief. On their way out one of the other warriors decided to take one of the bracelets.

The leader told him to leave the bracelet, as the cave was clearly the home of some great spirit. However, the warrior argued that he wanted to prove to the chief that they spoke the truth about the cave and its many wonders. The leader insisted that terrible trouble would follow the warrior and the rest of the group should the bracelet be taken. But the warrior scoffed at his leader. He placed the bracelet on his wrist and stepped out of the cave. When they arrived home the warrior flashed the bracelet before everyone as proof of what they had discovered.

The next day these same men were setting a trap to catch some wolves. They raised several heavy poles above a piece of meat that rested on a patch of leaves that covered a hole. When the wolf reached for the meat, he would fall in the hole. The men would pull strings, releasing the poles to trap the wolf. But as they prepared the trap, the warrior who had taken the bracelet accidentally slipped. He fell against the poles, which tumbled on top of him. When the others removed the poles they saw that the warrior was alive, but that his wrist was broken.

Frightened about further angering the cave's spirit, the warrior immediately took the bracelet back to the cave. When he entered he saw new paintings on the walls—paintings of a wolf trapped beneath a pile of poles. He also saw paintings of women cutting up buffalo meat and hanging it out to dry.

Since that day the villagers would often come to the cave to see the paintings, to seek direction about how they should live their lives.

Above **Pictographs, Seminole Canyon State Park, Texas.** Produced between 2,000 and 8,000 years ago, these paintings on the wall of a rock shelter may have originally had a specific religious purpose. There are pictorial symbols of humans, animals, warfare, dancing, and other rituals.

Above **Navajo rug.** This early twentieth-century rug features the swastika, an ancient symbol found in the art of many cultures from around the world. In Navajo mythology it represents abundance, happiness, and well-being.

Twins of the Goddess

NAVAJO PEOPLE

When the First Goddess was fully grown she drew the affections of the Sun God. He came up behind her and nuzzled her neck. The warmth of his breath was very pleasing to her, and they were immediately joined in union at that moment. Soon she bore him a beautiful son and they seemed to be forever happy.

But one day while she was resting below a cliff, a drop of dew fell upon her head. It was not long before she realized that she was with child. When the child was born she knew that the Water God was the father. Despite this she raised both boys as if they were twins. They were known as the Twins of the Goddess.

As time passed word spread that there was an evil giant roaming the land, devouring every human he could find. One day he came upon the First Goddess. He was so taken with her beauty he did not want to

In the beginning of all things, wisdom and knowledge were with the animals, for Tirawa, the One Above, did not speak directly to man.

CHIEF EAGLE (LETAKOTS-LESA), PAWNEE
(LATE NINETEENTH CENTURY)

kill her. But when he saw the footprints of her twin boys on the ground he became very jealous and was intent on eating them.

She quickly ran into her home and hid the boys in a hole that was dug in the ground. The giant stormed into the house and demanded to know where the twins were. The First Goddess told him she had no children. The evil giant accused her of lying, as he had seen their footprints. In a sad voice the First Goddess replied that the footprints had been made by her own hands to comfort her as she was so lonely and wanted children of her own. This seemed to satisfy the giant until the day he saw the boys. But the twins escaped and hid in the hills. Later, their mother came to them while the giant slept. She told them to travel to the west and find their fathers.

The twins did as she told them, but soon realized that their fathers were not in the west. They secretly returned home, and accused their mother of lying to them about where their fathers were. At that, the mother told the boys to go east and then south. And so they did, but they did not find their fathers. They returned only to hear that they must travel to the north to find their fathers. This they did as well but again, they could not find either of their fathers.

Finally the mother relented. She told her sons that in order to reach the place where their fathers were they would need to travel over a great canyon, an awesome place that they would never survive crossing. But the boys were determined to find their fathers, and so they journeyed toward the canyon.

Along the way they met Spider Woman who took pity on them. She gave them each a magic feather to hold up in the direction they wished to travel, and the wind would carry them across the canyon.

When the boys reached the canyon they held their feathers up. The wind carried them safely across the canyon to the Great Water. At the shores of the water a rainbow bridge appeared. The twins crossed the rainbow bridge and when they reached the other side they found their fathers, Sun God and Water God. They were warmly greeted and they stayed there, never returning to their mother.

ANIMAL RELATIVES: SOME OF OUR CLOSEST FRIENDS

There are numerous tribal myths that begin with a sentence like "Back in the days when animals used to speak." The ancestors truly believed there was a time when animals governed the world before the peoples arrived. In fact, many ancient ones would say that the peoples learned to create community among themselves because the animals taught them. These days the animals speak only to one another. But animal myths are still full of wisdom from Brother Wolf and other intelligent animals like him. Native Americans believe that some animals are wiser than even the smartest human in the land.

Day and Darkness
IROQUOIS PEOPLE

Porcupine seemed to be the best choice for leader over the other animals, given the constant division and arguments that always arose over particular concerns. Porcupine was greatly respected for his even temper, and was never one to be easily persuaded.

The first concern that was raised after Porcupine took up his post was a question about day and night. Many of the animals decided that daylight should be constant, while others insisted that darkness should rule the land. As expected, a huge debate erupted between the two sides during the special meeting porcupine had convened.

Chipmunk was the most vocal proponent for daylight. He intensely argued that the light of day afforded more time to gather food, as well as for play and relaxation. He believed that there was no productivity at all when night fell, and that the animals wasted a lot of time when it was dark.

Bear matched Chipmunk's argument with his own appeal. He said that fish were easier to catch during the darkness, and that the animals spent far too much time trying to snare the fish that dwell deep in the waters to escape the light.

Left **Elliptical gorget (throat pendant), Glacial Kame people.** Dating from the Archaic Period (over 3,000 years ago), slate gorgets were placed in Glacial Kame burial complexes as offerings. Gorgets are ordinarily plain, but this one has been engraved with the likeness of an animal still bearing its umbilical cord.

Left **False Face Society mask, Iroquois people.** Carved from the wood of a living tree, the False Face mask depicts a mythical being with the power to cure ills. When the owner "feeds" the mask tobacco and sings the sacred song, he becomes imbued with the ability to heal.

But no matter how hard Porcupine tried to maintain order it was no use. The animals were so fiercely divided they spent the rest of the meeting time yelling at each other. Nothing was resolved.

The next day Porcupine decided the best way to find a solution would be to speak privately with Chipmunk and Bear. Fearing the debate would result in warring divisions, Porcupine was bent on finding common ground with his fellow animals.

Chipmunk told Porcupine that Bear spent very little of his time trying to catch fish, and that if he wasn't so lazy he could have all the fish he needed. It was Chipmunk's belief that Bear only wanted to catch fish in the darkness because he did not have to work as hard then as he did during the day.

Bear presented a similar case to Porcupine. He thought that Chipmunk was deceiving them, that he had stored up enough food to last him an entire year. He merely wanted more time for frivolous play.

Of course Porcupine was quite disturbed at what appeared to be no resolution in sight, given the firm positions of the two animals. And so he decided that song and dance might be the way to soften the hearts of both parties. An evening of grand celebration would remind everyone just how much they need each other. Porcupine was sure that once the dancing and singing began they would reach a compromise.

That day Porcupine sent out word that there would be no

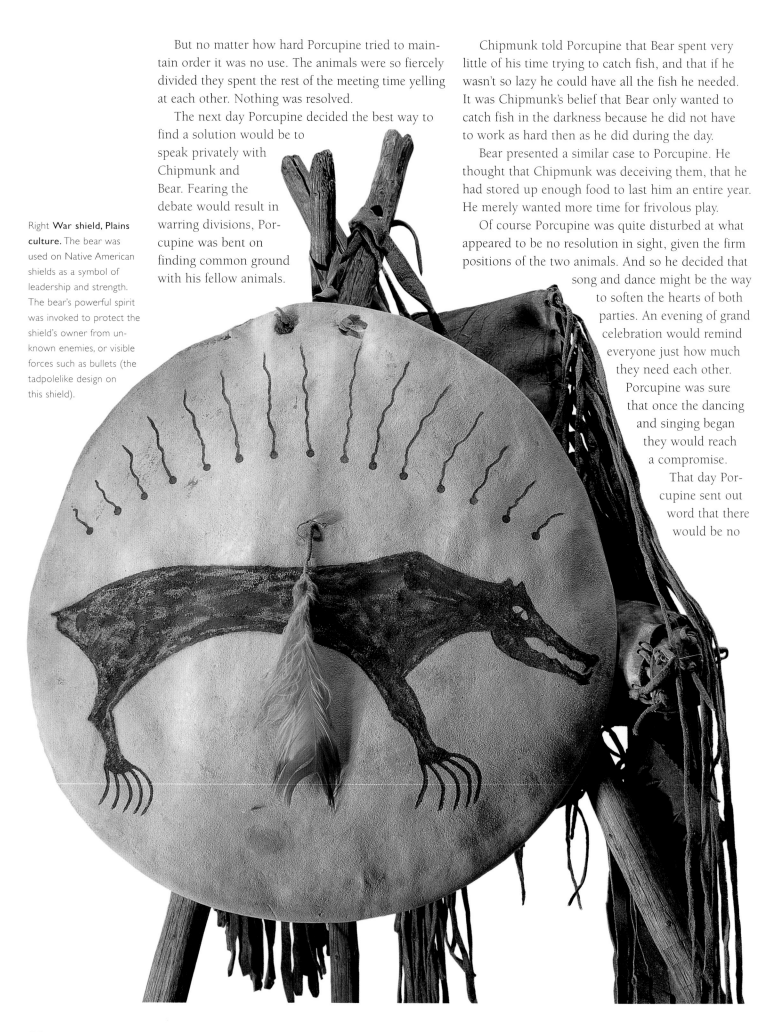

Right **War shield, Plains culture.** The bear was used on Native American shields as a symbol of leadership and strength. The bear's powerful spirit was invoked to protect the shield's owner from unknown enemies, or visible forces such as bullets (the tadpolelike design on this shield).

evening meeting—it would be an evening of song and dance. And as the evening progressed it seemed that Porcupine's plan was working, for Bear danced right alongside Chipmunk. You might never guess such friends could be so opposed to each other if you were there that night.

But the one thing Porcupine had forgotten about Chipmunk was how arrogant the animal could be. Out of nowhere Chipmunk broke into song, singing "We must have light, we must have light all day!"

Well, naturally, everyone was stunned. Furious, Bear broke into his own song, singing "We must have night, we must have night all day!"

In a matter of moments the singing gave way to yelling—each faction demanding Porcupine rule in their favor. In fact, things were so out of control that Bear lunged at Chipmunk. Chipmunk fled and Bear pursued. Just as Chipmunk was scaling a tree, Bear swiped at him with his paw—leaving a dark mark on his back that has stayed on the chipmunk to this day.

The only way Porcupine could settle the debate was to order that day and night would alternate. And that too remains to this day.

Alligator Wisdom
CHOCTAW PEOPLE

Among the people there was a hunter who was more skilled at the bow than anyone else. But despite this great skill he was terribly unfortunate during the hunt. He concluded that he must be cursed with bad luck.

Though he knew the forest well, and knew where to find huge herds of the most prized deer, something always happened, something that kept him from making the kill. For instance, one day the hunter spotted a large buck. Just as he aimed his arrow a flock of birds swept over the deer, frightening it away. The hunter could only grimace as he watched the animal fleeing deep into the woods.

The hunter's frustration was so great that he decided he would venture into the swamps and remain there until he succeeded. He decided he would not return to the village even if it meant facing his own death during the hunt.

He made his way through the swamps for a few days and finally came upon a very shallow pool. The hunter knew the long hot summer had reduced the ordinarily large pool to nothing more than a puddle. There, on the sand, was an alligator. The hunter was afraid of the beast, and he made sure he kept his distance.

The alligator told him not to be afraid, as he was too weak to harm the hunter. "My luck is worse than yours, friend," the alligator said.

The hunter replied by telling the alligator that there was a much deeper pool just to the east. But even the hunter knew that the alligator was too weak to travel that far east on his own. The alligator then proposed that if the hunter helped him get to the bigger pool, he would help the hunter make a great killing, thus reversing his hunting fortunes.

The hunter was suspicious about the alligator's motives, but the alligator convinced him that he would give him his word.

And, to be sure, the alligator let the hunter bind his legs and jaws.

Though the alligator was almost too heavy to carry, the hunter was desperate to put an end to his string of bad luck. He carried the beast to the large pool in the east, untied him, and watched him dive into the cool waters.

Above **Bronze plaque depicting American alligators.** These creatures are found in the southeastern states of the U.S.A., and influenced the mythology of many Native American cultures in the region. The Choctaw called them *chin-chuba* and respected their wisdom and survival skills.

Left **Wooden deer head effigy, Calusa people.** The Calusa inhabited Key Marco in Florida between A.D. 800 and 1400. Discovered by Frank Cushing in the 1890s, this effigy was described by him as having been produced by someone who "loved, with both ardor and reverence, the animal he was portraying ..."

Above **Deer pendant, Sin-agua people.** Made from abalone shell (obtained through trade) and turquoise beads, this pretty pendant may have been interred with the dead during burial as a symbol of the game that was hunted during life. The face of the deceased was stained or painted blue and green, and the body was clothed in cotton robes.

Right **Wooden mask with deer antlers, Mississippian Southern Cult.** Produced around A.D. 1200, this mask is made from cedar and inlaid shell. It was probably worn by a shaman during a special ceremony to promote good hunting. Deer meat was an important part of the Mississippians' diet, and a successful hunt was essential for the group.

After some time had passed, the alligator surfaced and swam to the shore. Making sure to keep his distance, the hunter waited for the alligator to speak.

Presently the alligator offered his reward for the help he received from the hunter. He told the hunter to go off into the woods, where he would see a small doe—but he should not kill it. Next he would find a young buck, but he must not kill that one either for the buck shall mate with the doe and she shall give birth to a fawn. If the hunter restrained from killing either animal, he would come upon an older buck, one that was ready to give itself to the hunter. That one the hunter may kill.

The hunter thanked the alligator and eagerly set out on his hunt. As the beast had told him he did indeed come upon the doe and young buck. And he did not shoot either of them. Finally he spotted the older buck and he raised his bow. His aim was perfect. The buck dropped to the ground as soon as the arrow plunged into his side.

Each time the man went out on a hunt he thought about the wise words of the alligator, which taught him about being patient. He never came back from hunting without a kill ever again.

Turned To Stone

NEZ PERCE PEOPLE

Long before the peoples arrived, the ants and bees used to live peacefully on a hillside. That peace was severely disrupted when the chief of the ants insisted on feasting on the chief of the bees' prized salmon.

Though he had plenty of food of his own, the chief ant was taken with jealous greed.

The chief bee liked to dry his salmon on a large rock on the hill. It was here that he returned to eat the fish. One day the chief ant called out as the bee was preparing to eat. He wanted to know what the chief bee was doing on that rock, as that spot was not his. The chief ant believed the chief bee had no right to it, and demanded that he leave at once. The chief bee replied that he ate at this rock all the time.

But the ant insisted the bee had no right to the rock. After a long exchange the chief bee realized the ant really only wanted his salmon. He knew that if he were to leave the rock he would have to leave some of his food as well for he could not carry it all.

Though the bee tried to ignore the ant it became impossible. The ant approached the bee and gave him one last warning to leave. When the bee refused, the ant engaged him in a fierce battle.

While the two were fighting, the coyote came along. He wanted to know why the ant and bee were fighting. But the bee and ant were too busy kicking and biting each other to respond to the coyote. It was only after the coyote roared his loudest that the two stopped long enough to hear the coyote out.

The bee told the coyote that he had always eaten his food on this particular rock, and that the ant knew it. He believed that the ant just wanted to steal his food. The coyote turned to the ant and said that there was plenty of food for all of them in this land.

But the ant was not interested in the coyote's words. He lunged at the bee, catching him off guard. The

bee then responded by biting the ant hard on his back leg. The coyote attempted to get the bee and ant to stop fighting. He warned them that if they did not stop they would cause great division between all ants and bees. If they became divided they would no longer be great throughout this land. But they refused to listen.

Fearing he had no choice, the coyote warned them that if they did not end their war he would be forced to turn them into stone. But the bee and ant were so caught up in their fighting they ignored the coyote's threat. The coyote warned them one last time to either stop fighting or be turned into stone. He knew that if that happened there would be great division between all bees and ants.

Every part of the earth is sacred to my people. Every shining pine needle, every sandy shore, every mist in the dark woods, every meadow, every humming insect. All are holy in the memory and experience of my people.

CHIEF SEATTLE (SEATHL),
DUWAMISH (1786–1866)

But his repeated threats were to no avail. The bee and ant continued to battle with each other. The coyote raised his paw and moved it in the air, calling upon some ancient magic. While the bee and ant continued to fight, the coyote pointed his paw toward them. The bee and ant turned to stone, just as the coyote had threatened.

And the fear of a great division growing between the bees and ants came true. By the time the humans came, the bees and ants were both reduced in power and greatness because of this division. Today, if you look carefully, you can still see the bee and ant locked in each other's arms on that rock.

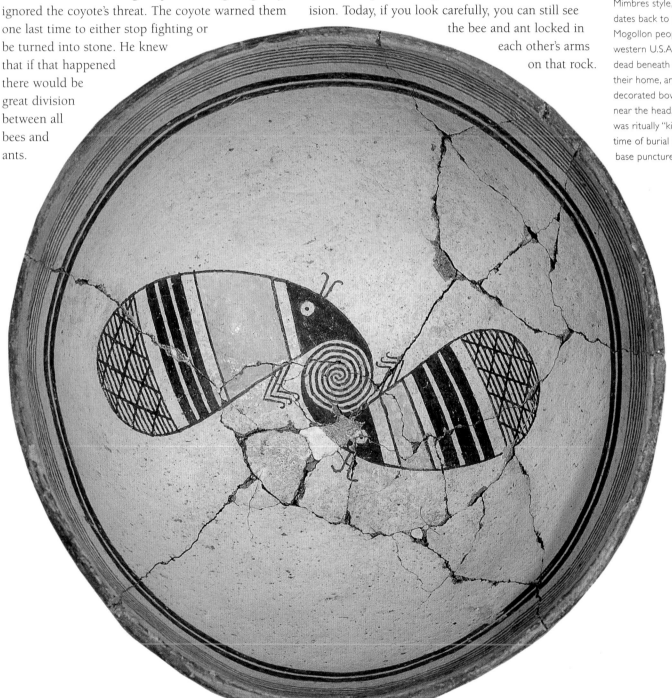

Left **Pottery bowl painted with insects, Mogollon people.** Painted in the Mimbres style, this bowl dates back to A.D. 950. The Mogollon people of south-western U.S.A. buried their dead beneath the floor of their home, and placed a decorated bowl over or near the head. The bowl was ritually "killed" at the time of burial by having its base punctured.

LOVE VISIONS: DEEP DESIRE WITHIN THEIR HEARTS

Not many people know that some of the most appealing tribal myths are, in fact, engaging stories about true love. Myths reveal that tribes have always honored rituals of courtship and marriage. But many tribes had no spoken rules for runaway love or unharnessed lust. Rarely, if at all, can one find tribal myths that punished someone who fell in love with a person other than the one he or she was supposed to be with. Like Native American hero tales, many myths that seem to be about wild love are often really about preserving the tribal village's health and wealth.

Certain things catch your eye, but pursue only those that capture your heart.

NATIVE AMERICAN PROVERB

The Star Lovers

OJIBWE PEOPLE

There once were two young women who longed to make love to the stars, as they thought that stars made the best lovers and they were eager for the experience.

They decided to dream about the stars in their sleep, and let their dreams carry them to the stars during the night. And so the young women put on their very best outfits and washed their hair in order to look their best for the stars. They covered themselves in heavy blankets of fur and drifted off into the dreamworld.

Suddenly they opened their eyes and found that they were among the stars. They were surprised to learn that they each had a new star husband. Excited by this, the young women wasted no time with small talk. They insisted on making love to their husbands immediately.

After many long hours of very intense lovemaking the men decided they had to escape from the voracious women, for they feared making love constantly for the rest of their lives. The star husbands found an opening in the sky leading to the earth below. In order to reach the world below, they lowered a long rope and began to climb down. But on the way down they got stuck in an eagle's nest.

Unable to free themselves from the prickly walls of the eagle's nest, the star husbands cried out for help to the animals that passed by beneath them. When no one was interested in helping them, the husbands tried to tempt the animals with promises of wild lovemaking sessions. However, the only one interested in their offer was the wolverine.

Thinking they would trade one night of passion with the wolverine for their freedom, the star husbands gave themselves to the animal. But when the wolverine was finished he refused to let them go. Instead, the wolverine stuck them back into the thick and prickly nest walls. "Now I shall make love to you whenever I like," he said with a devious grin.

Below *Algon Captures a Star-maiden* by James Jack. According to Shawnee legend, the constellation Corona Borealis is made up of 12 Star-maidens. The hunter Algon fell in love with the youngest Star-maiden and carried her off to his home. She fell in love with Algon but was homesick, and eventually returned to the sky. Algon followed her and became the star Arcturus.

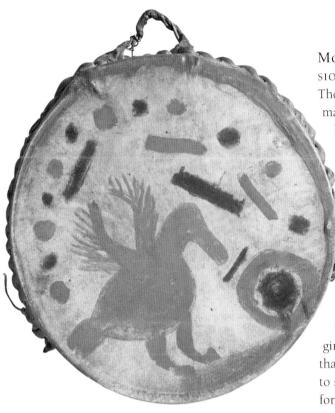

Moccasins of Love
SIOUX PEOPLE

The young hunter had never given much thought to marriage until he spotted the most beautiful girl he had ever seen. Just as he was returning from a hunt he saw her fetching water from the local stream. But even though he was a bold hunter he was very shy with women.

Unable to resist staring at her, the hunter hid in the bushes and watched the girl fill her bucket. After she was done she dried her feet in the warm grass. Then she put on her moccasins. The hunter was amazed at how superb the girl's shoes were.

The hunter lived with his grandmother, and when he returned he wanted to tell her about the girl at the river. He wished to tell his grandmother that he wanted to marry her. But he was even too shy to speak of his feelings to the woman who had cared for him his entire life.

Left **Hand drum with bird design, Ojibwe people.** As with other Native American cultures, the Ojibwe see the drum as the beating heart of the people. It plays a prominent part in social gatherings and religious ceremonies such as the Drum Dance, which is said to bring peace to the Ojibwe people.

The star husbands were furious with the wolverine and his trickery. After the wolverine left they once again called out to the other animals, pleading for their help. But they knew it was no use. They should have stayed with their wives—at least they would be free from the eagle's nest.

Not long after that a female wolverine came by and listened to the pleas of the star husbands. She promised to set the husbands free from the nest on one condition— that they help her in her quest to make passionate love to the male wolverine.

That night the male wolverine returned to the nest. The night was darker than most, and the wolverine had trouble seeing. But he concluded that he did not need his eyes to make love to the star husbands. After a long night of lovemaking, the wolverine woke up to the morning sun thinking that he had just had the best lovemaking he had ever experienced. But he also found that his lover was the female wolverine. Both wolverines were repulsed for they found each other to be terribly ugly.

But the wolverines were also practical animals. "Who else would have us," the female wolverine said. "Besides, I can't imagine either of us finding anyone who can make love as well as we can."

Above **Quilted moccasins, Sioux people.** Intricately decorated with colorful beads and porcupine quills, these leather moccasins feature a design of bear claws and buffalo heads. They may have been made for a Sioux hunter by his loving wife or proud grandmother.

THE SACRED PIPE

Often called "peace pipes" or "calumets," sacred pipes hold both religious and political significance for Native Americans. Tobacco symbolizes the wonder of creation, and in smoking it indigenous people show their respect for the Great Spirit who created all. As the smoke from the pipe rises, the thoughts, feelings, and prayers of the person holding the pipe travel upward to the Great Spirit. If the "keeper" of the pipe lives a good and righteous life, the pipe will reward him with honor and power.

Politically, the sacred pipe has played an important role in treaties between European settlers and Native American tribes. Smoking the sacred pipe signaled an agreement to seek out friendship and harmony between the cultures. To refuse to take part in the pipe-smoking ceremony was regarded by native people as a supreme insult.

Below **Pipe, Crow people.** The leader of a Crow war party would often sit apart from the other warriors to seek advice from the spirits by smoking his pipe. To this day the flag of the Crow nation features a pipe.

Below **Slate pipe, Santee people.** Many traditional Native American pipes were carved with figures of animals or people, who acted as spirit messengers between the earthly realm and the spiritual world. They carried the thoughts and prayers of the person upward in the smoke emanating from the pipe.

After supper the hunter's grandmother sat by the fire and started to sew up some holes in an old pair of moccasins. The hunter sat next to his grandmother, trying to work up the courage to tell her about the girl.

The grandmother knew something was on her grandson's mind, and asked him to tell her what it was. But he couldn't bring himself to confide in her. Instead he turned his attention to the moccasins. "Do women who make fine moccasins make good wives?" he asked. The old woman smiled, knowing exactly what was on her grandson's mind.

The next morning the young man again noticed the girl making her way down to the stream to fetch the day's water for her family. He looked at the pair of his grandmother's old moccasins. When she was not looking he grabbed the shoes, hid them in his shirt, and raced out the door.

Determined to meet the girl, he quickly put on the shoes and ran the entire way to the stream. Just as the girl had finished taking off her moccasins he slowed his pace and walked up to her, offering to fill the bucket for her.

Then he reached down and picked up her shoes, so he could give them back to the girl to put on again. But as he held her moccasins he could not help but admire how beautiful they were.

The girl looked at the hunter's old moccasins and noticed how worn they were. "You should have your grandmother make you a new pair," she said. But the hunter told her that his grandmother was nearly blind and could no longer sew.

Knowing the hunter was vying for her affection, the girl teased him by saying he should find a wife who could make him beautiful new moccasins.

Later the mother of the girl realized that her daughter had not returned from the stream. She set out to find her. When she arrived at the stream she saw the empty bucket. The mother was quite puzzled until she saw something in the sand that made her laugh. She saw two pairs of moccasin tracks leading toward the bushes.

Wolf Woman

DAKOTA PEOPLE

In the days and years that followed this story, the peoples remembered to replant the corn and to smoke the sacred tobacco. They did this to remember their First Mother and thank her for her sacrifice.

There once was a beautiful young woman who was not particularly interested in marriage. All the young men of the village attempted to court her, but none could win her heart. Finally she met a wonderful man to whom she found she could give herself in marriage. She had only one condition in accepting his proposal—he must always treat her kindly.

But not long after their marriage the man broke his promise. He often criticized her and he would beat her. Fearful for her life, the young woman ran away. The men of the village formed many search parties, but the woman was not found.

One day the woman came upon a strange man. Little did she know that he was not, in fact, a man at all.

He was the chief of the wolves. Feeling sure that he would not give her up to her cruel husband, she asked the wolf chief if he had any food as she was hungry. The wolf chief held out his hand and offered to take the woman to his village.

When they arrived at his village she found a pack of wolves gathered around a fire. It was then that she realized he was not a man after all. The wolf led her into a tipi and asked her what her pleasure for food was. The woman wanted buffalo meat.

The chief wolf ordered two in the village to go out and bring back some buffalo. When they returned the wolf asked her how they should prepare the meat, and the woman said the meat must be boiled. Then the wolf chief instructed that a large bundle should be opened up. The woman guessed that the contents of the bundle had been stolen from humans.

An iron pot and sharp knives were found inside the bundle. The wolf asked the woman what to do next. She replied that she sliced the meat.

And so she was given a knife and she began to slice away meat from the animal. She dropped the meat in the pot of boiling water. When the meat was ready, she prepared the meal for the entire pack of wolves. The woman stayed with the wild wolves for many months, always in charge of preparing each meal for them.

One night the chief wolf told the woman that her people were on a buffalo hunt, and if they continued in the direction they were heading, they would reach the wolves' camp by morning. The woman had to go to them and ward them off, as they would kill the wolves if they reached the camp.

Left **Wolf head effigy, Calusa people.** The Calusa were a highly religious people and believed in an afterlife. They used local shells and hardwood from nearby forests to create offerings to their ancestors in the form of statues and effigies of animals and birds.

Below *Mexican Coyote 1845* by Col. H. Smith, from Sir William Jardine's *The Naturalist's Library.* The coyote is related to the wolf, and is found from Alaska to Panama. Its wide distribution means that it has found a place in the mythology of many Native American peoples—mainly as a trickster.

Right **Wooden headdress, Nootka people.** Carved in the shape of a wolf and vividly painted, headdresses such as this were worn during the Wolf Society Ceremony (Tluukaana). As part of the ceremony, the elders would take the young men of the tribe away to teach them the heritage and rituals of the Nootka people. Legend has it that these rituals were given to the ancestor of the Nootka people by the all-knowing wolves.

The next day the woman went out to meet the hunting party. But when she neared the men she began to feel faint at the smell of the humans. One of the men recognized her. But the woman told them she had been living among the wolves and was not interested in returning to her people.

The men begged her to come back to the village. The woman was silent. Finally she told them to continue with their buffalo hunt. When they came back this way they had to give her the tongues and some of the best meat. The men agreed.

When they returned they brought her all the requested meat. The woman took the meat and spread it between two hills. Suddenly the hillsides were swarming with wolves who raced to the meat.

The woman returned to the village and eventually made up with her husband. She knew he would now treat her well for she had lived among the wild wolves.

HUMAN JOURNEY: STORIES OF DISCOVERY AND VICTORY

Two of the greatest gifts the Creator gave the peoples were the gifts of observation and humility. Native Americans have always paid close attention to the ways of the animals and plants. Many peoples found their way through famines and long, cold winters by watching how their relatives, the animals, managed.

But once in a while a human will be bestowed with special powers that can either be used for good or evil. Sadly, such humans can allow their pride to rise unchecked, causing great harm both to themselves and to others. But sometimes the gifted human does not allow their special powers to eclipse the simple gifts of observation and humility.

Buffalo Man
UTE PEOPLE

There once lived an old man and his wife. They were very frail and struggled to find food. They had no children to aid them with hunting and other food gathering activities because the woman was barren.

Facing starvation, the old man went out one last time to find some small game. Along the way he came upon some buffalo tracks. But he also noticed a small clot of blood that he guessed was something the buffalo had dropped. He wrapped it in a cloth and brought it home.

That night the old woman boiled some water and placed the blood clot in the pot. When she went to stir the pot she was shocked to see that a baby boy was inside. She lifted the boy from the pot and dried him in her arms.

THE IMPORTANCE OF THE BUFFALO

The buffalo, also know as the American bison, formed an essential part of the economy and culture of the Native Americans—particularly the tribes of the Plains—before the arrival of Europeans. They made use of virtually every part of the buffalo—from the hide and hooves to the bones and organs—and this bounty was believed to be a wonderful blessing from the Great Spirit above.

As well as being seen as a direct link to the Great Spirit, the buffalo was revered for its unique strength and power. Native Americans believed that incorporating "buffalo" as part of a child's name ensured that the child would grow up to be strong, while hunters who dreamed of buffalo regarded the beasts as their spiritual guides to successful hunting.

As befitting these important animals, there are many myths associated with the buffalo, such as "White Buffalo Woman" from the Sioux and Lakota tribes, and "Legend of the Buffalo Dance" from the Blackfeet people.

Left *Buffalo Hunt Under White Wolf Skin* by George Catlin (1796–1872). Men of the Great Plains tribes would hunt buffalo by either stalking them under wolf skins and using their bows and arrows, or by driving the herd over a cliff edge.

In only a few days the old couple noticed that the boy was growing very quickly. It wasn't long before the old man found the boy outside with his bow and arrow. The old man told his wife that the boy was an expert shooter, and he planned to send the boy out to hunt for their food.

The next day the old man instructed the boy to go on a hunt. The boy eagerly took the bow and left. Later that day he returned with nearly every kind of animal that lived in the land—from rabbits and deer to squirrels and birds. The old couple now had enough food to last them for many months.

Years later the boy had grown into a man. The old man soon realized that his adopted son needed to find his own tribe and live among his people. The young man agreed but before he left he wanted to make sure the couple had enough food to last them for their remaining days.

Not many days into his travels the man came upon a village, where he was greeted by the chief. The man told the chief he was looking for his tribe, for he didn't know where he came from. Feeling sorry for the man, the chief offered to let him live among his people.

It was not long before the young man fell in love with the chief's beautiful daughter. The chief allowed him to marry his daughter because he was such a great hunter.

One night the young man told the villagers that a great storm was approaching. He told everyone to fasten down their tipis. The next morning there was a dead buffalo in front of every tipi. It was then the young man realized that he was of the buffalo tribe. But he loved his wife deeply and he told her that in order for him to stay with her people she must not say the words "buffalo calf."

Many weeks later when the men were preparing for a buffalo hunt, the young man's wife forgot about her husband's words of warning in her excitement about the hunt. She cried out to the men, "Kill the buffalo calf!" At once the young man started to flee the village, turning into a buffalo as he ran. His wife called out to him to return, but he did not. He lived the rest of days among his own—the buffalo.

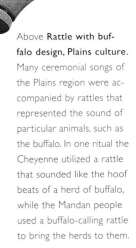

Above **Rattle with buffalo design, Plains culture.** Many ceremonial songs of the Plains region were accompanied by rattles that represented the sound of particular animals, such as the buffalo. In one ritual the Cheyenne utilized a rattle that sounded like the hoof beats of a herd of buffalo, while the Mandan people used a buffalo-calling rattle to bring the herds to them.

Raven Feast

APACHE PEOPLE

Long ago the peoples only had two kinds of seeds for food. They would grind the seeds in preparation for their meals. One day a raven noticed a woman and a man leaving their tipi. Not realizing that there were children inside the tipi, the raven hung his quiver on one of the poles.

Later, when the children came out to play they found the quiver hanging on the pole. They lifted it down and looked inside, seeing some meat. They eagerly ate the food and instantly became fat.

When their parents returned they were in awe at the strange sight of their fat children. While they were inside the tipi, the raven returned to fetch his quiver. The parents watched as the raven flapped his wings and flew away with his empty quiver.

When the rest of village heard the story of the raven's food, it was decided that a group of scouts should seek out the home of the ravens and discover where the birds got their special meat.

For four days the group traveled, and it was a distance that no one had ever traveled before. Finally they found the ravens' camp. They waited until the ravens left the camp, then discovered a bed of ashes where the birds prepared their meat. In order to get close enough to the ravens, a boy was changed into a puppy. They placed the puppy near the ashes, hoping the ravens would befriend him.

Indeed, when the ravens returned they felt great affection for the puppy and they wrapped him in a blanket. As night approached, the puppy watched as the ravens removed a large stone from the ashes, revealing a deep hole in the ground. The ravens descended into the hole and were away for a long time. When they returned they brought back a buffalo with them that was killed for supper.

The next day when the ravens departed, the boy turned himself back into his normal human shape. He found a black feather and a white feather near the ravens' camp. He removed the stone and climbed down the hole with the two feathers. Below he found four buffalo. He placed the white feather on the mouth of one of the buffalo, and commanded the animal to follow him to the world above.

But the buffalo told him he must go to the last buffalo among them. And so the boy went to the fourth buffalo, placed the feather on his mouth, and commanded it to follow him to the world above.

But the buffalo told the boy that he needed to stuff the feather in the first buffalo's mouth. And so the boy did, declaring to the first buffalo that it would be king of all the animals if it followed him to the world above.

Meanwhile the ravens had returned to find their puppy gone. Suddenly the stone in the middle of the ashes was overturned. The boy and a herd of buffalo

put it back in place at will. He could also turn himself into a pile of bones if he wanted.

Word spread throughout the village about the boy with the amazing special powers. Feeling threatened by his growing popularity, the chief attempted to belittle the boy and his powers. The boy refused to be treated in such a way, and soon a fight broke out between the two. The chief was no match for the boy, who was very strong. With a swift jab the boy managed to knock the chief down to his death.

The warriors were enraged and they raced to the boy. But the boy kicked a kettle of boiling water into the fire, causing a large cloud of steam to rise. The warriors were lost in the steamy cloud and the boy escaped from them.

For days the warriors tracked the boy but they never got close enough to capture him. The clever boy managed to elude the men at every turn. It seemed to the warriors that the boy could disappear into the rocks of the mountainside.

One day, after the boy eluded the party of angry warriors by slipping magically into the mountainside, he realized that he was not alone. He turned to see a council of old men. One of the old men told the boy not to be frightened, as they were not there to capture or harm him. They were there to help him and his people.

Trusting the wise men, the boy—who was tired of constantly being pursued—asked if he could stay among them. For four years the men taught the boy many mysteries and secrets about the universe. When they felt his training was complete they gave him a bundle of arrows with special powers.

As the boy, who was now a man, neared his home, he shot and killed a buffalo. He thought that this act of goodness might help the village forgive him for killing the chief. Little did he know that a great famine had come over his people while he had been away. They not only welcomed him home, but they made him their chief as well.

came rising from the world below. The ravens scrambled to close the lid but it was too late. The boy and buffalo escaped.

As the ravens watched the boy leading the buffalo to his people's camp, they cried out for the boy to save the eyes for the ravens when the beasts were killed.

When the boy returned home with the buffalo, the chief slit the throat of the first buffalo and a feast was prepared. And the boy saved the animal's eyes just for the ravens.

Boy in the Mountain
CHEYENNE PEOPLE

It was the longest pregnancy that anyone in the village had ever seen. The woman was with child for four years. The elders in the village talked among themselves, musing that when it arrived the child was sure to have special powers.

Indeed, when the woman finally gave birth to the baby, she found the boy to have supernatural skills. Amazingly, the boy could remove his own head and

Below **Detail of a hide warrior's cloak, Apache people.** This cloak features an image of a Gan, one of the mountain spirits who were responsible for teaching the first Apaches how to govern themselves, hunt for food, and heal the sick. The Gans eventually returned to the mountains, but they can still be prayed to in times of need.

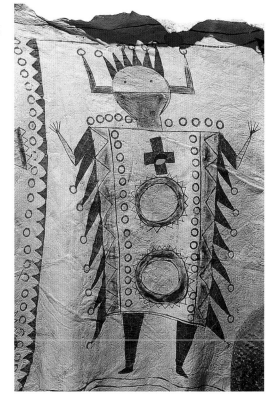

MOTHER EARTH: MYTHS OF LAND AND WATER

For many generations Native Americans have recognized that to truly live in balance with the world they needed to respect both the land and the water. For it is only in respecting and honoring Mother Earth that the peoples can be prosperous. Caring for the land and water has given tribes plentiful food and game. The stories and ceremonies of the peoples come from the land. Without a good relationship with the land and water, Native Americans believe there will be no world for their future generations.

Treat the earth well: it was not given to you by your parents, it was loaned to you by your children. We do not inherit the earth from our ancestors, we borrow it from our children.

NATIVE AMERICAN PROVERB

Monsters and Floods
CADDO PEOPLE

It was not uncommon for monsters to be born among the peoples. Usually they were killed immediately for fear of what they would do to the villagers. But on one occasion a chief's wife convinced her husband that the four monsters she bore him would make productive members of the tribe.

The chief, of course, was entirely opposed to his wife's desires. However, he relented after it was learned that she would not be able to have any more children. Convinced that she could raise the monsters to be good members of the tribe, she fed and nurtured them as any devoted mother would do.

Right *Nekumonta Collapses in the Snow* by James Jack. In this Iroquois myth, the warrior Nekumonta falls to the ground exhausted after searching for special herbs that will save his sick wife. As Nekumonta is a good person who respects the earth, the great spirit Manitou sends him a message in a dream, telling him of the healing waters that will cure his wife.

But it soon became apparent to everyone—as the monsters grew much larger than the rest of the villagers—that something had to be done to ensure the tribe's safety. It was decided that they would be banned from the village. But before they could be banished the monsters went on a rampage, devouring the villagers at will.

In just a few days the monsters killed nearly everyone in the village. Finally an old man in the village, who had been left alone by the monsters because of his skinny frame, heard a voice telling him that the monsters' parents needed to hide in a hollow tree trunk. A great flood was coming and the entire land would be covered with water, the old man told the monsters' parents. The mother wanted to know when this would happen.

"There will be a sign, a cloud of birds will form in the sky," the old man replied. "It will rain until the whole earth is flooded."

The old man was right. Just as the parents entered a hollow tree trunk near the village they saw a cloud of birds overhead. Suddenly the skies opened up with heavy rains that lasted for many days. The parents clung to each other in the floating trunk until the skies cleared.

Meanwhile a turtle was resting at the bottom of the flooded land when he heard a voice telling him to attack the monsters. The turtle thought he was no match for the monsters' great strength, but the voice assured him that the monsters were at a disadvantage in the deep, swirling waters.

The turtle took comfort in that, and he set out to ambush the monsters. He decided he would come right up under the monsters, who were staying afloat at the surface. The little turtle rammed the monsters and then with his sharp teeth he easily ripped them to pieces.

As the days continued the hot sun began to dry the land. Soon the parents were able to walk around again. It took some time but eventually the land was repopulated with a wealth of animals and plants. And

much to the joyous surprise of the woman she was able to have more children. So in time they repopulated the land with humans.

First Mother

PENOBSCOT PEOPLE

Before the time of the world's peoples there was only the All Maker. One day while standing on the shores of the great waters, the All Maker saw the unique shape of a young man emerging in the crashing waves.

He watched as the waves rolled up on the shore, tossing and turning the shape of the youth in the foam and sand. Finally the water yielded the young man. The sun dried his frame and the moist wind gave him breath. The All Maker decided to appoint the young man as his chief helper.

Above **Pottery bowl with hermaphroditic monster, Anasazi people.** Produced by women, the pottery of the Anasazi was made from smoothed coils of clay—which contained the spirit of Mother Earth—and was decorated with geometric designs, symbols of the artist's clan, or images of mythological creatures.

Left **Beaded buckskin pouch in the form of a turtle, Plains culture.** Associated with both fertility and long life, the turtle is a potent Native American symbol for women. This pouch held a female baby's umbilical cord, and was carried later in life to protect the woman from ill health.

Not many days later a young girl appeared to the All Maker and his chief helper. She said she was born from the earth, nourished by the plants, and given blood from the morning dew. She announced that she was the giver of life to all men and animals.

The All Maker thanked the Great Mystery for sending him the young girl. In time the young girl and young man were married. She conceived and gave birth to the peoples. She became the First Mother. The All Maker taught the peoples to live, and then he went north to live for the rest of his years. He returned only when called upon by the peoples for his help and guidance.

As the population grew in size, the hunger of the peoples also grew. There were not enough sources of food to feed all the world's peoples. The First Mother was saddened at the starvation facing her children, and promised to find food for all her young ones.

First Mother spent the evening alone, apart from the peoples, hoping that she could find a way to feed her children. As the evening wore on, her husband came to her, feeling her sadness and frustration. He asked her what he could do to help.

The First Mother knew that the only thing left to do was to have her husband kill her. But her husband refused. She looked her husband long in the eyes and he felt her sadness in a new way.

The next morning the husband traveled north to see the All Maker. The All Maker revealed to the husband that the First Mother would go on with her sadness forever unless he killed her—that the husband had no choice.

The First Mother was very specific about what her husband had to do after he killed her. He had to have his two older sons drag her body across a patch of land by her hair, until only her bones remained. They must then gather her bones and bury them in a small clearing nearby. They were to wait seven moons before returning to the spot, and when they returned they would find her flesh nourishing the land.

And so, with great sadness, the husband took his wife's life. The sons dragged her body across the land until her flesh covered every part of the ground. Her bones were buried and many tears were shed by the

Above **Stone sculpture of a nursing mother, Coast Salish people.** Found along the Pacific Northwest coast of the U.S.A. and into Canada, the Coast Salish people created bowls and tools from local stone, as well as sculptures that were used in shamanistic rituals.

Right **Mother and child sculpture, Nootka people.** Nootka mythology is rich in stories involving mothers. In one, Tihtipihin and Kwatyat are two brothers who rescue their mother from the stomach of a monster. A second tale tells of a woman whose children have been kidnapped by a malevolent forest deity named Malahas. As she cries, the woman's tears become a fully grown man, Andaokut, who saves the children by killing Malahas.

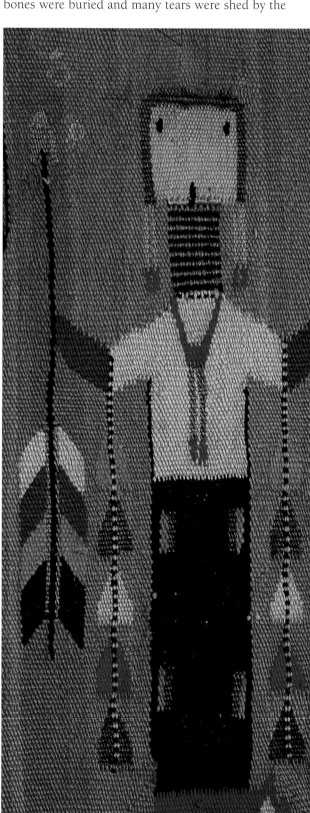

family. Seven months later they returned and found the land covered with tall green stalks bearing fresh corn. When they tasted it, they found that the corn was sweet. The husband instructed the sons to gather all the corn but to save some of the kernels so they could return them to the earth. He also found a new plant, called tobacco. Before they left they breathed in the sacred smoke of the tobacco plant and offered a prayer on behalf of the First Mother.

Traveling Tribes
CHOCTAW PEOPLE

There came a day when the people who dwelt in the west found their numbers had grown too big for the land. The land offered not enough food to support the tribe. Rather than face years of famine and death, the tribe sought the wisdom of their elders. The elders decided that the tribe needed to move from this land in search of a wealthier region to support them. And so two brothers were called upon to lead the tribe eastward in search of those more prosperous lands.

As the tribe prepared for the long journey, packing up their belongings, the elders called the brothers to a special council meeting. One of the elders presented the brothers with a magical rod that had been with the tribe as long as they could remember.

The elder told the brothers that the rod would guide them and the people to the right place. He warned the brothers not to rely on their hearts and minds, only to trust the rod. For if they did, they would find pleasant lands for the people, lands that would feed them for generations.

The brothers took great care of the magical rod as they led the tribe across the land. Like the elders had said, the rod guided the people on their journey. Each night during their long travels, the brothers would place the rod in the ground. Whichever direction it faced in the morning was the way the brothers would lead the people.

There were many tests along the way. Often many in the tribe liked certain places that they passed, and desired to settle there because there was a river and plenty of woods and animals.

But the brothers always reminded the people that they were not to settle on any lands unless the magical rod stood straight up. Though the people grew tired of the long journey and longed to end their traveling, they had faith in the brothers and in the wisdom of their elders.

Finally, after many weeks of traveling, they found a place that they hoped would be their new home. The land was rich with all the things they once knew in their old world. That night the brothers could only hope the magical rod would agree.

Above **Detail from an eighteenth-century sketch of Choctaw warriors.** The Choctaw myth of the two brothers and the magical rod that would only stand up in the land in which they were to settle is reminiscent of an origin myth of the South American Incas. The sun god Inti gave his son Ayar Manco Capac a golden rod, and told him to settle in the place where the rod disappeared when plunged into the ground—that place was Cuzco.

Left **Nineteenth-century blanket, Navajo people.** As a staple part of their diet, the maize plant featured prominently in the mythology of the Navajo. A deity called Estanatlehi (Changing Woman) created maize, which became the symbolic plant of the north. Later, the "Holy People" produced the first humans from the sacred maize.

THE THUNDERBIRD

One of the most well-known characters in Native American mythology, the Thunderbird is found in the stories of cultures right across present-day U.S.A., from the northwest coast through the Great Plains to the northeast. It is said to cause thunderclaps and windstorms by flapping its wings, while dazzling bolts of lightning are cast down from its eyes.

The Thunderbird is a creature of remarkable contrasts. It is sometimes viewed as a physical entity, with a number of researchers even believing that the myth is based on the existence long ago of enormous birds of prey, but is more often seen as a spiritual representation of nature's power. The Thunderbird can be benevolent—protecting Native Americans from monsters and evil spirits, and providing rain for crops—or malevolent—preying on people and animals, and destroying the land with hail storms and floods.

Below **Ghost Dance shirt with Thunderbird design, Plains culture.** The result of a vision beheld by Wovoka, a Paiute man, the Ghost Dance was said to bring peace, hope, and prosperity to the native peoples. The Thunderbird design may have symbolized protection for the owner of this shirt.

In the morning there was great joy in the camp. The rod was not pointing in any direction. It only faced straight up. But before they could settle in they knew that they must first honor their ancestors. A grand ceremony was performed and the tribe buried their ancestors' bones in a special mound.

But soon after making their home in this new land it was apparent that even this place could not support everyone. But the people did not want to leave the mound where they had buried their ancestors. It was decided that one of the brothers would lead half the tribe north to settle. In time it was reported that the people found prosperous land in the north and they became a tribe of their own. Even today one can find the northern tribe thriving. And one can find the southern tribe still alive and well, living close to the sacred mound where their ancestors remain.

SKY MYSTERIES: STORIES OF THE WORLD ABOVE

The world above has always enchanted and mystified Native Americans. Just about every star has been named, and there are a great many myths inspired by the celestial realm. Many tribal myths tell of great journeys across the skies to uncover hidden secrets of life below, above, and beyond. Some of the most sacred ceremonies and dances of Native American tribes have come to the peoples from the skies. But the world above is not an entirely safe place. For every kind spirit there is always a violent one eager to ambush any would-be sojourner.

Flying Sky Spirits
SEMINOLE PEOPLE

There once were five young men who were far too curious for their own good. They had many questions about their world that no one in the village could answer.

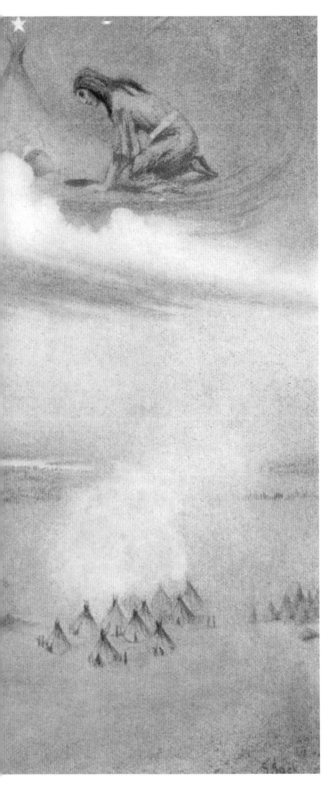

their own safety they would throw their bags over the edge to see if they could float. Much to their surprise the bags floated in the wind. The men did not hesitate in jumping over the edge.

And so they made their way across the sky for many days, looking for the Great Spirit. Finally they came upon an old woman living in a tiny lodge, who asked them why they had come there.

They told her of their journey to see the Great Spirit, and of their question about flying sky spirits, then asked her which way they must go.

The old woman answered that they could not see the Great Spirit at this time, and instructed them to stay with her for a few days.

During the first evening the curiosity of the men was too great. They did not want to wait with the old woman. The men decided to leave the lodge and continue on with their journey.

Not far from the old woman's lodge they came upon a band of angels. The angels were playing a game that the men used to play back in their village. The angels invited the men to join them. After the game, two of the men decided they wanted to become angels. Suddenly the Great Spirit appeared and promised to grant the men their wish.

A kettle of water was placed upon a fire. When the water began to boil, the Great Spirit placed the two men in the pot. They were boiled down to their bones. The Great Spirit removed the bones from the kettle and put them back together. The bones suddenly turned into angels dressed in white. The other men were in such awe, their strong curiosity about life's mysteries seemed fulfilled.

"What other mysteries would you like to know?" the Great Spirit asked.

The men looked at each other and could think of no other questions about life's mysteries for the Great Spirit. Instead they asked if they could return to their world. The Great Spirit instructed the men to sleep, and when they awoke they would find themselves back in their village. And indeed the Great Spirit's words proved true, for when the men opened their eyes after a deep sleep they were back in their village. The chief of the village was relieved when the men announced that they no longer wanted to know the secrets of the great mysteries.

Often they were seen doing nothing but staring into the sky, talking among themselves.

One day a question about flying sky spirits came up among the men. One of them suggested that the only way to get an answer was to travel to the sky and meet the Great Spirit.

The men packed their bags and started the long journey to the edge of the land, with hopes of learning about all the mysteries from the Great Spirit itself. When they reached the land's end they stared into the expansive sky. They decided that to be sure about

Left *Feather-woman Gazes Down From Sky Country* by James Jack. In this Blackfeet legend, Feather-woman marries a star-man and lives in the sky with him. He tells her of a place where she can dig up turnips, but warns her not to dig up the big turnip. One day, full of curiosity about the big turnip, Feather-woman digs it up—only to discover she has made a hole in the clouds, through which she can see her people down on earth. On seeing the Blackfeet camp, Feather-woman becomes sad.

Below **Buckskin chart of the night sky, Pawnee people.** The stars were held in great reverence by the Pawnee people, as they saw the stars as benevolent gods responsible for providing them with sacred ceremonial bundles. There were numerous rituals devoted to the stars, and homes were often laid out in the shape of important constellations.

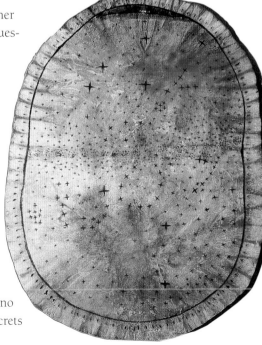

Above **Cave painting of the sun, Chumash people.** According to Chumash mythology, the sun lights the world by carrying a flaming bark torch across the sky. At the end of his long journey he causes the torch to throw many sparks up into the sky, which become the stars.

Sun's Daughter
CHEROKEE PEOPLE

While visiting her daughter and brother moon one afternoon, the sun complained about the people below. She did not care for the way they always squinted their eyes at her. Brother moon said he liked the people, as they always smiled at him. This, of course, made the sun jealous, and she decided to send a burning fever down to the people.

The sun made good on her promise. A terrible fever spread throughout the land below. Many people grew very sick and quite a few died. The people were bewildered as to why the sun was causing such sickness among their own. Those who were strong enough decided they needed to kill the sun if their people were to live.

It was decided that someone would need to use a bit of magic to turn into a snake. He would wait at the door of the sun's daughter's house, and when the sun visited he would bite the sun. Special magic was prepared and a volunteer offered to have a spell cast on him that would turn him into a snake. Once he was changed into a snake the volunteer went to the daughter's house and waited.

But during the wait the snake was startled when the daughter opened the front door. He accidentally bit her instead. The daughter fell dead, and the snake quickly returned to earth.

> *There is no death.*
> *Only a change of worlds.*
> CHIEF SEATTLE (SEATHL),
> DUWAMISH (1786–1866)

When the sun found her dead daughter she was distraught. She hid herself behind the clouds and grieved. This, of course, put an end to the fever, but also made the world turn cold and dark. The people feared the sun would never stop grieving and that eventually they would all freeze. They decided they needed to bring the sun's daughter back from the land of dancing ghosts.

The sun promised that if the people brought her daughter back, she would come out from behind the clouds and would not send another fever among them. And so seven people were selected for the mission of bringing the daughter back. It was a short journey, and they spotted the daughter right away. She was dancing with the other ghosts.

They made a plan to catch her off guard. Two men would strike her over the head with clubs, two would keep watch, and the rest of them would be prepared to place her in a box.

Once the men accomplished their goal of knocking the sun's daughter out and placing her in the box, they quickly made their way toward home. But along the way the daughter complained loudly that she was not able to breathe in the box. She wanted the men to open the lid a little.

But just as they opened the box's lid the daughter turned into a bird and flew out of the box and back to the land of ghosts. The men surmised that she had loved dancing more than life.

The men debated a long time about what to tell the sun. They feared greatly that the sun would never return upon hearing about their failure to rescue her daughter. But as the days passed the sun realized that the men had failed. She began to cry, which caused a great flood on the earth. The people were so desperate

NATIVE AMERICAN DANCE

Native American dance has many functions, including the expression of emotion, the promotion of cultural identity, the healing of ills, the influencing of nature, and the honoring of gods. Dances are thought to have been given to the tribes by the Great Spirit, animal friends, or even vanquished monsters, to be passed on from generation to generation to ensure the ongoing preservation of ancient beliefs and ways of living.

Many Native American dances are performed in a circular pattern, symbolizing the never-ending circle of life. Although the dances can be accompanied by a range of instruments—from rattles and whistles to rhythm sticks—the base drum beat is at the center of the dance and represents the beating heart of nature personified, Mother Earth.

Some of the most well-known Native American dances include the Ute Bear Dance, the Hopi Snake

Dance, and the Sun Dance and Ghost Dance performed by many of the Plains peoples.

Below **Hide painting showing Sun Dance, Sioux people.** The Sun Dance was held only once a year, at the time of the summer solstice. It brought the whole tribe together for a sacred ceremony celebrating renewal and regeneration, which lasted four to eight days.

they told the sun that all they could offer her was her daughter's special dance. When the sun saw how the people danced like her daughter she was immensely relieved. From that day forward each time the sun felt sad and began to cry—causing rain to fall—the people would dance like her daughter. And that would ease the sun's grief for her daughter.

TRIBAL PASSAGES: LOVE, DEATH, AND THE COMING OF AGE

Tribal myths were critical for keeping a sense of harmony and balance among the villagers. Roles were always made clear. Whether it was hunting or cooking, each person in the tribe contributed to this balance by fulfilling their designated role. And while having to leave the mother's bosom to cross into the difficult world of adulthood came with its share of trauma, and the sudden death of a loved one was not always immediately accepted, the recognition of natural and spiritual passages among community members was always steadfast. It was through hearing the traditional tribal myths that the villagers found their life's calling and the courage to face such necessary tribal passages.

Left **Pot decorated with images of severed hands, Hopewell people.** Used to hold funerary offerings, special mortuary pots were placed beside the deceased. The body and its grave goods were then buried under enormous amounts of earth—these earth mounds sometimes took the shape of animals such as snakes or alligators.

The Rattlesnake's Wife
POMO PEOPLE

When the clover was just right to eat, little girls loved to go into the fields and pluck it. Often they would pass by secret pits of rattlesnakes that lived in the rocks. The snakes kept to themselves because they feared the humans. Little did they know that the humans feared them as well.

One bright and breezy afternoon a rattlesnake happened to be slithering along through the grass when he noticed a little girl picking some of the clover. More than curious, the snake watched the young girl, noticing how beautiful she looked.

When the girl was finished picking the clover she started for home, and the snake followed her. Just as they neared her home he turned himself into a human, for he was overcome with desire. When he came to the door the family was surprised to see him, for they had never seen him before. The girl's village was very small and everyone knew everyone.

The rattlesnake told the girl's father that he had seen his beautiful daughter out in the fields, and wished to marry her. Not prepared to say yes or no, the family invited the stranger to stay the night. In the early morning he turned back into a snake. He realized he needed to leave before the family saw him. But upon arriving back among the other rattlesnakes his desire for the young girl grew. He went back to her home and just before he reached her door he turned back into a human.

Above **Carved coiled serpent with incised diamond pattern.** A pre-Columbian artifact from an unknown Californian tribe, this carving probably represents a western diamondback rattlesnake, which is found throughout southwestern U.S.A. This particular snake features in the art and mythology of the region as a symbol of power and sexual potency.

Right *The Monster Rattlesnake* by James Jack. In a Sioux myth, a war party is confronted by a monster rattlesnake, who rears up as if to strike. The men are afraid, but the chief bravely aims his arrow at the monster rattlesnake and kills it with one shot.

The family invited him to stay again for they still had not made up their minds. But in the morning he again turned back into a rattlesnake. This went on for four days straight. And, like the snake's desire for the girl, the little girl's affection for the stranger grew as well.

Finally on the fifth day the snake decided that he was not going to wait anymore. Should he stay a fifth night he would not leave in the morning. Sure enough, he was asked to stay the night and in the morning, as expected, he turned back into a rattlesnake. Instead of leaving he waited until the family awakened.

Once again he asked for the girl's hand in marriage. The mother of the girl looked around the room, not knowing where the voice came from. Then she looked on the ground and saw the rattlesnake beside her. She was terrified and ran out of the house. But the girl did not. She found the snake even more appealing, and agreed to become his wife.

The girl returned with the snake to his home in the rocks. They lived very well together for many years. The girl even bore four boys. As the children grew older they realized that their mother did not look very much like their father. Their mother explained that she was a human, not a rattlesnake like their father. She warned them that if they saw any humans they must not bite them, for they were their relatives.

She decided that she would let the snakes crawl all over her body to see that humans were not their enemies. The snakes slithered across her frame and were satisfied. They vowed that they would never strike out against the humans if they should ever meet them in the fields.

One day the woman realized that she needed to return home to tell her parents what had happened to her. And though her family was happy to see her again, they were equally sad to learn that she was going back to the rattlesnakes. It was the last time her family ever saw her again.

Dark Wind

MENOMINEE PEOPLE

In the thick woods surrounding the Great Waters there lived a little girl with her mother in their hut covered with birch bark. The girl's father was away on a hunt along the northern shore and would not return until autumn. For the women, summer was a time of gathering berries and herbs while the men hunted deer and other larger animals. This was a time to store up for the long, cold winter that would come upon the thick woods in just a few months.

But one morning the mother decided her little girl would have to stay home because the southern sky was the darkest it had been all year. The girl watched her mother staring at the black clouds, then begged to be allowed to go with her mother.

The mother just looked at her daughter and shook her head. She told the girl she would be back by suppertime, and instructed her to make sure the fire was started by the time she returned.

The little girl stood in front of her mother and stomped her bare feet into the grass, refusing to let her mother leave without her.

But the mother would not be swayed. She warned her daughter of the dark wind that was coming for her, the wind that comes for all girls her age, and told her to go inside. The girl clung to her mother's basket and burst into tears, as she was afraid and did not want to be left alone.

At that her mother relented. But before allowing the girl to gather food with her, the mother made her promise that she would never look at the southern sky until nightfall. The girl promised that she would keep her eyes on her work and not the sky.

Left **Native American Woman and Child, 1758.** In a Menominee myth, the dark southern sky signaled danger. However, in general the Menominee people saw the upper world as a good place ruled by the sun, a place that was separated from the evil lower realm by an island of earth inhabited by humans.

Below **Anthropomorphic bowl, Coast Salish people.** Bowls featuring seated human figures were used by shamans in the purification rites associated with the onset of female puberty. The figures often have a rattlesnake carved down the back, which is a symbol of fertility.

Right **Fetish bowl, Zuni people.** Fetishes were animal or nature spirits carved from stone, which offered the owner luck, protection, fertility, and more when they were looked after properly. The fetish was kept in a special decorated bowl, and was "fed" through a hole in the side of the pottery piece.

Later that afternoon as the entire sky began to darken, the mother grew very tired and said she needed to rest against a large pine tree. She warned her daughter again about not looking at the southern sky. But as soon as her mother fell into a deep sleep the little girl raced to the edge of the forest so she could get a clear view of the sky.

Suddenly the day turned to night. A huge wind came screaming out of the southern sky. It whipped around the girl, sweeping her off the ground, up into the clouds. But as quickly as she was swept up she came down again, landing softly on a bush of blackberries. She quickly got up and ran to her mother, who was still sleeping. Fearing that she would get in trouble for looking at the southern sky, the little girl did not tell her mother what had happened.

Later that night the mother awoke to the screams of her daughter. She held the girl in her arms, wiping the cold sweat from her forehead. Before she could say anything her little girl began to give birth to three children—Nanabozho, Brother Wolf, and a sharp stone. It was then the mother realized that her young daughter had looked into the darkness of the southern sky. Before she could scold the girl she saw that the sharp edges of the stone had pierced her daughter's womb. The mother tried to stop the bleeding, but the girl had lost too much blood. By morning her daughter was dead.

The mother cared for Nanabozho and Brother Wolf as her own children. When the two had grown up she placed the stone in her small pouch and led everyone to the edge of the forest. She watched as Nanabozho and Brother Wolf ran off to live on their own. The mother looked at the southern sky, which was bright blue. She reached into her pouch and held the sharp stone in her hand. Then she flung it toward the sky, and it never returned.

The Red Feather
ZUNI PEOPLE

It was the most unexpected thing to happen to any young man. One day, after returning from a long and tiring journey, he found his wife's body in her bed, icy cold with death.

He pleaded with his dead wife to come back from the spirit world and comfort him. That night she appeared to him, and told him she must go on a journey. She added that if he followed her he would have the chance to bring her back into the world of the living.

Then the wife reached for a bright red eagle feather and raised it slowly to her head. As she tied it to her long hair she told her husband that the feather would be his guiding light because spirits become invisible in the other world.

Eager to have his wife back, the man followed her. For many days he trailed, trying to keep up. Then one day they reached a deep ravine. But while she easily moved down the ravine without effort, the husband began to slip, almost falling to certain death. But a nearby squirrel called out to the man, and pointed out the safest passage to take. The man was grateful to the squirrel, as he managed to safely reach the bottom of the ravine.

Once at the bottom he followed his wife to a dark lake. She dove into the water, sinking beneath the

THE MAGNIFICENT EAGLE

Respected for its special strength and skill, and revered as sacred, the eagle played a prominent role in the lives of most Native American peoples. Many saw the eagle as a messenger, carrying prayers to the gods and conveying visions to the warriors and holy men. Their talons were considered powerful talismans that protected the owner from harm, and medicine men used the tubelike bones from the wings to extract the spirit of disease from the body.

But perhaps the most valued part of the eagle was its feathers. They represented the eagle's courage, power, and intelligence, and the special few who bore the feathers on their headdresses or weapons were thought to be imbued with those much-venerated characteristics.

There are many myths related to the eagle. Hopi people believed that the dead were transformed into clouds in the sky, where the eagle was the ruler, while the Delaware people tell the story of the chief who was able to lead his people safely through enemy territory with the help of an eagle's feather.

Below **Eagle wing fan, Crow people.** The feathered wing of the sacred eagle was used by the shaman of the Crow tribe during curing rituals, as the eagle was seen as a powerful medicine.

surface. Fearing he would drown if he pursued her, the man sat on the shore in despair. But then an owl noticed the man and felt sorry for him. He offered to help the man find his wife. The man had to follow the owl to his people's cave and listen to their instructions. He warned the man that if he did not listen to their words he would lose his wife forever.

The man promised he would do whatever the owls told him to do. As soon as they reached the cave, the owl offered some sleeping medicine to the man. He promised that when the man awoke, he would find his bride at his side.

Fully trusting the group of wise owls, the man drank the medicine. In minutes he was fast asleep. When he awoke he was overjoyed to see his wife next to him. But when he reached for her, one of the owls told him not to touch her until the couple reached the man's village. If the man touched his wife before then, she would be returned to the land of the dead forever.

The man believed the owl's words, and he fought the temptation to embrace his wife on their journey home. Just as they were nearing the outskirts of their village she grew very tired and begged her husband to let her take a short nap. While she slept the man was so taken by her beauty that he reached out and touched her brow. Suddenly she turned invisible, leaving the red feather in her place on the ground.

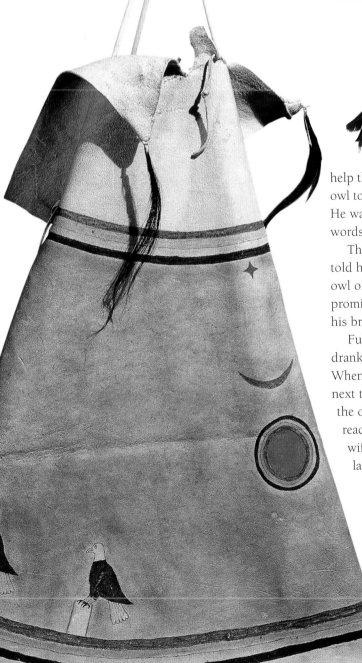

Left **Model of a medicine tipi, Cheyenne people.** Medicine tipis were usually erected for ceremonial purposes, and the exterior decoration came from a vision or dream. This tipi bears images of the sun, moon, and a star, as well as eagles ready to carry the owner's prayers from earth to the spirits in the sky.

INUIT MYTHOLOGY

As with the Native American cultures discussed elsewhere in this volume, Inuit peoples from the North American Arctic (which include peoples from Canada, Alaska, and Greenland) have had to adapt to the changes brought by European colonization of North America. These changes have affected their cultures, including their religions and mythology. However, the timing and the degree of change introduced in these cultures and their myths differ from region to region. For instance, Danish explorers, traders, and missionaries landed in Greenland over 300 years ago, causing great changes in religious practices. In contrast, although Russians first visited western Alaska in the mid- to late 1700s, it was not until the 1890s that a sustained U.S. presence, in the form of missionary-teachers and Revenue Cutter servicemen, forced great changes in Yup'ik and Inupiaq religions. In Canada, government educational and settlement programs were not instituted among the Inuit until the 1930s. This difference in timing has affected how many and what kind of traditional myths are still told in Inuit communities today.

Presenting traditional Inuit myths in published form has many inherent difficulties. The preferred method for retelling the stories is to refrain from editing them, in order to allow readers to hear the indigenous Inuit voices. In addition, contemporary folklore scholarship frowns upon retelling myths that mix several versions from different places and different storytellers. Such retellings would not allow readers to know which words came from the scholar and which from the storyteller, or where the myth or story originated. Contemporary folklore scholars also frown upon retelling myths that the scholar did not personally record, and if one does, proper attribution must be given. Finally, contemporary scholars now recognize indigenous intellectual property rights, so that, ethically speaking, scholars should always obtain permission from the native people before telling a particular story from that tribe or clan. The myths retold in this chapter are widely known, and fall under three themes important to Inuit peoples: creation, relationships, and animals. Where possible, all sources of information have been provided.

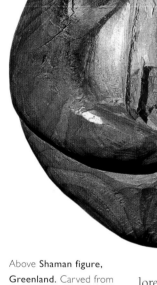

Above **Shaman figure, Greenland.** Carved from wood, this representation of a shaman may have been used by the medicine man of the village to communicate with the spirits and to seek their help during curing and divining rites.

Right **Female fertility figurine known as the "Okvik Madonna."** Produced during the Okvik period of indigenous Alaskan history—which occurred around 2,000 years ago—this simple sculpture was carved from the ivory of a walrus.

CREATION

The following three myths recount the origins of various things in Inuit cosmology. The first two stories reveal the origin of two of the three principal powers in Inuit thought. The first tale is based upon a myth found in Knud Rasmussen's *Report of the Fifth Thule Expedition* and tells the origin of the female sea spirit known as "Sedna." The second myth tells the origin of

Above **Walrus figurine, Ipiutak people, Alaska.** Marine mammals such as walruses and whales feature prominently in the myths of the Inuit peoples, especially those from seaside areas such as the Ipiutak culture (A.D. 1–800), which existed close to the Bering Strait.

the sun and moon (and thus, the "moon man," one of the principal spiritual powers) and is based upon tales found in Hinrich Rink's *Tales and Traditions of the Eskimo*, Lawrence Hennigh's "Control of Incest in Eskimo Folktales," and Knud Rasmussen's *The People of the Polar North*. The third myth tells the story of how the crane got blue eyes, and is a well-known tale from the Yup'ik people. The version included here is based upon a myth found in Lorraine Donoghue Koranda's *Alaskan Eskimo Songs and Stories*.

The Girl Who Would Not Marry

INUIT PEOPLE, POVUNGNITUK (QUEBEC)

There once was a girl who refused to take a husband, and in time her father grew angry and gave her to his dog. The dog took her for his wife and the girl soon became pregnant. The father left the girl on a small island and the dog joined her. From time to time, the dog would leave and come back with meat. The girl bore many children—some were in the form of dogs, and others in the form of humans.

After a while, the father felt sorry for his daughter. He took the dog, loaded him with stones and sand, and let him drown. After that, the father brought meat to the island to feed his daughter and grandchildren. However, the girl was angry with him, so she asked her children to attack him. The father escaped and decided not to come back to the island. Because they were hungry on the island, the girl put her dog-children into a boot sole and they drifted to land to become the ancestors of the white men. The human-children went into another boot sole and they became the ancestors of the Inuit peoples. Then the daughter returned home to live with her parents.

One day, while her father was hunting, a hunter in a kayak appeared at their house. The girl agreed to marry him because he seemed like a fine large man, but she eventually discovered that he was actually a very small bird with ugly eyes. They lived together and had a child. One day the girl's father set out in a boat to find her, and arrived while the girl's husband was out hunting. He took her away in his boat. The husband discovered them and caused a storm that almost capsized the boat. In fear, the father threw his daughter overboard, but she clung to the gunwale. He chopped off her first finger joints and they became seals. He chopped off her second finger joints and they became bearded seals. He chopped off the last joints and they became walruses. The girl then sank into the water and became Sedna, the mother spirit of the sea beasts.

Below **Seal-shaped snuff box, Inuit culture, Canada.** According to a popular Inuit myth, seals were created from the fingers of Sedna, the goddess of the sea. Sedna was also known as Arnarquagsag by indigenous Greenland people and Nerivik by native Alaskan cultures.

Right **Serving bowl, Eskimo culture, Alaska.** Decorated with a strange mythological creature, this bowl has been painted red and has had the rim steamed and bent into a rounded shape. Bowls like this were used by indigenous women to bring food to the men in their special house, known as a *kashim*.

The Sun and the Moon

INUPIAQ PEOPLE, ALASKA

Two orphans, a sister and a brother, lived together, although the brother always slept in the men's house. The sister did not want to get married. Many young men asked for her hand in marriage, but she refused. Her brother urged her to marry, but she still refused. One night, someone visited her in bed. She was very scared, but she let him go to bed with her. He left the room before daylight. This occurred for several nights. Finally, she decided to find out who it was. When the man next slipped into bed with her, she put soot on her hand from the lamp and marked the man on his cheek.

In the morning, the sister went to the men's house and looked through the skylight. She looked from face to face to see who her visitor might be. Finally, she looked at her brother and he had a soot mark on his cheek. She was surprised by this and went home. She took her *ulu* (women's knife) and a big wooden bowl. She cut off both of her breasts and put them in the bowl. Then she went back to the men's house without putting her parka on, and a great deal of deep red blood marked her tracks. When she got to the men's house, she went in and gave the bowl to her brother, stating that if he wanted her so badly, he could have her breasts. She turned and ran out of the men's house, and her brother chased her around the building. Presently, both of them rose higher and higher into the air. The girl kept running and became the sun. The brother became the moon.

Below **Mask of the moon spirit, Eskimo culture, western Alaska.** The moon "face" is surrounded by a painted white board that symbolizes the air, circular hoops that reflect the levels found in the cosmos, and a number of feathers that represent the stars.

How Crane Got Blue Eyes

YUP'IK PEOPLE, ALASKA

One day, as Crane was walking along, he decided to eat some berries. So he took his eyes off and put them on a stump. He told his eyes that if they saw someone, to yell and let him know. Crane started eating berries. Presently, his eyes shouted out that somebody was coming and they were going to take the eyes away. Crane went to his eyes, put them back on, and looked around. He told his eyes that it was only a piece of wood drifting in the river. He put his eyes back on the stump and told them not to tell him any more stories. He began eating berries again.

A few minutes later, his eyes yelled that somebody was coming and they were going to take the eyes away. Crane put his eyes back on and said that it was only a leaf floating to the ground. He took his eyes off again and continued to eat berries. He told his eyes not to tell any more stories. A few minutes later, the eyes started yelling that somebody was coming and they were going to take the eyes away. Crane ignored the eyes this time and soon the eyes' cries came from farther and farther away.

After he finished eating, Crane discovered that someone had stolen the eyes. So he decided to use cranberries for his eyes instead, and he put them in— but everything was much too red. He then put in blackberries for his eyes, but everything was much too dark. So he found some nice blueberries and put them in, and everything was just perfect. And, ever since then, the crane has had blue eyes.

RELATIONSHIPS

In the Arctic, immediate family and extended family relationships are very important. The following story relates the happy fate of family members who help each other and the terrible outcome for those that do not. Versions of this myth are told throughout the North American Arctic from Alaska to Greenland. This retelling is based upon the myth found in Howard Norman's *Northern Tales*, Edwin S. Hall's *The Eskimo Storyteller: Folktales from Noatak, Alaska,* Hinrich Rink's *Tales and Traditions of the Eskimo,* and Zebedee Nungak and Eugene Arima's *Eskimo Stories from Povungnituk, Quebec.*

The Blind Boy and the Loon
KALAALLIT (GREENLANDER) PEOPLE

There once was a boy who lived with his grandmother and sister. The boy was quite a good hunter, always bringing home plenty of game that his grandmother had to clean and prepare. Eventually the grandmother began to resent all the work that she had to do when the boy came back from hunting. Using magic, she took the boy's snow goggles and put them over a fire. When the boy next used his goggles, he slowly began to lose his sight. Soon he was no longer able to hunt, and he had to stay in the igloo.

By winter, the grandmother, brother, and sister were going hungry. One day, a bear started to eat their skin windowpane. The women were scared, but the boy asked his sister for his bow and arrow and then asked her to aim for him. He shot his arrow and killed the bear. However, the grandmother lied to him and told him that the arrow had missed the bear entirely. The sister whispered to her brother that he did indeed kill the bear. The grandmother butchered the bear and shared the meat with the sister, but only gave broth to the boy.

As spring approached, the boy asked his sister to take him outside. He decided to lie down and rest next to a lake while she continued gathering fuel. Loons noticed the blind boy by the lake. One of them flew to the boy and told him to climb on its head. The loon then dove into the lake several times.

Afterwards, the boy was able to see again, and when the sister arrived, they returned home.

Several days later, as they camped near the sea, they saw beluga whales offshore. The boy prepared to harpoon them and tied the end of his harpoon line to his sister so she could help haul in the heavy whale. He aimed and killed a small whale and they hauled it in. The grandmother then asked him to tie her to his harpoon line. He did so, but this time, he aimed for a much larger whale. This big whale was only wounded, and it began swimming far from shore, taking the grandmother with him. The grandmother was dragged underwater and her long, white hair became coiled into a thick braid. The whale pulled her down to the bottom of the sea and she became the black narwhal with a long, twisted, white tusk emerging from the top part of its mouth.

Left **Snow goggles, Eskimo culture, Alaska.** Carved from a piece of wood or bone, snow goggles were worn by people of the Arctic region to reduce the glare of the sun off the snow and avoid snow blindness. Unfortunately for the boy in the Kalaallit myth, his grandmother placed a spell on his snow goggles which made him lose his sight.

Left **Shaman's mask in the form of a whale, Eskimo culture, Alaska.** Whales are revered by Inuit cultures as they provide food such as meat and *muktuk* (skin)—which is said to taste like fresh coconut—and their bones have been used in the past to make tools and hunting implements.

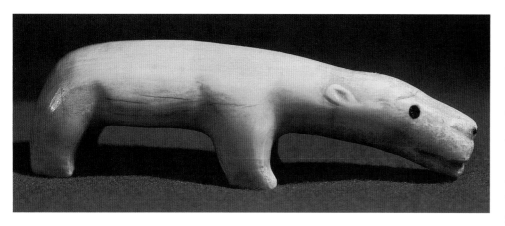

Above **Polar bear, Eskimo culture, Alaska.** The sheer size and power of the polar bear has made it the "king" of the Arctic animals. Called *nanuq* or *nanuk* by the Inuit peoples, legend has it that there was a race of polar-bear men that hunted in their white fur coats during the day, but returned to their igloos at night where they took their coats off.

ANIMALS

In the following myth, the origins of merrymaking and war are told. The story is the basis for Wolf Dance performances, which the King Island Inupiaq of Bering Strait performed in 1982 and in 1991. One of the central themes of Inuit cosmology—namely reciprocal relationships with animals—is prominent in this myth, in which a hunter and the eagles engage in several exchanges. This version of the myth was first recorded in 1924 by Knud Rasmussen, from a King Islander in Nome, Alaska.

The Eagle-Wolf Dance
INUPIAQ PEOPLE, KING ISLAND (ALASKA)
A hunter named Marten killed a giant eagle and distributed the meat to others in his community. He

We felt that all things were like us people, down to small animals like the mouse, and the things like wood. The wood is glad to the person who is using it, and the person is glad to the wood for being there to be used.

JOE FRIDAY, YUP'IK PEOPLE

then dried the skin and put offerings of meat into its claws, after which he became a better hunter. Some time later, he went hunting again and met two fox-men, who took him to a strange land. They flew swiftly through the air, going further and further into the country until the hunter heard a loud throbbing sound, which the fox-men said was the heart beat of the mother of the eagle that Marten had killed. He was frightened because he thought the mother eagle would hurt him in revenge for killing her son. Instead, the eagles greeted him kindly and held a feast for him outside the house—Marten had never seen such feasting before.

He then went into the house, where the eagle mother told him that she appreciated the care he gave her son's skin. She also told him she wanted to exchange gifts with him. He told her he wanted to return home and the eagle mother requested plaited sinew in exchange. Marten removed the plaited sinew from his arrow and gave it to the eagle mother, who was pleased. After another feast inside, she asked him to hold a great feast for her son's skin, for which he would need to send messengers to a neighboring village. The eagle mother also taught the hunter how to sing and dance and make merry, and in return for his feast, Marten would have to make a drum that sounded like her heart. The hunter

REINCARNATION AND RECIPROCITY

Inuit people believe that both human and animal souls are reincarnated after death. Death is not feared, necessarily, but is accepted as part of the ongoing cycle of life. In addition, humans and animals exist in equal and reciprocal relationships with each other. Animals are thought to be another class of people, as capable of intelligence and free will as humans, but wearing different "clothes" (their animal skins).

Animals are also believed to have special powers of observation, which they use to keep an eye on human beings. In other words, animals watch hunters and their wives and reward those people that are generous and industrious by allowing the hunter to kill them. In return, hunters have to perform certain rituals that return the spirits of dead animals to their world so they can be reborn. Animals do not give

themselves to hunters that do not follow proper rules for behavior.

Below **Arrow straightener in the shape of a caribou, Eskimo culture, Alaska.** This was an important tool for the Inuit hunter, as it both straightened the shaft of his arrows and served to soothe the souls of the caribou that he shot—ensuring that he would have continued hunting success.

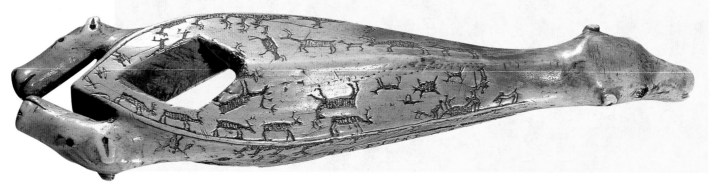

promised, and the eagle mother gave him two caribou heart sacks filled with the ear tips of caribou, wolverine, and wolf. She told him not to lay these down on the ground. The fox-men then returned Marten some distance from his home.

When Marten came to a river, he stopped to have a drink of water. In front of him, Marten saw a steep slope filled with holes. Suddenly, a flock of swallows disappeared into the holes. Then the heads of wolves peered out and began dancing. He was so surprised that he dropped his gifts. He heard a thunderous noise and all the ear tips were suddenly transformed into caribou skins, dried meat, and wolf and wolverine furs. He brought his bundle of gifts home and began preparations for a feast. He taught the other people how to sing and dance. Then Marten sent out messengers. To imitate the sound of the eagle mother's heart, he created a drum from a wooden box topped with sawlike teeth that represented the eagle's home.

He also created a large platform with holes in it to represent the vision of the swallows and wolves that he saw by the river bank. During the dancing at the feast, the dancers would slip into the holes and come out as dancing wolves.

Marten then went hunting for more food. He shot an arrow at a caribou but his arrow flew too high, and he soon discovered that he had accidentally killed one of his special messengers. He became sad and confused. He did not want to stop his festival, so he took the messenger's body home and dried it. Some days later, the guests arrived. After being entertained outside the feast hall, they all went inside. Marten brought in the dried body of the messenger. Songs and dances were performed, but without enthusiasm because of the corpse. When the festival was over, the other messengers decided to kill Marten, but he killed them first. Thus it is always so that merry-making and war go hand in hand.

Above *A Young Indian and his Totem Spirit* by James Jack. Falling exhausted to the ground, the northern Inuit man asks for help from his tribe's guardian or totem spirit, the she-wolf Utonagan. These days the name "Utonagan" has been applied to a breed of dog that closely resembles its ancestor, the wolf.

MESOAMERICAN MYTHOLOGY

Mesoamerica is a geographical and cultural region that takes in present-day Mexico, Guatemala, Honduras, Costa Rica, Belize, and El Salvador. It is thought that the first people arrived in this area about 15,000 years ago, having crossed the land bridge across the Bering Strait between what is now Russia and Alaska, and then moving south.

From about 2500 B.C. until the Spanish invasion in A.D. 1519, Mesoamerica was the center of several civilizations that were highly developed in terms of language, writing, art, architecture, mathematics, astronomy, and agriculture. Basically, these civilizations were known as Olmec (2000 B.C.–A.D. 250), Maya (A.D. 250–900), and Toltec and Aztec (A.D. 900–1500). There was no central or united government, but rather the area was separated into various individual city-states that were often at war with each other.

Right **Huehueteotl, god of fire, late Olmec culture.** This ceramic representation of Huehueteotl was used during religious ceremonies, when incense was burned in the brazier above the god's head. The Olmec people are considered the "mother culture" of Mesoamerica, as many of their gods and rituals were absorbed by later cultures.

ART AND ARCHITECTURE

The Mesoamerican societies were highly skilled in arts and crafts, and much of the knowledge that we have of their culture and spirituality has been gleaned from their murals, pottery, and sculpture.

Jewelry, masks, and carvings were beautifully crafted in gold, turquoise, obsidian, or jade. Brightly colored feathers, particularly the vivid green feathers of the quetzal bird, were used to decorate clothing and military uniforms.

The Spanish conquerors of the sixteenth century were amazed at the artistic accomplishments of these people. But they were even more astonished at the grandeur and sophistication of their cities, the most important of these being the Mayan cities of Palenque, Tikal, and Chichén Itzá, and the Aztec cities of Teotihuacan and Tenochtitlan.

The palace at Palenque took over two centuries to construct, and is an architectural masterpiece. The chambers in Palenque's Temple of Inscriptions were said to lead to the Underworld. Tikal, meaning "the place where the spirit voices are heard," was a great metropolis built in the center of the jungle. Chichén Itzá features the magnificent pyramid known as the Temple of the Warriors, the largest ball court in Central America, and the sacred well where sacrificial victims were offered to the rain god Chaac. Teotihuacan was an Aztec place of pilgrimage and an extremely significant sacred site, especially revered for the Pyramids of the Sun and the Moon. Tenochtitlan, the Aztec political and spiritual center, was built in A.D. 1325 on an island in Lake Texcoco ("the lake of the moon") and is now buried under the present-day Mexican capital, Mexico City. The Aztec city was built with the divine inspiration and guidance of the war deity Huitzilopochtli.

PEOPLE OF MAIZE

The economies of Mesoamerica were based chiefly on farming, especially of maize (also known as corn). The crops were grown by means of the slash-and-burn technique in the rain forests, in irrigated fields, or in the ingenious floating gardens known as *chinampas*. Beans, chilies, and squash—as well as cocoa pods, which were gathered in the wild—were also considered valuable crops for the people of Mesoamerica.

Due to the large-scale growing of maize, the Mesoamerican people evolved from a hunter-gather culture to a settled, agrarian society; this resulted in a population increase and development of larger villages and towns.

The success of the maize crop was so essential to physical and financial well-being that it permeated many Mesoamerican myths, symbols, and rituals. The Mayan creation story tells that

MAYAN AND AZTEC DEITIES

DEITY	MAYAN	AZTEC
SUPREME GOD	HUNAB KU, ITZAMNA	OMETEOTL
MOON GODDESS	IXCHEL	XOCHIQUETZAL
SUN GOD	KINICH AHAU	TONATIUH
WIND GOD	GUCUMATZ (KUKULCAN)	QUETZALCOATL (EHECATL)
RAIN GOD	CHAAC	TLALOC
MAIZE OR FERTILITY GOD	YUM KAAX, HUN HUNAHPU	XIPE TOTEC, CENTEOTL
FERTILITY GODDESS	AKHUSHTAL	COATLICUE
DEATH GOD	AH PUCH	MICTLANTECUHTLI

the first human beings were made from maize kernels that had been ground into meal. In an Aztec legend, the plumed serpent deity Quetzalcoatl changed himself into an ant to gather the seeds of what would become the first maize field.

Prayer, ritual, and sacrifice were performed for the deities of fertility, sun, and rain, in the hope that by appeasing the gods the Mesoamericans would in return receive a fruitful harvest.

SACRIFICE AND WAR

The belief in sacrificial offerings—of gold, flowers, and animals, but, most importantly, of human life—was an intrinsic part of Mesoamerican religion. The people thought that if they kept the gods well supplied with blood, the gods would then reward them with a good balance of sun and rain.

But there were deeper, existential reasons for these sacrifices. For the most part, the gods and goddesses were demanding and unpredictable. Both Mayan and Aztec creation myths explain how the world and the people in it could be annihilated on a divine whim, and it was the duty of the people to please the gods so fully that the world would not be destroyed again. The gods would suitably reward victims of sacrifice (especially self-sacrifice, or suicide) with an exalted place in the heavens.

The Maya, and particularly the Aztec, were militaristic nations, and prisoners of war provided a convenient supply of sacrificial victims. The main form of sacrifice was having one's heart cut out; beheading and being skinned (flayed) alive were also commonly practiced. Human sacrifice was also an important element of *pokatok*, the ritual ball game.

WHAT HAS REMAINED

The Spanish conquerors of Mesoamerica, led by Hernando Cortés in 1519, were to eventually abolish human sacrifice, but they practiced different forms of cruelty. They took over the farmlands and forced people into slavery. Many temples and pyramids were destroyed and, as a result, so were their histories and sacred texts. Thousands of Mayan codices were lost, and only a scant few (including the valuable *Popol Vuh*) survived.

Some visionary Spanish monks, such as Bernardino de Sahagún, felt it was important to preserve the ancient Mesoamerican manuscripts. The *Florentine Codex*, transcribed by de Sahagún, is the result of many years' work, and tells us a great deal about the Aztec worldview.

Today, despite centuries of Christianity, some of the old beliefs and ceremonies continue, often creatively blended with Catholic rituals. The surviving literature, art, and architecture are testament to these proud, fascinating, and complex people.

Above **Aztec human sacrifice.** It has been estimated that up to 250,000 people were sacrificed every year during the fifteenth century, when the Aztec civilization was at its most powerful.

Left **Cuauhxicalli, Aztec culture.** Elaborately carved from stone, the cuauhxicalli (or "eagle bowl") was an important vessel used by the Aztecs to store the hearts of human sacrifices.

113

MAYAN MYTHOLOGY

In what is now Guatemala, Honduras, and the Yucatan Peninsula of Mexico, the Mayan civilization reached its peak between A.D. 250 and A.D. 900. It was a highly organized, sophisticated society, as evidenced at the sites of Palenque and Chichén Itzá on the Yucatan Peninsula, and Tikal in Guatemala.

Most of what we know about the spiritual life of the Mayan people comes from the few books (known as codices) that were not destroyed by the Spanish conquerors, and the *Popol Vuh*, the major sacred text of the Maya. The Maya believed in unseen powers that were present in all of nature, the balance between darkness and light, and the eternal cycle of death and regeneration.

Going to your sacrifice as the winning stroke of your life is the essence of the early sacrificial ideal.

JOSEPH CAMPBELL (1904–1987)

MAYAN COSMOLOGY

The Mayan universe consisted of three parts: heaven (the Overworld), earth (the Middleworld), and the Underworld, and each of these parts was connected to the others by the World Tree.

The Overworld

Unlike the afterlife of many belief systems, the Mayan Overworld was not a heavenly reward for being virtuous. The only way one could gain entry to the Overworld paradise was through a violent death. The most exalted levels were reserved for sacrifice victims. Then there were levels for those who died in battle, those who died in childbirth, and those who died in fire or flood. Those who took their own life were sent to a heavenly realm ruled by Ixtab, the suicide goddess, who is often depicted as having a noose around her neck.

The Middleworld

It was thought that the Middleworld came into existence when the gods spoke the word "earth," and it arose gently, like a mist out of the ocean.

After the earth was created, it was organized in the same way as the Mayans arranged their maize fields, with the process being described in the Mayan book of creation, *Popol Vuh*, as "the fourfold siding, fourfold cornering, measuring, fourfold staking … of the earth, the four sides, the four corners."

The Underworld

The Underworld was known as Xibalba ("The Place of Fright"), and, like the Overworld, it also had many levels; it was the place where everyone went unless they experienced a violent death. The only way out of Xibalba was by passing a series of grueling tests in which mortals matched wits against the many Underworld inhabitants (as seen in the *Popol Vuh* story of the Hero Twins).

Artists' interpretations about Xibalba vary. Some depict it as being underground; others portray it as being underwater. The demons of the Underworld are shown to be hideous, foul, and grotesque, and are quite often adorned with necklaces made of human eyeballs.

THE BOOK OF MAYAN CREATION

The ancient hieroglyphic *Popol Vuh* (meaning "Book of Counsel") is the creation story of the Guatemalan Quiche Maya people.

Through their complex mathematical calculations, the Mayans concluded that the earth (Middleworld) came into being in 3114 B.C. (on August 13, to be exact). The beginning of the *Popol Vuh* sounds remarkably like the Bible's Book of Genesis, possibly because the original sacred text was transcribed by Spanish monks, who saw the value in preserving the manuscript but could not escape their religious background:

> There was nothing standing; only the calm water, the placid sea, alone and tranquil … then came the word.

Together, the gods Gucumatz and Hurakan uttered the word "earth," and the world came into being, rising up from the sea.

Although the two gods were happy with what they had created, the earth seemed very empty and quiet. So they filled it with animals—birds, reptiles, mammals, and fish—in the hope that these creatures would sing their praises. But when Gucumatz and Hurakan instructed the animals to speak, the gods were horrified at the crude and sacrilegious sounds that the animals emitted. "We shall fashion other creatures to obey us. Accept your lot. Your flesh shall be torn apart."

Below **Mayan sacrifice.** This carved stone relief from the ball court at El Tajin, Veracruz, depicts the ritualistic sacrifice of the losing ball-game competitors. According to Mayan cosmology, victims of sacrifice would occupy their own special level of the Overworld.

The First Humans

Disappointed at the animals' lack of eloquence, the gods set about trying to come up with a being who would support them by worship and sacrifice. But unlike the animals, trees, waterways, and landforms—which came into existence merely by thought and word—the gods realized that these special human beings would have to come from the solid substance of the earth itself.

In their first attempt to make a person, the gods used mud and clay. However, these creatures either fell apart because they were so soft, or hardened into useless rocks with human shapes. The gods then decided to enlist the help of the grandfather god Xpiyacoc and the grandmother goddess Xmucane. These wise elders suggested that wood might be a more suitable material. The wooden mannequins—made from the coral tree and the fiber from the bulrush—were certainly an improvement over the ones made from mud. But they lacked the intelligence and refinement necessary to appease the gods. In a fit of rage, Hurakan sent a wild storm to destroy the wooden creatures.

Finally, they found some yellow, white, black, and red maize kernels. Xmucane ground the kernels into a meal that she mixed with water, and the resulting dough formed the first human beings (four men and four women), in whom the gods were satisfied. Their main flaw was that they were too intelligent and curious—so the gods caused a cloud to form over their vision and perception, so that they would never have perfect knowledge, and would always be dependent on the deities to help them solve life's mysteries.

Above *The Creation of the Earth* by Diego Rivera (1886–1957). According to the *Popol Vuh*, the sacred text of the Maya, in the beginning there was only water. When the gods Gucumatz and Hurakan spoke the word "earth" the waters receded, revealing the world.

THE WORLD TREE

Central to the Mayan belief system is the World Tree *(Wakah-chan)*, which literally means "raised-up sky." The tree joins the Overworld, Middleworld, and Underworld into a unified cosmic whole.

The World Tree (whose color is green) is the central axis of the universe, along which souls of the dead migrate. Its roots reach down to the depths of the Underworld, and its crown extends to the top of the heavenly realms. It was believed that the souls of

people who committed suicide were sent to rest in the shade of the World Tree under the protection of the goddess Ixtab.

Four special trees in the Middleworld correspond to the four directions, and each has a different color: north (white), south (yellow), east (red), and west (black). Each direction has symbolic birds and animals of the same colors. White, yellow, red, and black are also the colors of the maize kernels that were used to create the first humans.

THE HERO TWINS

As well as the story of creation, the *Popol Vuh* includes many tales of the exploits of the Hero Twins, the most well-known of all the Meso-american mythological figures.

The First Hero Twins: One Hunahpu and Seven Hunahpu

Xpiyacoc and Xmucane, the god and goddess who were later instrumental in creating the first human beings out of corn, had twin sons known as One Hunahpu and Seven Hunahpu.

The twins loved to play *pokatok*, a popular ball game that was very swift and often violent, and that became a ritual central to Mesoamerican culture. The object of the game was to get a solid rubber ball into a stone ring at the end of a special court, using only knees, elbows, or hips. It happened that their stone ball court was just above the entry to Xibalba, the Under-world. Not only were the Underworld lords annoyed by the loud noises that accompanied the ball games, but they were also extremely envious of the twins' awesome athletic prowess. Two of the lords, One Death and Seven Death, summoned the twins to the Underworld to play ball, with the view to killing them and stealing their playing court. The twins' mother, Xmucane, suspected foul play and tried to persuade them not to go, but they disregarded her warnings.

116

To get to Xibalba the twins succeeding in crossing three loathsome and dangerous rivers: the first was full of blood, the second was full of pus, and the third was full of sharp spikes. After a series of arduous and humiliating tasks that they were tricked into failing, the brothers were sacrificed, their bodies buried under the ball court, and the head of One Hunahpu hung in a calabash tree. (Some versions of the story say that the head was transformed into a gourd, and it was forbidden for anyone to look at the tree or eat of its fruit.) The lords sent back the twins' ball-playing equipment, which Xmucane sadly hid away in the rafters of her house.

One day a young Underworld maiden by the name of Xquic ("Blood Moon") stopped to look at the tree. The head of One Hunahpu, or gourd, spat in her hand, and she became pregnant. Banished by her father, she retreated to the Overworld to the home of Xmucane to give birth to the next generation of Hero Twins.

The Second Hero Twins: Hunahpu and Xbalanque

When the twins Hunahpu and Xbalanque were born, Xmucane took them into her family, which included the first sons of One Hunahpu: One Monkey and One Artisan.

Like their father and uncle, Hunahpu and Xbalanque were bright and adventurous. They were also expert hunters and had magical powers. Because they were so handsome and clever, they aroused the jealousy of their half brothers, who would steal their food and try to get them into all kinds of trouble. Although One Monkey and One Artisan could be bad-tempered and lazy, they were also highly artistic and musical. Eventually Hunahpu and Xbalanque had enough of their brothers' tormenting, and they trapped them in a tree and changed them into monkeys.

The Ordeals of Hunahpu and Xbalanque

One day when the Hero Twins were out hunting, they caught a rat. They were just about to throw it into a fire, when the rat told them what had happened to their father and uncle in Xibalba. He also told them about the ball-game equipment (including helmets, belts, wrist-guards, and knee-guards) that was stored in their grandmother's house.

The second generation of twins loved the ball game, just as One Hunahpu and Seven Hunahpu had done. And they resolved that as soon as they could, they would avenge their father's death. Before long, the noise of their constant playing began to anger the Xibalba lords, and they summoned the twins to the Underworld.

Like their father and uncle before them, the brothers traversed the three dreaded rivers, and once they reached the Underworld, a series of tests awaited them. They bravely survived the dangers of each successive night in the House of Gloom, the Razor House, the Jaguar House, the House of Cold, and the House of Fire, outwitting the dark lords' traps and trickery. Their last—and hardest—night was to be spent in the House of Bats. The most vicious bat bit off Hunahpu's head, and, to add insult to injury, the lords forced Xbalanque to play a game of *pokatok* using his brother's head as a ball. Xbalanque was quick-witted, however; he found a rabbit to impersonate the ball, and quickly retrieved Hunahpu's head and attached it to his brother's body.

After all that, the Hero Twins allowed themselves to be sacrificed by fire, but several days later they emerged from a river as fishlike beings. They traveled throughout the Underworld, entertaining people with their songs, dances, and magic. Eventually the twins were summoned to a command performance by the two most powerful dark rulers, and were ordered to sacrifice themselves yet again. They obeyed the order, and instantly came back to life. The lords wanted the twins to perform the same magic on them, which they did, but they did not reverse the spell to bring the lords back to life. Xibalba became merely a shadow of its former self, and the victorious Hero Twins ascended into the heavens, eventually becoming the sun and moon.

Above **Ball-game player, western Mayan culture.** *Pokatok* players could not use their hands or feet to touch the ball, but they could employ the yokes and *palmas* (stone accessories) they wore, or stone *manoplas* (hand-held objects), to hit the ball. The first team to score was usually declared the winner—and the losing team were almost always sacrificed by decapitation.

MAYAN DEITIES

The Maya had approximately 170 gods and goddesses in their pantheon, whose presence permeated every part of their daily lives. There were gods for all aspects of nature—animals, earth, wind, rain, sun, and moon—who required continuous homage and frequent offerings (which occasionally took the form of bloodletting or human sacrifice).

Hunab Ku: the God Behind the Gods

Meaning "only spirit" or "the single god," Hunab Ku is unusual in that he is the only Mayan god that is totally abstract and invisible. Some believe him to be the creator of the gods, earth, and sky. He is the father of Itzamna, the supreme god.

There is another version of the Mayan creation story that goes like this: Hunab Ku first created a world that he populated with little people, and then destroyed by flood, assisted by a great serpent who spewed forth the raging waters from his mouth. He then created a world inhabited by a strange race of people known as the Dzolob, which was destroyed by flood as well. But the third time Hunab Ku created the world, he filled it with the Mayan people, in whom he was very pleased.

Itzamna: the Supreme God

Itzamna, some believe, is the visible manifestation of Hunab Ku, and he is certainly a multitalented and multifunctional deity. Firstly, he is the moon god, husband of the moon goddess Ixchel, and the patron

god of royalty. Itzamna loved his people, and bestowed on them the gifts of books, writing, calendars, and medicine. His name means "Iguana House" or "Lizard House," reflecting the Mayan view that the framework of the earth was formed by the bodies of lizards.

Itzamna is a benign patriarch, often pictured as an elderly man with square eyes, a prominent jaw, and a hawklike nose. The ceremonies of the Mayan New Year honor Itzamna, as does the Temple of the Cross located at Palenque.

Ixchel: the Moon Goddess

Ixchel is a formidable goddess, associated with the moon, tides, and floods. In some accounts she is the wife of the supreme god Itzamna, whereas other stories have her married to the sun god Kinich Ahau (her husbands may even be considered to be two aspects of the one deity).

As a young wife, Ixchel was very unhappy because she was barren—in fact, she had no reproductive organs whatsoever. One day a deer came and stepped on her abdomen, thus enabling her to bear children, who were known as the Bacabs.

Ixchel is capricious and, like the moon, she is also ever-changing. She is the benevolent rainbow mother

Below *Head of Itzamna* by **Frederick Catherwood (1799–1854)**. Originally located at Izamal in Mexico, this stucco stone head no longer exists. But it was described by John Lloyd Stephens, during his 1841 expedition to the Yucatan region with Catherwood, as having a "stone one foot six inches long [that] protrudes from the chin, intended, perhaps, for burning copal on, as a sort of altar."

or Ah Hoya ("he who urinates"), Chaac was essentially a benevolent god, but one whose continued goodness depended on regular rituals and sacrifices. He sometimes instructed his people to abstain from either food or sex, but when he was in a harsher mood, he could order them to be tied up and thrown into the sacred well at Chichén Itzá.

Chaac appears in many faces and guises. Some images show him with a curled, snoutlike nose, and sometimes he is seen with scales or catfish whiskers, or with tears flowing from his eyes. Often he is seen painted blue and wielding an axe, which he uses to create lightning and thunder. Chaac is closely aligned with the maize god Yum Kaax, and still features prominently in the ceremonial life of the people living in the Yucatan region today, especially at the coming of the important wet season. When a frog croaks, signifying the onset of rain, it is thought to be the voice of Chaac.

Left **Mask of the Mayan rain god Chaac.** The Codz Poop building at Kabah in the Yucatan region of Mexico features 250 masks of Chaac. One of the many beliefs about Chaac is that he uses his hooked nose to penetrate the clouds, causing rain to fall.

patron goddess of both childbirth and weaving. But she is also depicted as a fierce hag, her helmet and skirt adorned with snakes (very much like the Aztec goddess Coatlicue). She holds a jug of water that she could either sprinkle kindly on the crops, or pour down in a devastating flood.

The Bacabs

Itzamna the supreme god and Ixchel the moon goddess had four sons, collectively known as the Bacabs. Coming from such exalted parents, the Bacabs were indeed very important deities. Because the earth was thought to be flat, the Bacabs' function was to stand at each corner of the earth and hold up the thirteen layers of the sky like a canopy; they are often seen depicted with upraised arms, and are sometimes represented as jaguars. The Bacabs are associated with the four directions, as illustrated in the Mayan World Tree: north (white), south (yellow), east (red), and west (black). The most well-known of the Bacabs is the rain god Chaac (in fact, some academics believe that the four Bacabs are simply four aspects of the one god—Chaac).

Chaac: the Rain God

Because life cannot exist without water, Chaac (or Chac) the rain god is the most revered of all the Mayan deities—his Aztec counterpart is Tlaloc. Also known as Ah Tzenul ("he who gives food to others")

THE MAIZE GOD

Maize, or corn, was the Mayan staple crop, and was grown not only in fields, but in valleys and on rocky hillsides. It was prepared and consumed in a variety of ways, such as tortillas, tamales, and atole, a hot beverage. Because maize was so essential to the Mayans' very survival, it featured prominently in their mythological, religious, and ceremonial life.

The Mayan creation myth tells how the first human beings were fashioned out of ground maize meal. And one of the most revered deities was the maize god, who was called by many names: Hun Hunahpu, Ah Mun, or Yum Kaax (Lord of the Forest). This was a benign, passive god often portrayed as a young man with a ripe ear of maize sprouting from his head. Rituals and offerings to the maize god were of great importance and were performed regularly.

Right **Mayan maize god.** So popular was the maize god that it is believed the Maya performed cranial deformation on infants so that their head grew elongated like the shape of an ear of maize.

Gucumatz: the Feathered Serpent

Like his Aztec counterpart Quetzalcoatl, Gucumatz (also known as Kukulcan or Kukulkan) is the god of wind and is thought to have come from the west, bringing with him all the secrets of the universe. Sometimes he is pictured as moving through the water, and he may be yet another manifestation of the supreme god Itzamna.

At Chichén Itzá there is a magnificent temple dedicated to Gucumatz. At both the spring equinox and autumn equinox, Gucumatz appears as a large, serpent-shaped shadow across the steps of the temple.

Below **Mayan stone sculpture of Gucumatz.** In association with Hurakan, Gucumatz was responsible for the creation of the Mayan world and human beings. He taught the people about civilization and agriculture, and is often portrayed as a snake.

Hurakan: the Storm God

According to the Mayan book of creation, *Popol Vuh*, the god Hurakan collaborated with Gucumatz in creating the Earth, and fashioning the first humans out of mud and wood.

Hurakan was a harsh god. Displeased because he found the wooden folk so dull and witless, he destroyed them in a flood. However some survived, and those that did were tormented mercilessly. Hurakan employed wild dogs and violent monsters with names like "Gouger of Faces" and "Crunching Jaguar" to terrify and mutilate his poor wretched mistakes. Most of the wooden people were destroyed, but some fled into caves, never to be seen again.

Kinich Ahau: the Sun God

Having both a light and a dark aspect, Kinich Ahau is the sun by day, but at night he becomes the jaguar lord Balam, prowling the lower regions of the Underworld. Kinich Ahau is protector of the city of Izamal, and, in the name of Ah Xoc Kin, the sun god is also the patron of poetry and music.

Left **Terracotta relief of the Mayan sun god.** Situated on a temple wall at Campeche in Mexico, this decorative relief of Kinich Ahau shows the sun god in his rising and setting forms. As patron of Izamal, he was believed to visit the people of the city at noon every day in the guise of a macaw.

Ixtab and Ah Puch: the Deities of Death

Only people who have died a violent or suicidal death can enter the heavenly realms. Ixtab, the goddess of suicide, escorts into paradise the souls of people who have died by their own hand, and serves them food and drink in the shade of the World Tree. Ixtab is portrayed as rather a fearsome creature hanging from a noose.

As a beautiful young goddess Ixtab took great delight in luring men into the forest, seducing and bewitching them, and then vanishing. Some men stayed lost in the forest, and those who found their way home went insane, forever longing for her love.

Ah Puch (or Yum Cimil), the lord of death, is the ruler of the lowest level of the Underworld and takes many different forms: as a skeleton, as a distended gangrenous corpse, or as an owl.

AZTEC MYTHOLOGY

The Aztec civilization of Mexico existed between A.D. 1325 and A.D. 1521. It was a militaristic empire, whose spiritual belief system encompassed over 1,000 deities. The Aztec universe was multilayered, and its creation stories complex. Many of the ancient texts were destroyed by the Spanish, and much of our knowledge of Aztec religion comes from the *Florentine Codex,* transcribed by Franciscan monk Bernardino de Sahagún.

A THREE-PART UNIVERSE

In the Aztec belief system, the universe was tripartite, or composed of three parts: Earth, Heaven, and the Underworld.

Earth

At the center of the Aztec universe—the meeting place of Heaven, Earth, and the Underworld—was the capital city of Tenochtitlan. According to legend, the local people were known as the Tenochca, but the war god Huitzilopochtli renamed them the Mexica, and instructed them to build their capital on an island in the middle of Lake Texcoco. At the heart of the city stood the magnificent Great Temple, which was dedicated to both Huitzilopochtli and the Aztec rain god, known as Tlaloc.

Heaven

Heaven was a huge dome comprising 13 levels that reached upward from the surface of the Earth. In the highest of the heavens lived Ometeotl, the Supreme Being and the god of duality—no other god or mortal could enter this exalted realm.

Then there were the afterlife levels, which varied according to the status of one's spiritual life at the time of physical death. The House of the Sun in the east was the ultimate reward—souls could stay there forever and would never have to return to Earth. In the west was a peaceful afterlife reserved for those who died in battle or during childbirth. Other good souls could end up in remarkable places such as the Land of Clouds, the Land of the Fleshless, or the Land of Water and Mist.

The Underworld

Only those who died in battle or during childbirth could go straight to Heaven. Everyone else had to first go to the Underworld known as Mictlan, which means "that which is below us." The fearsome lord of the Underworld, Mictlantecuhtli, is often portrayed as a squatting, skeletonlike creature with a pointed hat and rather large, bulging eyes.

When a soul reached the Underworld, they were met by Black Tezcatlipoca, who sent them on their journey through Mictlan's nine levels. The soul would have to complete a series of challenging tests within a period of four years, traversing a frightening landscape of quaking mountains and treacherous rivers. If they passed, the souls were allowed into one of the heavenly realms, but if they failed, they had to stay in the lowest level for eternity.

Above **Aztec gods from the *Florentine Codex*.** Produced by Bernardino de Sahagún (c.1500–1590) in the 1570s, the *Florentine Codex* contains encyclopedic information and 1,846 illustrations that reveal the beliefs, rituals, and lifestyle of the Aztecs.

Left **Mictecacihuatl, Aztec goddess of the dead.** Known as the "Lady of the Dead," Mictecacihuatl is the wife of Mictlantecuhtli, lord of the Underworld. Mictecacihuatl presides over the Dia de los Muertos (Day of the Dead) festival, when the souls of ancestors are thought to return to visit their families.

CREATION OF THE FOUR DIRECTIONS

The Supreme God Ometeotl went by many epithets: Tloque Nahuaque, God above All, the Lord of Two, Lord of Duality, and Lord of the Ring. Although sometimes referred to as "lord," Ometeotl actually had both masculine and feminine attributes, and encompassed both good and evil. As a male he was known as Ometecuhtli, and as a female, Omecihuatl.

From the timeless void, Ometeotl created him/herself, and then gave birth to four sons, who went forth to create the universe at the four points of the compass. These four sons (who are often compared to the Bacabs in Mayan mythology) were different aspects of the god Tezcatlipoca.

East

The direction associated with the rising sun was created by Red Tezcatlipoca, who was also known as Xipe Totec, the much-revered god of agriculture and fertility, as well as regeneration.

North

The North was ruled by Black Tezcatlipoca, generally known as Tezcatlipoca, or "Smoking Mirror," the Lord of the Night Sky. He had a rather malevolent nature and could be capricious and manipulative.

West

Quetzalcoatl, the "Plumed Serpent," is White Tezcatlipoca, and connected with the west and the setting sun. He was the best-known and most-loved deity in the Aztec pantheon, and chief rival of his brother Tezcatlipoca.

South

There seems to be more than one Blue Tezcatlipoca. Some sources say that the South was created by Tlaloc, the rain god. Others attribute this direction to Huitzilopochtli, the god of war. Both of these deities were highly revered by the Aztecs.

CREATION OF THE FIVE SUNS

We have seen how the world was created by four gods at the four sacred directions. There is another Aztec story of creation, which focuses on the five successive ages, or "suns." But it is a story of destruction as well as creation: the Aztecs believed that the world was created and destroyed four times, and each age was ruled by a particular deity and its corresponding element.

The Sun of Earth

The First Sun was known as the Sun of Earth, whose creator and ruler was Tezcatlipoca. This age was inhabited by mighty giants. However, Tezcatlipoca's brother, Quetzalcoatl, was displeased with the giants, and he sent jaguars down to annihilate all of the giants and the earth itself.

Above **Ehecatl, Aztec god of the wind.** One of the many manifestations of the god Quetzalcoatl, Ehecatl is often shown with a mouth in the form of a bird's beak. As god of the wind, his breath is said to move the sun and bring rain clouds.

Right **Tonatiuh, Aztec god of the sun.** In this detailed illustration from the *Codex Vaticanus*, Tonatiuh watches over a priest who is burning incense. Tonatiuh rules the Fifth Sun—or present era—and the Aztecs believed that any weakness in him would lead to the end of the world. So sacrifices and offerings were regularly made to keep the sun god happy and strong.

The Sun of Air

After the First Sun was destroyed and Tezcatlipoca returned to the sky to become the constellation Ursa Major, the world was re-created by Quetzalcoatl, in one of his many aspects—the wind god Ehecatl. Many years passed, and the gods felt that the people were too sinful and needed to be destroyed yet again. Tezcatlipoca came to Earth, sending a violent wind, and those who survived were changed into monkeys.

The Sun of Rain

Tlaloc, the rain god, presided over this Third Sun. Quetzalcoatl eventually punished the people for not fulfilling their sacrificial duties by sending a rain of ash. The survivors of this fiery storm became birds.

The Sun of Water

The Fourth Sun—the Sun of Water—was both created and destroyed by the powerful water and fertility goddess Coatlicue (or Chalchiuhtlicue), sister of the rain god Tlaloc. Those who came through the flood were turned into fishes.

THE CALENDAR STONE

The Aztecs placed great value on the study of mathematics and astronomy, and developed complex timekeeping systems. Their concept of time was cyclical rather than linear; it was dependent on and controlled by divine forces. The Aztecs had two concurrent calendars: one of 260 days running clockwise (coinciding with the human gestation period), and one of 365 days, running counterclockwise.

Constructed in the fifteenth century, the famous Calendar Stone (also known as the Sun Stone) was discovered in 1790 at the Aztec capital of Tenochtitlan, now Mexico City. The stone is 12 ft (3.5 m) in diameter, weighs 25 tons (25.5 tonnes), and is elaborately carved out of basalt.

At the center of the Calendar Stone is the recognizable face of the sun god Tonatiuh, creator of the Fifth Sun. The four squares that surround Tonatiuh depict the four previous ages (or "suns") that were destroyed by either animals, wind, fire, or water. At the outer edge of the stone are two sacred serpents, which symbolize both the cyclical and spiraling nature of the dance of life.

Below **Aztec Calendar Stone.** Now the centerpiece of Mexico's National Museum of Anthropology, the Calendar Stone was commissioned by the Aztec ruler Axayacatl in 1469. There are indications that the basalt surface was originally painted.

The Fifth Sun

The Fifth Sun is the present era, and the Aztecs believed it to be the final sun. After the sky had collapsed, the four sons of Ometeotl—Xipe Totec, Tezcatlipoca, Quetzalcoatl, and Tlaloc—were transformed into trees, and in a spirit of cooperation, they raised the sky once again. The fifth age is ruled by the sun god Tonatiuh.

It was thought that after each cataclysm the world progressed to a higher level of spirituality, and the Fifth Sun is the most highly evolved era so far. However, the Aztecs believed that unless mortals worked in harmony with the gods, through worship and sacrifice, the Fifth Sun would eventually be devastated, never to be created again.

QUETZALCOATL: THE PLUMED SERPENT

Quetzalcoatl has many different aspects—both human and divine—and he has been likened to both King Arthur and Jesus Christ. His name is derived from the two words: *quetzal*, a beautiful green-feathered bird from the mountains of Central America, and *coatl*, meaning snake. He is most often portrayed as "the plumed serpent," a creature that links Earth with the heavens. The temple of Quetzalcoatl is one of the most magnificent architectural features of the ancient city of Teotihuacan. Quetzalcoatl's symbol is the conch shell, which has associations with both the wind and the sea.

Thought to be a reincarnation of an older Toltec deity, Quetzalcoatl is also linked to the Mayan god of wind, Gucumatz (Kukulcan) and the Aztec wind god Ehecatl. He is also White Tezcatlipoca, creator and ruler of the Second Sun, the Sun of Air. Legend even weaves the Quetzalcoatl figure into a real-life historical personage, Topiltzin, a visionary and compassionate tenth-century Toltec ruler who abolished the ritual of human sacrifice.

The following two stories demonstrate the nurturing, life-affirming qualities of Quetzalcoatl.

Below **Circular temple of Quetzalcoatl, Calixtlahuaca, Mexico.** The shape and form of this temple is reminiscent of the spiral of a conch shell, the symbol of Quetzalcoatl. The pattern of whorls also imitates the motion of the wind, as Quetzalcoatl is associated with the wind god Ehecatl.

The Compassionate Creator

After the Fourth Sun was destroyed, it was Quetzalcoatl's responsibility to create a new race of human beings. Accompanied by Xolotl, his dog-headed twin brother, Quetzalcoatl made the journey down to Mictlan, the Underworld, and gathered the bones of the people who had been drowned in the flood.

Right **Quetzalcoatl, the feathered serpent.** This modern representation of the wind god as a man reflects the legend of Topiltzin, the fair-skinned Toltec ruler who was said to be the wise and peaceful earthly incarnation of Quetzalcoatl.

The Lord of the Underworld, Mictlantecuhtli, was not pleased—he wanted to keep the bones to himself, so he sent his nasty pet quails to chase Quetzalcoatl and Xolotl away. When Quetzalcoatl dropped the bones, breaking them into many pieces, he was disheartened. But the old snake goddess, Cihuacoatl, came to his aid. She gathered the broken bones and ground them up in a jade bowl. Quetzalcoatl mixed his blood with the ground bones to form the first human beings of the Fifth Sun.

The human population eventually grew so large that their food supply dwindled. Quetzalcoatl needed to come up with a clever plan to feed them. One day he happened to be watching an ant coming out from a rock, carrying a kernel of maize. Quetzalcoatl had never seen maize before, and when he tasted it, he realized that it would be the perfect food for his people. He soon discovered that there were quite a lot of maize kernels under the rock, so he transformed himself into an ant, and moved a great many kernels—enough to fill a whole bag—which would be planted to become the first maize field.

Quetzalcoatl was also instrumental in developing the intoxicating drink from the maguey cactus known as pulque, which he thought would bring much pleasure to the world. But in a strange irony, the alcoholic beverage that was meant to be enjoyed by his people would also lead to his undoing.

Descent and Ascension

Because of Quetzalcoatl's many great achievements and contributions, he had become the most popular Aztec deity. His brother Tezcatlipoca was extremely jealous of Quetzalcoatl, and he conspired with Tlazolteotl, the wicked goddess of lust and intoxication, to get rid of him. She prepared a special brew for Quetzalcoatl and his sister and got them both drunk—so drunk, in fact, that they ended up sleeping together.

Quetzalcoatl!
Who knows what he meant
to the dead Aztecs, and to the older
Indians, who knew him before the
Aztecs raised their deity to the heights
of horror and vindictiveness?

D.H. LAWRENCE (1885–1930),
THE PLUMED SERPENT

Tezcatlipoca and Tlazolteotl told all the other gods what had happened. Quetzalcoatl was so mortified by what he had done that he sailed off to the east on a raft made of serpents, promising one day to return to his people. Eventually the other gods realized that Quetzalcoatl had been tricked, but by then it was too late—he was gone.

It was prophesied that Quetzalcoatl would return in the year Ce-Acatl, or 1519 in the Christian calendar. As it turned out, that was the year that Hernando Cortés arrived in Mexico. Because Cortés was such an imposing presence, many of the Aztecs thought that he was Quetzalcoatl, and due to that strange coincidence, the Spanish were quite easily able to conquer the Mexicans.

Another version of the Quetzalcoatl legend says that he burned himself on a funeral pyre, and his ashes flew up to the sky as rare and colorful birds, which then became the planet Venus.

Above **The birth of Quetzalcoatl.** Stories of this remarkable event vary. Topiltzin–Quetzalcoatl was born to Chimalman after a spear-throwing competition made her pregnant. The god Quetzalcoatl–Ehecatl is believed to have been fathered by the supreme Aztec god Ometeotl (also known as Tonacatecuhtli).

125

Above **Mixcoatl, Aztec god of hunting.** The husband of Coatlicue, Mixcoatl is called the cloud serpent as he symbolizes the nebulous Milky Way. He is the god of hunting, war, and the North Star, and was responsible for creating fire by spinning the heavens around a central point.

Right **The dismemberment of Coyolxauhqui.** This stone monolith, measuring 10 ft (3 m) across, shows Coatlicue's daughter Coyolxauhqui after the fight with her half-brother Huitzilopochtli. Coyolxauhqui was decapitated and torn limb from limb during the battle.

TEZCATLIPOCA: LORD OF THE NIGHT SKY

Sometimes compared to Jupiter and Lucifer, as well as to the Mayan god Hurakan, Tezcatlipoca is perhaps the most enigmatic and impressive of all the Aztec deities. As the son of Ometeotl, the Supreme Being, he is one of the four creators of the universe and the ruler of the First Sun (the Sun of Earth) and destroyer of the Second Sun (the Sun of Air).

The animal associated with Tezcatlipoca is the mighty jaguar. The Aztecs thought that the pattern of the jaguar skin resembled the night sky, and pictures of Tezcatlipoca usually show him wearing the animal's skin.

So vast is Tezcatlipoca's importance and influence that he is the patron of royalty, sorcerers, and criminals, and is a prototype for other war deities such as Huitzilopochtli. And, like Huitzilopochtli, he advocated and encouraged human sacrifice.

The Smoking Mirror

As well as the jaguar, Tezcatlipoca is inextricably linked with his "smoking mirror" of obsidian, a cloudy black stone. In fact, the Aztec word for obsidian is "tezcat." Tezcatlipoca had a mirror attached to the back of his head that he used as a tool of divination, with which he could predict events of the future, and tell what was in people's souls.

Tezcatlipoca also has one foot made of obsidian, and stories vary as to how he lost his real foot. One version tells how he fell in love with Xochiquetzal, the moon and flower goddess and wife of Tlaloc, the rain god. When Tezcatlipoca tried to seduce the goddess, her enraged husband threw him off their heavenly mountaintop and Tezcatlipoca's foot came right off. Tezcatlipoca replaced the foot with an obsidian mirror.

Another version tells how Tezcatlipoca and his brother Quetzalcoatl were sent to Earth to fight Cipactli, the crocodilelike Earth Monster who lived under the water. Tezcatlipoca stuck his foot into the water, trying to lure the monster out, and as he did so, Cipactli bit his foot off.

Rival of Quetzalcoatl

Although not as popular as his brother Quetzalcoatl, some consider Tezcatlipoca to be second in greatness only to their father Ometeotl, with Quetzalcoatl venerated more as an Aztec cultural hero.

The brothers had always been rivals, and would demolish each other's creations. One day, in a fit of jealousy, Tezcatlipoca got his brother drunk and then tricked him into sleeping with their sister, an event that led to Quetzalcoatl's dramatic fall from grace.

Tezcatlipoca and Quetzalcoatl represent the dualities of the universe—night and day, light and dark, good and evil, creation and destruction—the opposing forces that are necessary for regeneration and the maintenance of cosmic balance.

COATLICUE AND HUITZILOPOCHTLI: GREAT MOTHER AND WARRIOR SON

The foremost Aztec female deity, Coatlicue (also known as Chalchiuhtlicue), was both the creator and the destroyer of the Fourth Sun (the Sun of Water). As well as being a fertility goddess, she is also the patron of all bodies of water including oceans, rivers, lakes, and waterfalls.

From all accounts, Coatlicue has an awesome presence: her face is bloody and fleshless, she has clawlike hands and feet, her breasts are wrinkled and pendulous, and she wears a necklace formed from human body parts (a reminder of the necessity of sacrifice). Her skirt is made of live snakes, from which she gets the names "She of the Jade Skirt" and "She of the Serpent Skirt."

How Coatlicue Became Pregnant

Coatlicue had borne 400 children and, understandably, she did not want any more, so she ceased having sexual relations with her husband Mixcoatl, the cloud serpent. One day as Coatlicue was sweeping, a colorful feather ball fell out of the sky, which she caught and placed inside her blouse. After her work was finished she decided to have another look at the ball, but it had disappeared.

Months passed, and Coatlicue discovered she was with child. She was mystified, since she hadn't slept with her husband, or anyone else for that matter, for quite some time; she reasoned that it must have been the ball that made her pregnant. When her body could not keep the pregnancy a secret any longer, her children were disgraced, since they knew Mixcoatl could not have been this baby's father. One of Coatlicue's daughters, Coyolxauhqui ("Golden Bells"), arranged with her siblings to kill their mother and her unborn child, to save face and retain their supremacy.

Birth of Huitzilopochtli

Just as all 400 of Coatlicue's offspring gathered to attack her, an amazing thing happened. The child—Huitzilopochtli—emerged forth from the womb, fully grown and fully clothed, with leather sandals on his feet and carrying a spear and shield.

He killed most of his brothers and sisters, including Coyolxauhqui, their mother's favorite, who he beheaded and dismembered. Huitzilopochtli then threw Coyolxauhqui's head up into the sky, which became the moon.

Blue Hummingbird on the Left

As a result of his bold and bloody massacre, Huitzilopochtli gained the respect of all—including his surviving siblings—and he became the god of war. He also became the revered national deity of the Aztec people.

His name means "Blue Hummingbird on the Left" (left was thought to be south), since Huitzilopochtli guided the exodus of the Aztecs south from Atzlan to establish the capital at Tenochtitlan. Hummingbirds are particularly significant, since it was believed that they carried the souls of dead warriors. A temple was built in Huitzilopochtli's honor at Tenochtitlan, where many human hearts were offered to appease the deity.

Below **Coatlicue, Aztec goddess of fertility.** At over 8 ft (2.4 m) in height, this imposing statue of Coatlicue is one of the most famous sculptures from the Aztec era. It clearly shows Coatlicue's skirt of writhing snakes, which were popular Aztec symbols of fertility.

DEITIES OF FERTILITY, WATER, AND WINE

The Aztecs worshipped well over 1,000 gods and goddesses, who watched over and participated in every aspect of their lives. Here are a few of the most revered and feared.

Xipe Totec: the Flayed Earth God

Associated with the young shoots of spring maize, Xipe Totec is the god of fertility and regeneration.

Because maize was the staple crop of the Aztecs and essential to life, many people were sacrificed to Xipe Totec and other deities so that the gods would ensure a good crop. One of the favored forms of sacrifice was being flayed (skinned alive). The captors of the victims, as well as the priests, sometimes wore the skins over their naked bodies to symbolize the maize seeds, which lose their outer covering when the new growth appears.

Xipe Totec is often pictured as wearing a flayed human skin. It is also believed that he allowed his own skin to be peeled off to set an example to his people, and as a sign of renewal and regeneration.

Tlaloc: the Rain God

As creator of the Sun of Rain, the Third Sun, Tlaloc is one of the most important deities in the Aztec pantheon, and corresponds to the Mayan rain god Chaac. He is sometimes said to be the brother-consort of Coatlicue ("She of the Jade Skirt").

Tlaloc has four jugs, from which he pours down rain onto the Earth; some rain is benign and helpful for crops, and some is destructive. He is assisted by a sky serpent, which holds a vast amount of water inside its huge belly.

Sometimes pictured as a fierce creature with tusks and circles around his eyes, Tlaloc is a demanding god, requiring many sacrificial victims. In times of drought, people would sacrifice their babies, whose tears were said to help the rain fall. The rituals to appease Tlaloc often necessitated that the priests eat the flesh of the victims.

Anyone who was struck by lightning, or died by drowning or infectious disease, was welcomed into a paradise known as Tlalocan ("Place of Tlaloc").

Xochiquetzal: "Feather Flower"

Xochiquetzal also goes by the name of "Richly Plumed Flower," and is depicted as being adorned in quetzal feathers. She is a versatile deity, being the goddess of the moon, flowers, marriage, and children, and is patron of artists and weavers. Xochiquetzal is renowned for her beauty, youth, and sex appeal, but is also a great upholder of family values. When she was married to Tlaloc the rain god, Tezcatlipoca desired her so greatly that he ended up losing his foot when fighting for her affections.

Tlazolteotl: Goddess of Filth and Excrement

Presenting another side of female sexuality, Tlazolteotl is an important deity. She is the goddess of fertility, lust, and intoxication—of human abasement and the darker side of human sexuality—and encourages and pardons infidelities. Sometimes pictured as having

spindles in her hair, she is the patron of spinners, as well as of witchcraft and even steam baths.

When the jealous Tezcatlipoca got Quetzalcoatl drunk and tricked him into sleeping with his sister, he had enlisted the help of Tlazolteotl.

Whereas the flower goddess Xochiquetzal never ages, and is only ever portrayed as a beautiful young woman, Tlazolteotl is often depicted as an old crone in a squatting position.

Mayahuel: Goddess of Pulque

Pulque is the alcoholic drink made from the maguey cactus. After he created the first humans, Quetzalcoatl felt that they were too serious, and that they needed something to bring them cheer.

Quetzalcoatl traveled up to the heavens to persuade the virgin goddess Mayahuel to come to Earth and help him create a pleasurable substance. When they arrived on Earth, the god and goddess transformed themselves into a tree, the branches entwined in a lovers' embrace.

Mayahuel's enraged grandmother Tzitzimitl swooped down to Earth and tore the tree apart, feeding the pieces of what was Mayahuel to her entourage of star demons. Quetzalcoatl buried the fragments that were left, and from that planting sprouted the splendid maguey cactus.

Above **Tlalocan, paradise of Tlaloc.** Souls who came here were looked after by Tlaloc's servants, the Tlaloques. After four years the souls were reincarnated as human beings again.

THE SHAMAN

In ancient Mexico, the shaman was considered a highly respected member of the community, and served a vital function as an intermediary between the spirit world and the natural world.

Shamans did not choose their career—they were either born into it, or were called through special dreams and visions. An important part of the Aztec belief system was the interconnectedness of all things—living and dead—and it was the role of the shaman to work with the energy of the world beyond everyday perception.

Pulque, an alcoholic drink made from the maguey cactus, was widely used in ceremonies, as were hallucinogens such as peyote and datura. Masks, chanting, drums, rattles, and other instruments were also employed to help the shaman reach an altered state of consciousness.

The modern-day shaman practices within the ancient cultural tradition, invoking the myths and deities of old. They may prescribe herbal medicines, retrieve lost souls, read the future, or perform cleansings on a home or individual who has been bewitched.

SOUTH AMERICAN MYTHOLOGY

The ancient civilizations of South America thrived in diverse landscapes of intense natural beauty, encompassing the towering Andes Mountains, the surrounding plains and valleys, and the magnificent Amazon rain forest.

It is thought that the first people traveled to this continent from Siberia between 9000 and 5000 B.C. The earliest Andean culture—the Chavín—is estimated to have thrived between 900 and 200 B.C., and for centuries civilizations changed and progressed, culminating in the Inca empire.

The Inca ruled from A.D. 1400 to 1532, and were a highly organized, disciplined, and stratified society. They made great advances in both agriculture and building construction, and had a sophisticated network of roads and communication.

Most of our knowledge of Andean civilizations comes from archaeological evidence, as they had no writing systems. The Inca had a record-keeping system known as *quipu,* involving knotted string. Myths were held by the *quipucamayoqs* (the knot makers), as well as the *amautas* (the court poets), and the *mamacunas* (the virgins of the sun temples). As the Inca took over other civilizations, they adopted their deities, sacred sites, and legends.

The people of the Amazon had a purely oral tradition. Their myths varied from tribe to tribe, focusing on the natural world and the balance of power within human relationships and between humanity and nature. Most of what we know of the Amazonian myths is due to the work of anthropologists.

COMMON THREADS

Several common themes recur in the myths and histories of the South Americans, and the stories generally fall into the following categories: the origin of the world, the great flood, the creation of human beings, the cultural hero, and the animal story.

All of the civilizations tell of a belief in a creator deity, and in many cases there is an endless cycle of creation and destruction. This is seen very clearly in the Inca concept of *pachacuti.*

The Andean cultures tried to make sense of the cosmos, setting up astronomical observation posts so that they could study the celestial bodies. The sun, moon, and often the stars were deified, and were inextricably linked to the agricultural and ceremonial life of the people.

Human sacrifice (especially of young children) was deemed to be a necessary part of religious life, especially in times of adversity. Artwork of the Moche people graphically depicts ritual scenes of strangling and beheading, and the great sun gods of the Inca and Chibcha—Inti and Bochica respectively—were especially demanding of human blood.

Naturally occurring drugs such as coca and the hallucinogenic *ayahuasca* were regularly used in rituals and ceremonies to enable the priests and shamans to communicate with the spirits. During festivals and other important events the people of the Andes enjoyed drinking *chicha,* an alcoholic beverage made from maize fermented with human saliva.

Cultural heroes featured prominently in all the mythologies. Sometimes semi-divine, they were traveling teachers who brought civilization, law, living skills, and morals to less advanced people.

Right **Sun god mask, La Tolita culture.** Well-known for working with gold, the people of Ecuador's La Tolita culture (which existed from 500 B.C. to A.D. 500) created masks for special occasions. The wearer of the mask was said to take on the power of the deity represented by the mask— in this case the sun god.

Right **Detail from an eighteenth-century carpet showing an Incan person with flora and fauna.** The indigenous South Americans lived in harmony with their natural environment, and treated the animals and plants with respect. There are many myths involving native creatures such as llamas, jaguars, and anacondas, which reveal the importance of these animals in everyday life.

THE NATURAL WORLD

The people of the Andes and the Amazon lived closely with the natural world, and their myths are dominated by flora, fauna, and natural disasters.

In South America, the jaguar was considered the king of beasts, and was thought to once control the earth. The city of Cuzco was designed in the shape of a puma. Llamas were revered for their many practical uses, and they were also believed to have the gift of prophecy. In the Andean view of the universe, the souls of the dead were reincarnated as llamas, and the serpent ruled the underworld, the puma was the lord of the middleworld, and the condor presided over the upperworld.

Natural disasters such as floods and earthquakes occurred regularly throughout history and mythology, and were thought to be acts of the gods: either as punishment, or for purification and renewal.

SACRED PLACES

There are several places throughout South America that are considered by the native inhabitants to be very sacred, and some of them are connected with the stories of creation and human origin.

Tiahuanaco in the Bolivian Andes was a major pilgrimage center, and the highest city in the ancient world. Pachacamac was another revered pilgrimage site in central Peru, an amazing place with a temple built on an artificial hill. According to Inca legend, the first humans emerged from Lake Titicaca; within the lake lie the Island of the Sun and the Island of the Moon. Machu Picchu was a beautifully designed city set high in the Andes, and was used as a spiritual retreat for the royal family. Cuzco, the Inca capital, was considered to be the navel of the world, and the meeting place of the earth and sky. The focal point of Cuzco was the complex of temples at Coricancha.

ANCESTOR WORSHIP

Throughout the South American continent, people honored the spirits of their ancestors in various ways. Human bodies were preserved as mummies, and were brought out to worship during ceremonial occasions. There were certain features in the landscape (such as rocks, caves, and hills) that had special significance because it was believed that the souls of the ancestors departed the earthly realm from these places, and left a small part of their spirit behind. These places were called *paccariscas*. Some tribes of the Amazon rain forest practiced cannibalism to preserve the revered qualities of their forebears.

SOUTH AMERICA

SPANISH CONQUEST

Francisco Pizarro arrived in South America in 1532, and in just 20 years the entire continent was under Spanish control. They came in search of gold, and even tried to drain Lake Guatavita in Colombia where the myth of El Dorado originated.

The Catholic priests were often relentless in their zeal to convert the natives. They took over or demolished temples; destroyed idols, mummies, and *quipus*; and abolished rituals and festivals. One priest, Francisco de Avila, made a thorough inquiry into the old religious practices to prove their inferiority. These chronicles were known as *Idolatrias*, and record many of the beliefs and legends of the conquered people.

Many of the old ways have become amalgamated within the Catholic tradition. In addition, many Westerners are now making pilgrimages to places such as Machu Picchu, and traveling to the Amazon to learn the wisdom of the shamans.

EARLY PRE-INCA ANDEAN CULTURES

Several civilizations thrived in the Andes region for many centuries prior to the emergence of the Inca empire. These include the ancient Chavín, Paracas, Moche (Mohica), and Nazca cultures.

Chavín

The Chavín culture existed during the Early Horizon Period (900–200 B.C.) in present-day north-central Peru. It has been described as the "mother culture" of the Andes, and was named after the site where the culture was first discovered, the religious center of Chavín de Huántar in the Ancash highlands.

The temple is the oldest and, some say, the most beautiful in South America. It was believed to be the center of the cosmos, and features a carved stone monolith known as the Lanzon, a half-human/half-monster oracle figure. Many images of the Staff Deity also endure from this period: a fertility god/goddess with birdlike, snakelike, or catlike characteristics (often with fangs), holding a staff in each hand.

Paracas

Also from the Early Horizon Period, the Paracas culture occurred along the southern coast of Peru. The Paracas people created some superbly colored textiles made from llama wool and cotton, and were pioneers in the art of mummification. Archaeologists have noted from studying their textiles and other craftwork that the Paracas people worshipped a deity who has become known in modern times as the Oculate Being because of its large, penetrating eyes. The Oculate Being incorporates features of several different creatures: feline, bird, killer whale, and fox.

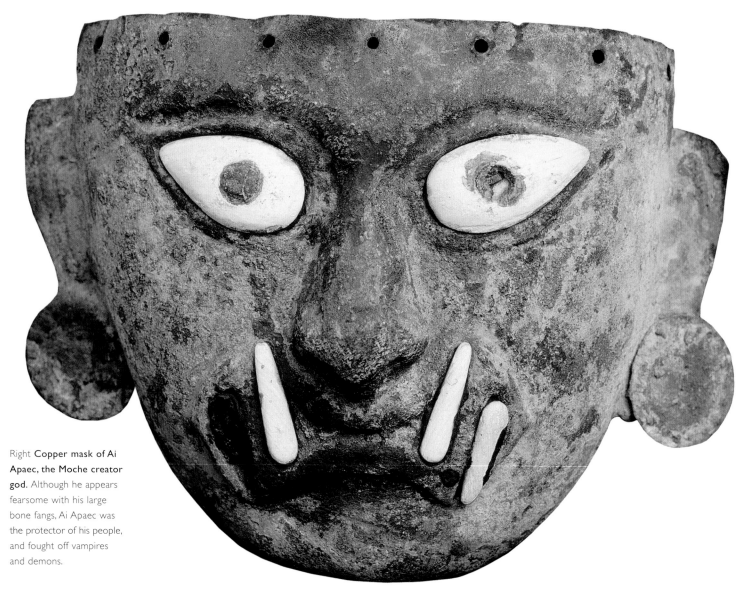

Right **Copper mask of Ai Apaec, the Moche creator god.** Although he appears fearsome with his large bone fangs, Ai Apaec was the protector of his people, and fought off vampires and demons.

Moche

The Moche (or Mohica) culture existed between A.D. 1 and 700 (in the Intermediate Period) throughout the coastal valleys of northern Peru. As their artifacts clearly demonstrate, the Moche people were both skilled and prolific artisans in a variety of mediums: ceramic pottery, metalwork, gold and silver jewelry, textiles, murals, and friezes.

Moche artwork indicates that they were a warlike people, and that the wars were often motivated by the need for sacrifice victims to appease the gods. The Moche experienced floods and earthquakes, signs of the gods' displeasure, and the more violent the weather conditions, the greater the need for sacrifice.

The most favored form of sacrifice was slitting the throat, and then presenting the victim's body and blood to the deities. There is a terrifying statue that shows a rather Satan-like figure (perhaps a deity or an executioner) pulling a man's hair, preparing to cut his throat. Ritual burial sites have revealed the skeletons of young girls who had been beaten on the head by clubs, and then had their legs pulled off.

Ai Apaec, the god of creation, is one of the most important deities in the Moche pantheon, and the precursor to the Inca god Viracocha. He is a distant and impersonal god of the sky and mountains, and features prominently in Moche iconography. Ai Apaec is often pictured in fearsome warrior mode, with slanted eyes, a fanged mouth, and a belt and head-dress made of snakes.

Si is the Moche word for moon, and is the name of the unisex moon deity, who was also in charge of fertility, rain, and the sea. Unlike Ai Apaec, who was

fairly remote, Si seemed to be more involved in the activities of mortals. The Huaca de la Luna (Temple of the Moon) was built in honor of Si.

In Moche culture, the moon was more important than the sun. The harsh desert sun was seen more as an enemy than a friend, and many of their religious ceremonies were performed at night.

The most feared and bloodthirsty Moche deity goes by the name of Decapitator God. He is portrayed as half-human and half-spider, or half-human and half-jaguar, and his likeness is seen on every type of artwork, especially around ritual sites. He has four sharp fangs protruding from a contorted mouth, piercing eyes, and a beard.

Unfortunately, no myths or stories seem to have survived from this interesting era.

Nazca

The Nazca culture also flourished during the Intermediate Period (from 200 B.C. to A.D. 500) in Peru's southern coastal desert valleys. This culture developed a sophisticated underground irrigation system, and had excellent textiles and ceramics. But the Nazca culture is most well known for the incredible system of geoglyphs (symbols scored into the earth) known as the Nazca Lines, which cover a total area of 190 sq miles (500 sq km) and have been carbon-dated to A.D. 350.

NAZCA LINES

The Nazca Lines are South America's greatest mystery. They are a complex of close to 300 geoglyphs that are found mainly in the Pampa de Ingenio desert of Peru.

As well as lines and geometric shapes, the images also include humanlike figures, flowers, fish, insects, and various animals and birds. They were made by etching, or scraping, the surface pebbles of the desert floor so that the lighter rock underneath could show through. Some of the drawings on hillsides can be seen from the plains below, but most can only be viewed from the air.

There are several theories about the origins of the Nazca Lines. Some think that they were of astronomical and astrological significance. Others believe that they were used for ritual walks. According to Erich von Daniken in his 1970 book, *Chariots of the Gods*, the lines were the work of UFOs. It is also possible that the drawings were a form of visual prayer to the sky and mountain deities in the hope that they would bestow rain on the arid desert landscape.

Left **The Oculate Being, Paracas culture.** Made from alpaca wool, this fine example of a Paracas textile shows the Oculate Being in human form. He is wearing a golden diadem (ornamental headband) and holding a snake. A snakelike creature also hovers above his head.

Above **Shaman on painted vessel, Nazca culture.** As with most South American cultures, the shaman played an important role in the lives of the Nazca people. It has been suggested that the spirits of the shamans were able to soar above the landscape and direct the people to create the immense Nazca Lines for religious purposes.

LATE PRE-INCA ANDEAN CULTURES

The centuries leading up to the Inca empire were known as the Middle Horizon Period (A.D. 500–1000) and the Late Intermediate Period (A.D. 1000–1400). During the Middle Horizon Period, the major political, cultural, and religious centers were Huarí in the Peruvian highlands, Pachacamac on the coast, and Tiahuanaco in the Lake Titicaca Basin. Chan Chan was the capital of the Kingdom of Chimor (or Chimu) during the Late Intermediate Period, in the area previously ruled by the Moche (or Mochica) people in the north Peruvian coastal valleys.

Below **Passage of Fish and Birds, Chan Chan.** The extensive ruins of Chan Chan are located near the present-day Peruvian town of Trujillo. Many of the adobe brick walls still show the fascination of the original inhabitants with the fauna of the region, and the designs may have had both a religious and an aesthetic function.

[They] commonly acknowledge a supreme lord and author of all things, which they of Peru called ... Pachacamac, or Pachayachachic, which is the creator of heaven and earth ...

JOSÉ DE ACOSTA (1540–1600), JESUIT MISSIONARY

Pachacamac: Sacred Place and Sacred Being

Not only was the coastal city of Pachacamac an important cultural center, it was also a place of worship and pilgrimage in honor of the deity of the same

name, which means "earth-maker" or "the one who animates the world."

The complex of temples and pyramids at Pachacamac (near present-day Lima) was an awe-inspiring sight, built on top of an artificial hill made of adobe bricks. These buildings were adorned with beautiful murals and frescoes and held many treasures. The major focus of the sacred site was the oracle of Pachacamac, as represented by a wooden idol. Priests that had been specially ordained would act as mediums between the pilgrim and the oracle—as no ordinary human being was deemed worthy of direct contact— and even the priest was not able to gaze at the idol uncovered.

When the Incas later took over Pachacamac, they were so impressed with the temple's grandeur that the only change they made was to add a chapel in honor of their sun god, Inti.

Pachacamac, the creator deity, was the son of the sun and moon, and the god of earthquakes and fire, and he was worshipped by the people of the Andes for close to 1,000 years. There are several myths illustrating just what a harsh and mighty deity Pachacamac could be.

Before Pachacamac existed, he had a half-brother named Con, who was also the son of the sun, and an imposing deity in his own right. Con arrived from the north, and as he traveled the land, he would move mountains or fill up valleys to make his journey easier. He designed a beautiful fertile land, but became lonely, so he decided to create some people to share the land and its bounty with him. Con soon became displeased with the people he created, thinking them lazy and ungrateful. He turned their lush farmlands into barren rocky ground, thus making life much harder for them.

One day Pachacamac appeared, and decided he wanted his brother's creation all to himself. He challenged and defeated Con, and changed the people into monkeys. All the crops withered away and died. Pachacamac then set about creating people of his own—one man and one woman. But because he neglected to provide food for them, the man died, and the woman knew that she would soon die herself if she did not get help. So she approached the sun for assistance, and the sun obliged her by making her pregnant through the force of his rays. After her son was born, Pachacamac became extremely jealous. He killed the boy, then chopped the body up and scattered the pieces. The boy's teeth became maize

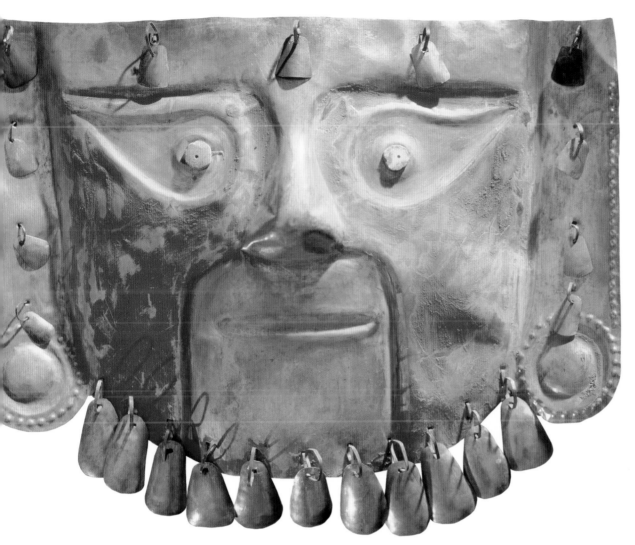

Left **Gold funerary mask, Chimor (Chimu) culture.** Elaborate funerary masks were usually buried with wealthy or noble Chimor people. This gold mask has traces of red cinnabar paint, and may even have been originally decorated with brightly colored feathers, shells from the local area, or prized semi-precious stones.

and his bones became the yucca plant. This story seems to be a parable about the importance of human sacrifice (especially the sacrifice of children) to ensure a bountiful harvest.

The *Huarochirí Manuscript*

This seventeenth-century text was written in the Quechua language under the direction of Spanish priest Francisco de Avila. It has been likened to the Mayan *Popol Vuh*, and details the myths, culture, and beliefs of the Huarochirí (or Warachirí) people of the western Andes. The purpose of the manuscript was to compare the indigenous beliefs with Christianity—rather unfavorably, one would think, judging from the manuscript's original title: *A Narrative of the Errors, False Gods, and Other Superstitions and Diabolical Rites of the Indians* (1608).

PARIACACA AND HUALLALLO CARUINCHO

One of the many stories of the *Huarochirí Manuscript* tells of the rain god Pariacaca, who was an important deity of the region. During a flood, five eggs were found on Mount Condor Coto. Falcons emerged from these five eggs, flying in all directions, and transforming themselves into men, who became the five aspects of the divine Pariacaca.

The most powerful deity of the Huarochirí people was Huallallo Caruincho, known as the "Man Eater." He was the god of fire and volcanoes, and was very demanding and autocratic. Huallallo Caruincho had a rule that there could only be two children per family, and one child had to be eaten by the god.

Pariacaca decided that he wanted to challenge the vile supremacy of this tyrannical god. His weapon would be water and Huallallo Caruincho's would be fire. A long battle ensued. Because Pariacaca was a multiple deity, he could attack Huallallo Caruincho from five different directions at once. Although he was a formidable opponent, Huallallo Caruincho eventually surrendered, fleeing toward the jungles of the Amazon.

Below **Textile from the Late Intermediate Period.** Produced by the Chancay culture (A.D. 900–1450) of coastal Peru, the design of this textile shows the typical Chancay motif of an unnamed deity with a large, decorative headdress composed of a number of writhing "sky serpents."

Above **Stele (sculpted upright slab) of pre-Incan god Coniraya Viracocha.** Dating from the period A.D. 600–1200, this simple stone sculpture of the creator deity was found at the ruins of Tiahuanaco in Bolivia. Coniraya Viracocha's influence was such that the Incas absorbed the myths and characteristics of the deity into their own creator god, Viracocha.

a kindly woman brought him a cup of maize beer and some food. After he was refreshed, he told the woman to take her family and leave the village, because something terrible was going to happen in five days. And he warned her not to tell anyone else, or she would be destroyed too. The woman followed Pariacaca's instructions. Five days later, Pariacaca caused torrential rain to fall from the mountain, which washed everyone in the village out to sea.

CONIRAYA VIRACOCHA

The second chapter of the *Huarochirí Manuscript* contains the story of Coniraya Viracocha, a pre-Inca deity who was later taken up by the Incas and incorporated into their creator, Viracocha. This chapter details the exploits of Coniraya Viracocha as he journeyed throughout the universe on foot, dressed as a penniless beggar.

While visiting a village by the sea, Coniraya Viracocha fell in love with a beautiful virgin named Cavillaca, but she was not interested in him because he was old and poor. But Coniraya Viracocha was mad with desire, and he shape-shifted himself into a bird so he could follow her around and watch her without being noticed.

One day as Cavillaca was weaving a tapestry underneath the shade of her favorite lucuma tree, Coniraya Viracocha flew to the tree and ejaculated some sperm into one of the orange fruits, causing the fruit to drop to the ground. Cavillaca saw how lovely and ripe the fruit was, so she picked it up and ate it.

Because she was a virgin, Cavillaca was absolutely horrified to find herself pregnant—especially as she did not have a clue as to who the father could possibly be—and in due course she gave birth to a son. When the baby was about six months old Cavillaca was determined to learn the identity of the father. She gathered together all the men of the village, and

Another version of the story tells that while he was on his journey to fight Huallallo Caruincho, Pariacaca stopped at a village during a festival, and sat down at a banquet table. Because of Pariacaca's bedraggled, road-weary appearance, nobody offered him anything to eat or drink. Pariacaca was outraged—didn't these people realize who he was? Finally, after many hours,

For when the Indians worshipped it they said, "Coniraya Viracocha ... thou art Lord of all ...

TRANSLATED FROM THE *HUAROCHIRÍ MANUSCRIPT* BY CLEMENTS R. MARKHAM (1830–1916)

MUMMIES

The practice of preserving bodies as mummies *(mallquis)* was carried out from the very earliest Andean civilizations, and was a very important aspect of ancestor worship.

The mummy bundles were wrapped in alternating layers of cloth and sand, and then tied up with fiber rope. Sometimes clothes, jewelry, or other personal belongings were wrapped in the bundle. Often a mask or head was added, made from wood or copper, and decorated with feathers, shells, or fabric. The mummies were not actually buried, but were stored in special buildings or caves, and became preserved by the hot, dry, desert atmosphere.

At *mallqui* rituals, the mummies were brought out of storage, put on display, and given offerings of food and *chicha* (maize beer). During the ceremonies, the people would relate myths about the history of the clan, and share their knowledge. These rituals were thought to please the gods, and bring prosperity and spiritual merit.

Above right **Death mask from a Chimor (Chimu) mummy bundle.** In the Chimor (Chimu) culture, the deceased were placed in a sitting position before being wrapped in layers of cloth. The mask was placed over the head area of the bundle.

her baby reached the ocean near Pachacamac, they were turned into stones. Not one to give up easily, Coniraya Viracocha traveled on, asking each and every creature he passed along the way if they had seen his beloved.

Now you can choose the ending to this story, depending on how cynical or how romantic you are. In one version, when Coniraya Viracocha reached the coastal city of Pachacamac he came across two beautiful daughters of the god Pachacamac. Being the lustful god that he was, Coniraya Viracocha seduced one of the goddesses and wanted to bed her younger sister as well, but she became a bird and flew away from the god. The other ending tells that Coniraya Viracocha was so heartbroken not to have found his beloved Cavillaca and his son, that he made a raft out of his golden cloak and, like the Meso-american deity Quetzalcoatl, sailed away to the horizon, promising one day to return.

asked whoever was responsible for making her pregnant to come forth and admit their cruel deed. Quite a few young men were eager to accept the responsibility for her baby, just so they could marry the gorgeous Cavillaca.

But Cavillaca was confused. How could so many men be this baby's father? So she decided to let her son choose. She placed him on the ground and told him to crawl to the man who was his true biological father. He was a bright little lad, and she trusted that he would know what to do. As it turned out, Coniraya Viracocha, dressed in his beggar's garb, was hanging around on the sidelines. Without any hesitation, the baby crawled right up to Coniraya Viracocha, and put his arms around the deity's leg.

Disgusted at the prospect of marrying this filthy itinerant, Cavillaca snatched the baby away and ran as fast as she could toward the sea. She did not look back to see Coniraya Viracocha remove his shabby gray cloak and transform himself into a handsome young god in golden finery. When Cavillaca and

Below **Human head effigy, Inca culture.** Carved from wood, with startling eyes made from inlaid shell, this head was probably part of a mummy bundle. Placing the realistic head near the cloth-wrapped mummy ensured that the deceased retained human form in the afterlife.

Right **Pachacuti Inca Yup-anqui, eighteenth-century Cuzco School painting.** The ninth emperor of the Incas officially ruled from 1438 to 1471, but legend has it that he became the sovereign of the Incas at age 22, and ruled his people for 103 years.

Below *Inca Sun Worship* by **Bernard Picart (1673–1733).** The Incas believed they were descendants of the sun god, Inti, and many temples and other sacred sites were devoted to wor-shipping the sun. A rock on Lake Titicaca's Island of the Sun is said to be the birthplace of the sun.

THE INCAS

By the time the Spanish arrived in South America in the sixteenth century, the Inca empire was the size of the Roman empire, extending 2,600 miles (4,186 km) throughout the Andes and beyond. The guiding force of this highly organized society was the ruler Pacha-cuti Inca Yupanqui.

Inca means "people of the sun," and the major deity of the Inca people was the sun god Inti. How-ever, their belief system also absorbed the deities of the people whom they conquered.

The spirituality of the Incas had much in common with that of the Mesoamerican peoples in that it was focused on fertility and agriculture, especially the growing of maize (also known as corn). As in Meso-america, human sacrifice was practiced, but not on such a grand scale. The Inca people also believed in honoring and worshipping their ancestors.

INCA COSMOLOGY

Similar to the Aztec worldview, the Incas believed in cycles of creation and destruction. Each "age" or "sun" lasted 1,000 years, and was known as a *pachacuti,* named for the ruler Pachacuti Inca Yupanqui. *Pachacuti* virtually means the turning over of time and space. Each cycle was thought to be the reversal of the previous one, and the Inca civilization was in the cycle of the Fifth Sun, which ended at the time of European invasion.

Linked to the concept of *pachacuti* is the belief that the Spanish would one day be conquered and the Inca would rise again. Legend has it that the last Inca emperor, Atahualpa, was beheaded by the Spanish conqueror Francisco Pizarro, and that his head was buried at Cuzco. But the head never died, and over the years a body has been growing. When Atahualpa becomes a complete person again, he will rise from the earth and restore the ancient empire to its former glory.

Peruvian shamans have prophesied that in the twenty-first century a new *pachacuti* will evolve in which order will emerge out of chaos and peace will come from turmoil. In this golden age, the indigenous people of the world will take their rightful place, and the Eagle of the North will fly with the Condor of the South.

Heaven, Earth, and Underworld

The Inca believed that all of nature was permeated with a divine force, and that there were three levels of existence: the upperworld, *Hanaq Pacha,* which was inhabited by the gods and goddesses; *Kay Pacha,* the earth plane; and *Ukhu Pacha,* the land of the dead.

Inti, the sun god and father of the Inca emperors, was the most powerful deity. It was to Inti that most of the sacrifices, offerings, and rituals were performed. The Inca believed that if they led a virtuous life, they would join the sun god in the heavens.

Mama Quilla (or Mama Kilya), the moon goddess and wife of Inti, was also revered, and there is a temple at Cuzco in her honor.

As well as the sun and moon, the stars also had special significance. The Inca used the Milky Way to help them devise their calendar system and predict seasonal and weather changes. The stars in the Milky Way (or Mayu, the celestial river) were afforded the status of minor deities. The Pleiades, for instance, was the celestial patron of agriculture.

The earthly plane, too, was full of sacred meaning. There were supernatural forces associated with rocks, mountains, lakes, rivers, and trees. These forces were known as *huacas,* and the places they inhabited inspired great reverence.

People also had their own little *huacas* that they carried around with them. These could be stones or pebbles, or perhaps pieces of wood or stone carved

INTI RAYMI

Inti Raymi is the Inca festival of the winter solstice (which is in June in the Southern Hemisphere). It is held at Cuzco to honor the sun god, Inti, and celebrates the resurrection of the sun. Traditionally people fasted and abstained from sex for three days before the festival, and the proceedings lasted for nine days. A black llama was sacrificed, and the celebratory feast included cornmeal (*zancu*), round bread, and maize beer (*chicha*).

The essence of Inti Raymi is expressed in this prayer: "Oh creator and Sun and Thunder, be forever copious, do not make us old, let all things be at peace, multiply the people and let there be food, and let all things be fruitful."

After the Spanish conquest, the old rituals were considered sacrilegious and abolished, but Inti Raymi was revived in 1944, and moved to June 24 to coincide with the feast of St John the Baptist.

Today Inti Raymi attracts thousands of people from all over the world. It is a blend of reverence and revelry—a colorful carnival of singing and dancing in traditional costume.

Left **Gold llama, Inca culture.** Llamas were important to the Incas, and were often sacrificed during religious festivals. At other times they were used as sure-footed pack animals.

into the shape of a person, animal, or plant. A special type of *huaca* would be placed in a maize field or irrigation canal to ensure a good harvest. Many of these agricultural *huacas* were destroyed by the Spanish conquerors.

Paccariscas were not unlike *huacas,* and were generally found near natural formations like caves, rocks, mountains, and springs. But *paccariscas* were considered even more important because the people believed that it was at these sacred places that their ancestors departed for the spirit world, and where a bit of their soul was left behind. When people arrived at the *paccarisca,* they would utter the prayer: "Thou art my birthplace, thou art my lifespring. Guard me from evil. O Paccarisca!"

The Inca underworld was a cold and inhospitable place where immoral people went after death. It was ruled by Supay (or Cupay), a demonlike being.

INCA MYTHS OF ORIGIN

Pachacuti Inca Yupanqui, who reigned between A.D. 1438 and 1471, led the Inca empire into a golden age of prosperity and expansion. Among his many achievements were a national taxation system and a sophisticated road and communications network.

As a result of a spiritual experience, Pachacuti believed that he was the child of the sun god, Inti, and set about reorganizing the religious structure of the empire. Religious unification meant political unification, and the myths that were created served to support and reinforce Inca supremacy.

Major Inca Deities

Pachacuti's improvements extended to the Coricancha, the magnificent center of the capital city of Cuzco and one of the major sacred sites of the Inca empire. He dedicated special areas to each of the most important deities within the extensive Inca pantheon, including Viracocha, Inti, and Mama Quilla.

IMPORTANT INCA DEITIES

NAME	REALM
APO	GOD OF THE MOUNTAINS
APOCATEQUIL	GOD OF LIGHTNING
APU ILLAPU	GOD OF THUNDER
CHANTICO	GODDESS OF GOLD
CHASCA	GODDESS OF VENUS
CHASCA COYLLUR	GOD OF FLOWERS
COCOMAMA	GODDESS OF HEALTH
CONIRAYA	GOD OF THE MOON
COPACATI	GODDESS OF THE LAKES
EKKEKO	GOD OF PROSPERITY
EPUNAMUN	GOD OF WAR
ILYAP'A	GOD OF THE WEATHER
INTI	GOD OF THE SUN
KA-ATA-KILLA	GODDESS OF THE MOON
KON	GOD OF THE RAIN AND THE SOUTH WIND
MAMA ALLPA	GODDESS OF THE HARVEST
MAMA COCHA	GODDESS OF THE SEA
MAMA OCLLO	GODDESS OF SPINNING
MAMA QUILLA	GODDESS OF THE MOON
MANCO CAPAC	GOD OF FIRE
PACHACAMAC	GOD OF THE EARTH
PACHAMAMA	GODDESS OF PLANTS AND ANIMALS
SUPAY	GOD OF DEATH AND THE UNDERWORLD
URCAGUARY	GOD OF BURIED TREASURE
URPIHUA-CHAC	GODDESS OF FISH AND FISHING
VIRACOCHA	SUPREME DEITY, THE CREATOR
ZARAMAMA	GODDESS OF MAIZE

VIRACOCHA: CREATOR AND SUPREME GOD

This remote, impersonal, and invisible deity was called by many names, corresponding to the many roles he played in the cycle of creation. Some of his epithets were Callya ("the ever-present one"), Pachayachachic ("world teacher"), Illa ("Light"), and Tici ("the beginning"). It was believed that he rose from Lake Titicaca to create the sun, moon, and stars.

There is a stone statue at the sacred site of Tiahuanaco in which he is represented as a weeping god. When someone died, special prayers were offered to Viracocha so that the soul would find a peaceful resting place. Small children were sacrificed to Viracocha at his temple in Cuzco and in places high in the mountains in the hope that the Inca people would be victorious in war.

In certain myths, Viracocha appears in various disguises—often as a pale-skinned man with a beard. In this human aspect he is both a teacher and a cultural hero.

INTI: THE SUN GOD

Although Viracocha was the highest-ranking god, Inti was the most popular deity, and was believed to be the ancestor of the royal family and the father of the Inca race. It was through Inti that the Inca received their name "people of the sun."

Inti was a benevolent god, and is honored at his own special temple in Coricancha at Cuzco, and at the "hitching post of the sun" at Machu Picchu, among other sacred places. The ancient festivals of the winter solstice (Inti Raymi) and summer solstice (Capac Raymi) pay homage to Inti and are popular celebrations with South Americans even today.

The Inca believed that if they lived a virtuous life, their spirits would join with the sun god in

the heavens. Inti is associated with the element of gold, and he is often represented as a large golden mask with a humanlike face.

MAMA QUILLA: THE MOON GODDESS

Mama Quilla, or Mama Kilya, is the highest-ranking female deity, the mother of the Incas, and protector of women. As the moon goddess, she governs the calendar and the passing of time. Originally she shone brighter than the sun, so the jealous Inti threw ashes in her face so he would be the more luminous.

Mama Quilla is associated with the element of silver, and there is a temple in her honor at Coricancha in Cuzco as well as at Machu Picchu. Because she is the wife, as well as sister, of the sun god Inti, this relationship set a precedent for brother-sister marriages within the royal family.

How Viracocha Created the World

One of the myths of creation that may even pre-date the Inca period centers on Viracocha, the supreme god. Viracocha and his wife Mama Cocha (goddess of the sea) lived in the sacred lake, Titicaca. One day Viracocha took mud from the bottom of the lake and created all the formations of the earth: the valleys, fields, and mountains.

Although he was pleased with his achievement, Viracocha felt that the earth needed people who could worship him, so he took blocks of stone and sculpted them into human beings. But he was unhappy with his first attempt: he had created ugly, shapeless giants who were stupid and disobedient, so he immediately destroyed them with a torrent of water.

Viracocha decided that before he endeavored to make any more people, he would create the Island of the Sun and the Island of the Moon within the lake itself; the sun and moon rose up from these islands, and Viracocha set them on their celestial course. Now that the sun was in the sky, Viracocha could actually see what he was doing.

Feeling more confident now, Viracocha then set about finding some clay from which to fashion a new group of humans. He shaped them into male and female, child and adult, and painted on clothes and hair. Viracocha was happy with these new folk, and led them underground where they were dispersed throughout a labyrinth of caves. The creator breathed into them his life force, and they went forth into the world to people the land.

Above **Silver maize plant, Inca culture.** Silver was associated with the moon goddess Mama Quilla (also known as Mama Kilya), as the color of the metal is similar to the glow of the full moon. This silver maize cob may well have been created specifically as a symbolic offering of food to the moon goddess.

Left **Inca temple of the sun god, Island of the Sun, Bolivia.** The Island of the Sun (also known as the Isla del Sol) sits amid the cool, blue waters of Lake Titicaca, the highest navigable lake in the world. Even today the indigenous population believes that the lake collects water sent by the nearby mountain deities, and offerings are made to ensure good fishing and safe sailing.

Below *Cuzco, Peru* by Georgius Braun (1541–1622). The great Inca capital, Cuzco was founded in the twelfth century by Manco Capac, son of the sun god Inti. From the majestic temple dedicated to Inti—the Coricancha—41 imaginary lines radiated outward, linking a number of shrines, small temples, and other sacred places.

Several years passed, and Viracocha couldn't help but wonder what had become of his creatures on earth. So he took on human form, dressed as an old beggar, and wandered the countryside near Lake Titicaca, searching for his people. When Viracocha arrived at the first village, the people were intimidated by this wandering stranger, and tried to kill him. Viracocha was so angry that he took a thunderbolt from his bag and threw it into the forest, causing all the trees to catch on fire. The villagers realized that this man who could make fire was a powerful being indeed, and they got on their knees and begged for

mercy. Because Viracocha was compassionate, he forgave the people and called rain down from the heavens to quell the flames.

When he came to the next town, the people there recognized Viracocha for the divine presence that he was, and offered to build a golden throne for him to sit on whenever he passed through. Viracocha was delighted by this reception, and bestowed upon the people many blessings.

And so Viracocha traveled from place to place, rewarding the people who recognized him and paid homage, and punishing all those who ignored or

mistreated him. He finally arrived in Cuzco, which at that time was just a humble village. But the people were so industrious and hospitable that Viracocha told them he would send a great ruler, and their city would be known far and wide as the wondrous capital of the Inca empire.

The People of the Sun

There are several versions of this story, which tells of Manco Capac, the founder of the Inca dynasty, and the origins of the capital, Cuzco. The myth serves to clearly illustrate the divine origin and superiority of the Inca people, and outlines their basic social order.

After the first people were created by Viracocha, they were pretty much left to fend for themselves. They lived like beasts in caves: going naked or wearing animal skins, mating indiscriminately, and having no religion or education. For sustenance they ate game, grasses, roots, or wild berries, and when times were hard, they would be forced to eat each other.

Inti the sun god looked down from the heavens and despaired at the wretched state of humankind. So he sent his four sons and four daughters, collectively known as the Ayars, to travel the countryside and teach the people to be civilized. The sons' names were Ayar Manco Capac, Ayar Auca, Ayar Cachi, and Ayar Uchu, and the daughters Mama Ocllo, Mama Huaco, Mama Cura, and Mama Raua. Like Inti and Mama Quilla the moon goddess, these brothers and sisters were allowed to marry each other.

The Ayars entered the world through a heavenly window in Mount Tambo Toco near Lake Titicaca. However, not long after they began their journey, Ayar Cachi began to annoy everyone with his pride and destructiveness. His siblings lured him into a cave, and then pushed rocks against the opening so that he could not escape. Then Ayar Auca and Ayar Uchu displeased the gods with their disobedience, and were turned to stone.

Inti had given the leader, Ayar Manco Capac, a rod made of gold, and told him to plunge the rod into the earth wherever they stopped to rest. The place where the rod disappeared into the ground in one thrust was where they were instructed to settle. Trying several spots, eventually the rod disappeared into the earth at a place that they called Cuzco, which literally means "the navel of the world."

Following Inti's strict instructions, the remaining Ayars stayed in Cuzco to begin their ministry. The people had never seen anyone like Manco Capac and his sisters before. They were beautiful beyond words, and wore shining golden cloaks and large gold discs in their ears. They were so wonderful that the local people wanted to emulate these children of the sun. Manco Capac taught the men how to plant seeds, till the soil, irrigate the fields, and make and use weapons. Mama Ocllo and her sisters taught the women how to spin and weave cotton and wool, and how to cook and sew. And as the people learned new ways and prospered, they went out and taught others. That is how the Inca empire began.

Left **Mama Ocllo, eighteenth-century Cuzco School painting.** Sometimes known as Mama Coya, Mama Ocllo was the sister–consort of Manco Capac, and was responsible for teaching women how to spin fiber, cook, sew, and weave. In one myth, Inti sent his children Mama Ocllo and Manco Capac to earth to civilize the people, while in another story the moon goddess Mama Quilla allowed her daughter Mama Ocllo to become Manco Capac's bride.

KNOTS OF HISTORY

Although the Incas had no system of writing as we know it, they had an efficient system of record-keeping known as *quipu*, which is the Quechua word for "knot."

Quipus were knotted strings made of cotton (or occasionally wool) which Inca rulers used to monitor taxes, population, military action, and the economy. As well as statistical information, *quipus* were also devices for keeping the stories, myths, poems, and history of the Incas. The people responsible for both encoding and decoding the information were known as *quipucamayoqs* ("knot makers"), and teams of messengers would swiftly transport the *quipus* from one city to another, covering as many as 150 miles (240 km) in one day.

Color, type of knot, and placement of knots on the string were all significant factors in interpreting the messages. For example, red would refer to the army, and white indicated peace. Only a handful of *quipus* survived the Spanish conquest, because the Catholic priests thought them to be the devil's handiwork.

Below *Quipus*, **Inca culture.** The information contained in *quipus* was lost to the modern world until Leland Locke deciphered their meaning in the early 1920s.

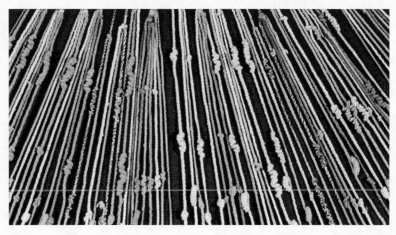

WOMEN OF THE SUN

The major Inca centers such as Cuzco, Lake Titicaca, Pachacamac, and Machu Picchu all had
temples dedicated to the sun god, Inti. Each
of these temples contained a cloistered section known as an *acllahuasi,* the "house of
the chosen women."

These "chosen women," or
acllas, were young girls selected
by a special committee that traveled
throughout the empire searching for the
most beautiful and unblemished eight-
year-olds, preferably with pure Incan
lineage. If a girl became an *aclla,* it was
considered a great honor for her family
and indeed for her entire village.

Acllas performed various duties, but
their primary purpose was to be of service
to the sun god. The highest class of *aclla,*
known as the *mamacunas,* had to be of the
purest bloodline, and were widely revered
as saints. *Mamacunas* lived in celibacy their
entire lives, and were thought to be able to
communicate directly with the gods. They were
responsible for looking after the temple, tending
the sacred fires, and assisting the priests in their
rituals (including sacrifices), and were the
custodians of Inca history.

The young *acllas* learned how to weave,
how to make the ceremonial *chicha* (maize
beer) and *canca* (maize pudding), and
how to care for mummies. When a girl
reached the age of fourteen, the committee decided if she would return
home or if she would proceed to the
next stage. Some girls would be trained
to look after the principal and secondary
idols, and some would become the servants of the nobility and the priesthood.
Others were earmarked as sacrificial
offerings to the sun god, which was
considered to be a great privilege. The
girls of the lowest class, the *Pampa
Aclla Conas,* either became concubines
of the nobility and high-ranking military officers, or were given away in marriage
for political purposes.

144

The Virgin and the Shepherd

There was once a virgin named Chuquillanto who lived at the *acllahuasi* in Cuzco. All the maidens there were selected for their impeccable beauty, but Chuquillanto was the most special, because her hair was the color of the sun.

The virgins had to follow a strict set of rules, including a rigorous regimen of personal hygiene. However, in the afternoon, once the work had been done and the bathing ritual completed, the girls were free to wander outside of the cloister, as long as they traveled in pairs.

One fine summer's day Chuquillanto and her friend were walking in a meadow, and were enchanted by sweet music that they could hear in the distance. They kept following the music, and finally arrived at the source of the sound—a handsome young shepherd named Acoynapa, playing the flute to his herd of llamas. When the shepherd laid eyes on Chuquillanto, he thought she must have been a goddess. Never before had he seen a girl whose hair was the color of gold, or who smelled as fresh as flowers. And never before had she heard such wondrous music.

That night, neither Chuquillanto nor Acoynapa could sleep a wink; both of them were burning with desire. But they knew what the punishment would be if Chuquillanto were to lose her virginity—she would be buried alive, and her partner would hanged by his feet. Days passed, and Acoynapa could not eat, sleep, or even play his flute—he was languishing for love. His mother, who was a skilled sorceress and clairvoyant, realized what was going on, and knew she had to do something or Acoynapa would die.

Chuquillanto could bear it no longer—she had to see her beloved again—and once more she took her friend along to Acoynapa's farm. Acoynapa's mother told the girl and her companion that her son was dead, but gave her his staff to remember him by. That night, Chuquillanto took the gift to bed with her, and was amazed when Acoynapa emerged from the staff; he was not dead at all, but placed in the enchanted staff by his mother. Thus hidden, Acoynapa stayed in the cloister, and the couple spent several nights together in blissful love.

But disaster soon struck—a plague of smallpox descended upon the land, and the priests decreed that the golden-haired virgin was to be sacrificed to Inti. How could Chuquillanto offer herself to Inti now

that she had been deflowered? If she told the truth, Acoynapa would be hanged. But if she let herself be sacrificed, Inti would be so displeased that he would bestow even further misery to the people. Chuquillanto and Acoynapa decided to run away to the jungle. They arrived at the border, and just when Chuquillanto and Acoynapa thought they were safe, they were suddenly turned into stone pillars, which will remain there for all eternity.

MACHU PICCHU

Situated high in the Andes, Machu Picchu (meaning "manly peak") was a royal estate and center of spiritual retreat thought to have been built by Emperor Pachacuti Inca Yupanqui in A.D. 1470.

Hiram Bingham of Yale University accidentally discovered the site in 1911, and when all the vegetation was cleared away, a magnificent city was revealed. Archaeologists discovered many bodies of young women there, leading them to believe that the settlement contained an *acllahuasi* ("house of the chosen women").

Machu Picchu was laid out in what we would call today an "eco-friendly" design, as the 200 stone buildings blend harmoniously into the features of the environment. Because of its cultural and natural significance, Machu Picchu was awarded World Heritage status in 1983 and has since become a major tourist destination within South America.

Below **Machu Picchu, Peru.** Two of the main features of Machu Picchu are the Temple of the Three Windows and the "hitching post of the sun" (*intihuatana*). Comprising a pillar of stone set in a stone base, the *intihuatana* was used by Inca priests to "tie" the sun down as the winter solstice approached and the hours of daylight shortened.

THE CHIBCHA OF COLOMBIA

The Chibcha people (who are also known as the Muisca people) lived in the central highlands of present-day Colombia between A.D 900 and 1450. Their civilization was basically contemporary with the Inca, and comprised three tribes: the Iraca, the Zaque, and the Zipa.

Both the lifestyle and the economy of the Chibcha people revolved around metallurgy: copper, silver, and especially gold. To the Chibcha, gold was imbued with mystical qualities, and this is exemplified in the story of the gilded man, who later became known by the Spanish—and the rest of the world—as El Dorado.

El Dorado

The well-known legend of El Dorado was based on a Chibcha ritual that was performed when a new chieftain was appointed.

Prior to the inauguration ceremony, the prospective chieftain spent several days in fasting and contemplation. Thus purified, he traveled to Lake Guatavita. At the sacred lake, he removed all of his clothing, and his attendants painted his body with an adhesive resin, and then sprinkled gold dust all over his body.

The appointed ruler stepped onto a raft, which was heaped with treasures made of gold and other precious materials. The raft drifted across the lake amid music and fanfare. When it reached the center of the lake, everyone became silent as the chieftain and his entourage each tossed the objects into the water as offerings to the gods. Another version of the story tells that as well as throwing valuable objects into the lake, the chieftain dove into the lake and washed the gold dust from his body as a further gift to the gods.

As well as this special ritual, the Chibcha people would regularly throw valuables into Lake Iguaque as part of their devotional practices to honor the goddess Bachue. When the Spaniards heard these stories, they thought that they must have entered a land of unlimited wealth, and their lust for gold was heightened even further. The name El Dorado has since become synonymous with a utopian fantasy of riches and power.

The Creation of the World

Chiminigagua was the supreme being and creator deity. The Chibcha believed that before creation, the universe was in total darkness. Chiminigagua, who held all the light of the world within him, decided to unleash it. He transformed himself into a flock of black birds which dispensed light from their beaks as they flew over the mountain peaks. After the world was illuminated, Chiminigagua then created the sun and moon to brighten the sky.

Although Chiminigagua was the all-powerful creator, he was not revered as highly as other deities such as Bachue, the mother of the Chibcha race, or Bochica, the bringer of civilization.

Bachue: the Mother Goddess

Bachue ("she of the large breasts") was the goddess of fertility, water, and agriculture. She was also known as Furachogue ("beneficent woman"). One day she appeared as if by magic from Lake Iguaque, carrying her little son. When the boy reached puberty, Bachue began to mate with him, and they produced many children. Bachue was so prolific that most of her pregnancies resulted in multiple births.

Bachue and her partner lived in the village of Iguaque long enough to see their great-grandchildren. But the time came when they had to return to the lake, their spiritual home. So they gathered their tribe together and urged them to lead a good life and perform their religious duties.

They transformed themselves into snakes, and went back to the sacred lake from whence they came.

The Chibcha loved the goddess Bachue so much that they would make pilgrimages to Lake Iguaque and make offerings of gold and precious jewels to her. Occasionally, devotees would be rewarded with dreams and visions of the divine serpents.

> *He [the chieftain] went about all covered with powdered gold, as casually as if it were powdered salt. For it seemed to him that to wear any other finery was less beautiful ...*
>
> GONZALO FERNÁNDEZ DE OVIEDO (1478–1557), SPANISH HISTORIAN

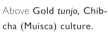

Above **Gold *tunjo*, Chibcha (Muisca) culture.**

Tunjos were figures used as religious or votive offerings by the Chibcha people. They were mostly anthropomorphic (in human form), and may have represented past rulers of the civilization. Other *tunjos* portrayed animals, or depicted scenes of political or social significance.

Bochica: the Bringer of Civilization

Bochica is sometimes designated as the Chibcha sun god, but he is more often thought of as a cultural hero who brought living skills and high moral standards to the Chibcha. Like other cultural heroes of mythology, Bochica was portrayed as a wise old bearded man. He traveled around the country, teaching the grateful people metalwork, weaving, building, and how to use a calendar.

Bochica was married to Huitaca (or Chia), the moon goddess. While Bochica advocated sobriety and fidelity, Huitaca promoted drunkenness and promiscuity, so naturally, many people were eager to follow her example. This caused Bochica great heartache, after all his hard work in trying to bring laws and refinement to his people.

Huitaca used her powers of enchantment to help Bochica's main rival, Chibchacum, to flood the plains of Teguendama. Bochica became so enraged that he turned his wife into an owl, condemning her to live forever as a nocturnal creature. He then changed himself into the sun to evaporate the water. With his magic staff he created channels in the rocks into which the water could drain— these are known as the Teguendama waterfalls.

As punishment for causing the flood, Bochica sent Chibchacum down into the bowels of the earth and forced him to carry the world on his shoulders. When Chibchacum moves the world from one shoulder to the other, an earthquake occurs.

Above **Gold model of the raft used in the Lake Guatavita ceremony.** The raft used by the Chibchas in the ritual that formed the basis of the El Dorado legend was made from local rushes. It was richly decorated and carried four braziers that burned highly perfumed incense.

Left *El Dorado, the Golden Man* by Theodore de Bry (1528–1598). As part of the ritual to make him the chieftain, the naked Chibcha man would be covered in a sticky resin and then have fine gold dust blown over his body. He would then sail out onto Lake Guatavita, to make offerings of gold to the god who lived at the bottom of the lake. In another myth, the offerings were made to a monster who was holding the spirit of an earlier chieftain's wife captive in the depths of the lake.

147

MYTHS OF THE RIVERS AND RAIN FORESTS

The Amazon region of South America features the largest rain forest—and one of the largest rivers—on the planet. For thousands of years, the people of this region have lived intimately with nature in small tribal communities.

The myths of the Amazon are localized, and focus on plants and animals, the river, the daily activities of the people (such as hunting and cooking), and their rituals and ceremonies. Shamans feature prominently in the myths, and in many cases are the myth-keepers of their tribes.

Shamanism is not a religion, per-se, it is a set of techniques, and the principal technique is the use of psychedelic plants.

TERENCE MCKENNA
(1946–2000), AUTHOR

Uaica and the Sleep Tree

From the late nineteenth century to well into the twentieth century, teams of anthropologists lived among the people of the Xingu River region of Brazil and recorded their myths. Here is just one of the many fascinating Xingu River stories.

Uaica was a hunter from the Juruna tribe. One day while exploring in the rain forest he came across a gigantic tree, the like of which he'd never seen before, and he was awe-struck by its unique beauty, immense age, and majestic grandeur.

Uaica also noticed something very peculiar—a pile of animals lying motionless beneath the tree. At first Uaica thought the animals were asleep, but when he looked more closely, he realized they were dead. He began to feel dizzy and drowsy and feared he might have been bewitched and would meet the same fate as the animals, but no matter how hard he tried he could not stay awake.

Sinaa, the jaguar ancestor of the Juruna people, appeared to Uaica in a dream, and taught him the secrets of healing and divination. Uaica awoke feeling blissful and refreshed, and returned to the tree many times, to enter the dreaming trance and to receive the jaguar's teachings. But one day Sinaa instructed Uaica that never again should he return to the tree, although he told Uaica that he could take away some of the bark.

When Uaica returned home to his village, he discovered that by brewing a tea from the sacred bark

Below **Dance festival of an Amazonian tribe.** Deep within the Amazon rain forest, tribespeople used the sound and movement associated with age-old sacred dances to worship their deities, to empower warriors, and to honor the spirits of their ancestors.

and drinking it, he could re-enter the dreaming state and communicate with Sinaa once more. He also learned that the special tea had curative properties, and he soon became known throughout the land as a great healer and cultural hero.

The villagers had great love and respect for Uaica, and thought he should be married. Someone so good and wise should have a child, so that his knowledge would be passed down. However, Uaica was not so wise in choosing a wife. They were not married very long when Uaica's wife became unfaithful, and she and her lover plotted to kill Uaica.

One night the lover snuck up behind Uaica and attempted to strike him on the head with a club. But because Uaica had the spirit of the jaguar ancestor within him, he had eyes in the back of his head, and was able to get out of the way of the club. However, the club left a huge hole in the ground, and Uaica fell into it, disappearing down into the center of the earth, never to be seen again.

How the Jaguar Lost His Fire

This engaging myth, from the Kayapo tribe of tropical Brazil, tells of how mankind acquired fire.

A young boy named Botoque was out hunting for birds with his older brother when they spotted a large macaw nest at the top of a cliff. The older brother soon persuaded Botoque to climb up a pole and steal the eggs from the nest.

Botoque was quite jubilant when he found two eggs, which he promptly threw down to his brother. However, as the eggs fell downward, they turned into stones and broke the brother's hand as he tried to catch them. The older boy was so furious that he stormed off, deliberately knocking the pole down to the ground and leaving Botoque stranded up on the cliff for two days without any food or water.

Poor Botoque began to despair when, from his clifftop, he saw an amazing sight. It was a jaguar, walking upright on two legs, carrying a bow and arrow and a big basket of freshly killed meat. The jaguar spotted Botoque, and with a deep and kindly voice, asked the boy if he would like some help. Botoque was terrified and shook his head, but the jaguar replaced the pole and eventually Botoque slid down.

The jaguar sensed that Botoque hadn't eaten for days, and invited him home for a meal of roasted meat. Botoque did not know what roasted meat was (they ate raw meat in his village), but he was so cold and hungry that he accepted the invitation. When they arrived home, the jaguar's wife was roasting meat over an open fire and Botoque was amazed—he had never seen fire before, or felt such incredible warmth. And he had never tasted anything as wonderful as the tender roasted boar meat.

Botoque stayed with the jaguar for many days, and the jaguar treated him like his own son. He taught him how to use the bow and arrow, and how to build fires and cook food. Botoque would have been happy staying with the jaguar, except for one thing: the jaguar's wife. She was jealous of Botoque, and was cruel to him at every opportunity.

Because of this harsh treatment, Botoque soon became very homesick—he was even starting to miss his older brother—and told the jaguar that he needed to return to his village. Wiping a tear from his eye, the jaguar said farewell to Botoque, and gave him a basket of cooked meat. Then he very sternly told Botoque that under no circumstances should he let his tribespeople know about fire.

Botoque's mother was thrilled to have her son home again and invited her neighbors around for

Left **Funerary urn, Marajo Island, Brazil.** Marajo Island is located in the mouth of the Amazon and Tocantins Rivers, and the ceramics from this area date back over 1,600 years. This red, black, and white funerary urn depicts a crouching female fertility deity with large eyes and a protruding tongue. The bones of the ancestors were kept in urns so the spirits of the deceased remained close to the family.

Below **Gold feline figure, Chavín culture, Peru.** Felines played an important role in the mythology of many South American peoples. Cults devoted to the jaguar existed in Peru, while Amazonian peoples believed in the jaguar spirit—a powerful symbol of strength, athleticism, and dark magic.

149

SPIRITS AND VISIONS

To the people of the Amazon region, the spiritual world was just as real as the physical world around them. In fact, the features of the natural world—such as the rivers, plants, stones, birds, and animals—were all believed to contain their own unique spirit essence.

Shamans are the intermediary between the earthly and the divine realms. Often with the assistance of a mind-altering substance such as *ayahuasca* (a native plant), they would enter a trance and would be able to see and communicate with the gods, the ancestors, as well as the spirits that move through all things. In their altered state, they could shape-shift into the body of another creature, such as a snake or jaguar.

To this day, shamans are respected members of their Amazon communities. They diagnose and cure illnesses, exorcise demons, see into the future, and help dying people make the transition into the next life.

Left **Gold Darien pectoral representing a shaman, Colombia.** The Tukano people of Colombia's Amazon region believe shamans cause lightning to streak across the sky when they throw special crystals at their foes.

a feast of the delicious roasted meat. They were all extremely curious about how the meat was cooked, and eventually Botoque broke his promise to the jaguar and told them about fire, and what a wonderful thing it was. The next day Botoque brought two tribesmen to the jaguar's cottage when he was out hunting, and they were so impressed with the marvelous fire that they decided to take away all the logs that were burning in the jaguar's hearth.

When the jaguar returned from hunting, he was angry and disappointed that Botoque had betrayed him. From that time on, the jaguar became a wild and vicious creature, as he was forced by Botoque's treachery to live in the cold and dark, to hunt with his teeth and claws, and to eat his meat raw. Botoque became a cultural hero, having gained supremacy over the animal kingdom and brought the bow and arrow and the knowledge of fire to his people.

Below *Making Curare in the Brazilian Forest* by François-Auguste Biard (1798–1882). Curare, a deadly poison used for hunting, was carefully prepared by the shaman of the tribe.

Recommended Reading

Mythology of Oceania

Beckwith, M. *Hawaiian Mythology*. Bishop Museum: Honolulu, 1940.

Berndt, Ronald and Catherine Berndt. *Man, Land and Myth in North Australia. The Gunwinggu People*. Ure Smith: Sydney, 1970.

Best, E. *The Astronomical Knowledge of the Maori*. Government Printer: Wellington, 1925.

Best, E. *Maori Religion and Mythology, Volumes 1 and 2*. Government Printer: Wellington, 1925.

Buck, P. *The Coming of the Maori*. Polynesian Society: Wellington, 1949.

Charlesworth, Max, Howard Morphy, Diane Bell, and Kenneth Maddock (eds.). *Religion in Aboriginal Australia: An Anthology*. University of Queensland Press: St. Lucia, 1984.

Davis, Stephen. *Man of all Seasons: An Aboriginal Perspective of the Natural Environment*. Angus & Robertson: Sydney, 1989.

Handy, E.S.C. *Polynesian Religion*. Bishop Museum: Honolulu, 1927.

Hemming, Steven and Philip Jones, with Philip Clarke. *Ngurunderi: An Aboriginal Dreaming*. South Australian Museum: Adelaide, 1989.

Hiatt, Lester (ed.). *Australian Aboriginal Mythology: Essays in Honour of W.E.H. Stanner*. Australian Institute of Aboriginal Studies: Canberra, 1975.

Holden, Robert. *Bunyips: Australia's Folklore of Fear*. National Library of Australia: Canberra, 2001.

Isaacs, Jennifer. *Australian Dreaming: 40,000 Years of Aboriginal History*. Lansdowne Press: Sydney, 1980.

Keen, Ian. *Knowledge and Secrecy in an Aboriginal Religion: Yolngu of North-east Arnhem Land*. Oxford University Press: Melbourne, 1994.

Mowaljarlai, David and Jutta Malnic. *Yorro Yorro, Aboriginal Creation and the Renewal of Nature: Rock Paintings and Stories from the Australian Kimberley*. Inner Traditions: Rochester, Vermont, 1993.

Orbell, M. *The Illustrated Encyclopedia of Maori Myth and Legend*. Canterbury University Press: Christchurch, 1995.

Smith, Heide. *Tiwi: The Life and Art of Australia's Tiwi People*. Angus & Robertson: Sydney, 1990.

Tregear E. *The Maori–Polynesian Comparative Dictionary*. Lyon and Blair: Wellington, 1891.

Tunbridge, Dorothy. *Flinders Ranges Dreaming*. Aboriginal Studies Press: Canberra, 1988.

Walker, R. *Ka Whawhai Tonu Matou: Struggle Without End*. Penguin: Auckland, 1990.

White, J. *Ancient History of the Maori, Vols. 1–6*. Government Printer: Wellington, 1887–1890.

Mythology of the Americas

Bierhorst, J. *The Mythology of North America*. William Morrow: New York, 1985.

Burrin, Kathleen (ed.). *The Spirit of Ancient Peru*. Thames & Hudson: New York, 1997.

Fagan, B. *Ancient North America*. Thames & Hudson: London and New York, 1995.

Hall, Jr., Edwin S. *The Eskimo Storyteller: Folktales from Noatak, Alaska*. The University of Tennessee Press: Knoxville, 1975.

Hardin, T. (ed.). *Legends and Lore of the American Indians*. Barnes and Noble Inc.: New York, 1993.

Hennigh, Lawrence. "Control of Incest in Eskimo Folktales." *Journal of American Folklore 79 (312): pp356–369*.

Jones, David M. and Brian L. Molyneaux. *The Mythology of the Americas*. Lorenz Books: London, 2001.

Josephy, Jr., Alvin M. *500 Nations: An Illustrated History of North American Indians*. Hutchinson/Pimlico: London, 1995.

Koranda, Lorraine Donoghue. *Alaskan Eskimo Songs and Stories*. University of Washington Press: Seattle, 1972.

Laughton, Timothy. *The Maya: Life, Myth, and Art*. Duncan Baird Publishers: London, 1998.

Nicholson, Irene. *Mexican and Central American Mythology*. Paul Hamlyn: New York, 1967.

Norman, Howard (ed.). *Northern Tales: Traditional Stories of Eskimo and Indian Peoples*. Pantheon Books: New York, 1990.

Nungak, Zebedee and Eugene Arima. *Eskimo Stories from Povungnituk, Quebec*. The Queen's Printer: Ottawa, 1969.

Osborne, Harold. *South American Mythology*. Hamlyn: London, 1968.

Rasmussen, Knud. *The Alaskan Eskimos. Report of the Fifth Thule Expedition 1921–1924 10(3)*. Gyldendalske Boghandel, Nordisk Forlag: Copenhagen, 1952.

Rasmussen, Knud. *Intellectual Culture of the Iglulik Eskimos. Report of the Fifth Thule Expedition 1921–1924, 7(1)*. Gyldendalske Boghandel, Nordisk Forlag: Copenhagen, 1929.

Rasmussen, Knud. *The Netsilik Eskimos: Social Life and Spiritual Culture. Report of the Fifth Thule Expedition 1921–1924, 8(1-2)*. Gyldendalske Boghandel, Nordisk Forlag: Copenhagen, 1931.

Rasmussen, Knud. *The People of the Polar North: A Record*. Kegan Paul, Trench, Trubner & Co. Ltd: London, 1908.

Rink, Hinrich. *Tales and Traditions of the Eskimo*. Dover Publications, Inc: Mineola, New York, 1997.

Roberts, Timothy R. *Gods of the Maya, Aztecs, and Incas*. Friedman/Fairfax Publishers: New York, 1996.

INDEX

Italic numbers refer to illustrations and maps, while **bold** numbers refer to break-out boxes and family trees.

PICTURE CREDITS

The Publisher would like to thank the following picture libraries and other copyright owners for permission to reproduce their images. Every attempt has been made to obtain permission for use of all images from the copyright owners, however, if any errors or omissions have occurred Global Book Publishing would be pleased to hear from copyright owners.

Key: (t) top of page; (b) bottom of page; (l) left side of page; (r) right side of page; (c) center of page.

The Art Archive, London: 22(b), 40(b), 55(b), 76(c), 90(b), 121(t), 147(b); Album/Joseph Martin: 120(b); Antochiw Collection Mexico/Mireille Vautier: 116(b); Archaeological Museum Lima/ Dagli Orti: 133(c); Archaeological Museum Lima/Mireille Vautier: 139(c), 143(b); Archaeological Museum Tikal Guatemala/Dagli Orti: 128(t); Biblioteca Nacional Madrid/Dagli Orti: 142; Biblioteca Nacional Mexico/Dagli Orti: 118(b); Bibliothèque des Arts Décoratifs Paris/Dagli Orti: 10–11; Bibliothèque des Arts Décoratifs Paris/Dagli Orti (A): 144(b); Bill Manns: 80, 92–93(t); British Museum/Eileen Tweedy: 58–59, 119(b); Dagli Orti: 30(b), 124, 129, 134, 141(b), 144(t), 145; Dagli Orti (A): 37(t), 148; Mesa Verde National Park Museum/ Mireille Vautier: 63; Mexican National Library/Mireille Vautier: 122–123(b), 126(t); Mireille Vautier: 5, 72; Musée des Arts Africains et Océaniens/Dagli Orti: 29(t); Musée des Arts Africains et Océaniens/Dagli Orti (A): front cover (b), 25(t), 26(r), 28(b), 29(b), 33(t); Musée de la Marine Paris/Dagli Orti: 19; Musée du Nouveau Monde La Rochelle/Dagli Orti: 138(b), 150(b); Museo de Arte Colonial de Santa Catalina Cuzco/Dagli Orti: 130(b); Museo Banco Central de Quito Ecuador/Dagli Orti: 130(t); Museo Ciudad Mexico/Dagli Orti (A): 113(t), 125(t); Museo Larco Herrera Lima/ Album/J. Enrique Molina: 132(b); Museo del Oro Bogota: 147(t); Museo del Oro

Bogota/Dagli Orti: 146; Museo del Oro Lima/Dagli Orti: 135(t), 149(b); Museo Pedro de Osma Lima/Mireille Vautier: 138(t), 140(t), 143(t); Museo Regional de Oaxaca Mexico/Dagli Orti: 128(b); Museo del Templo Mayor Mexico/Dagli Orti: 126(c); National Anthropological Museum Mexico/Dagli Orti: 1, 112, 113(b), 117(c), 118–119(t), 121(b), 122(t), 123(c), 125(c), 127; Neil Setchfield: 2; Nicolas Sapieha: 114, 120(t); Private Collection Paris/Dagli Orti: 110(t); Stephanie Colasanti: 6–7.

Art Resource, New York: 79; Smithsonian American Art Museum, Washington DC: 70(t).

Bridgeman Art Library, London: Kakadu National Park, Australia: 28(t); Museo Casa Diego Rivera (INBA), Guanajuato, Mexico/Index: 115; Natural History Museum, London: 89(b); Private Collection/The Stapleton Collection: 75(b).

Corbis: 103(t); Bob Rowan, Progressive Image: 73(t); Bowers Museum of Cultural Art: 102(t); Burstein Collection: 87(t), 97(t); Christie's Images: 104; David Muench: 100; Kimbell Art Museum: 116(t); Patrick Ward: 83(t); Peter Harholdt: 107(c); Tom Bean: 66(t).

Global Book Publishing: front and back cover (t), 8–9.

Mary Evans Picture Library, London: 67, 76(t), 77, 78(t), 86, 94, 98–99(t), 102(b), 111.

National Library of Australia: 17(r), 38(b).

Werner Forman Archive, London: 15(t), 15(b), 135(b); American Museum of Natural History, New York: 106–107(b); Art Gallery of New South Wales, Sydney: 20(b), 21(t), 22(t), 25(b), 34(t), 34(b), 35, 36, 39; Auckland Institute and Museum, Auckland: 40(t), 43, 49(b), 54; British Museum, London: 16(b), 16–17(c),

18(b), 55(t), 65(t), 71; Canadian Museum of Civilization: 96(b); Canterbury Museum, Christchurch: 12(br), 57; Centennial Museum, Vancouver: 96(t); Dallas Museum of Art: 137(t); David Bernstein Collection, New York: 132–133(t), 149(t), 150(t); Denver Art Museum: 90(t); Edmund Carpenter Collection: 109(t); Courtesy Entwistle Gallery, London: 44, 51(b); Eugene Chestow Trust: 60(b); Field Museum of Natural History, Chicago: 60(t), 75(t), 92(b), 99(b), 105(b); Glenbow Museum, Calgary, Alberta: 74; Haffenreffer Museum of Anthropology, Brown University, Rhode Island: 101(t); Jeffrey R. Myers Collection, New York: 109(b); Maori and Pioneer Museum, Okains Bay: 12(bl), 50; Mesa Verde National Park Museum: 95(t); Museum of the American Indian, Heye Foundation, New York: 62(b), 84(b), 88(b), 98(b); Museum of Mankind, London: 62(t), 110(b); Museum of Northern Arizona: 73(b), 84(t); Museum für Völkerkunde, Basle, Switzerland: 13; Museum für Völkerkunde, Berlin: 45(r), 47, 52–53(b), 56(b), 69(b), 105(t), 136, 137(b), 141(t); National Museum, Denmark: 106(c); National Museum of New Zealand, Wellington: 52(t), 53(t); Ohio State Museum: 70(b), 81(t); Otago Museum, Dunedin: 16(tl), 42(b); Peabody Museum, Harvard University, Cambridge, Massachusetts: 85; Plains Indian Museum, Buffalo Bill Historial Center, Cody, Wyoming: 68, 69(t), 82, 87(b), 88(t), 95(b); Private Collection: 12(t), 24; Private Collection, London: 27; Private Collection, New York: 30(t), 31, 37(b), 38(t), 81(b); Private Collection, Prague: 23, 32, 33(b); Provincial Museum, Victoria, British Columbia: 64(b), 103(b); Schindler Collection, New York: 65(b), 96–97(b); Sheldon Jackson Museum, Sitka, Alaska: 108(b); Smithsonian Institution, Washington DC: 61, 66(b), 91(t), 93(b), 101(b), 108(t); Tara Collection, New York: 21(b), 26(l); Taranaki Museum, New Plymouth: 46(t); Te Awamutu Museum: 46(b); University Museum, Alaska: 106(t); University Museum, Philadelphia: 83(b), 89(t).

New World
MYTHOLOGY

Produced by Global Book Publishing
Level 8, 15 Orion Road, Lane Cove,
NSW 2066, Australia
Ph: (612) 9425 5800   Fax: (612) 9425 5804
Email: rightsmanager@globalpub.com.au